Crisis Communication
in a Digital World

Crisis Communication in a Digital World provides an introduction to major crisis communication theories and issues management, using practical examples from Australia and New Zealand.

The book examines how public relations can influence the nature of a crisis and the impact of its aftermath. It explores the role of PR specialists in different crisis situations – including natural disasters and morphing crises – and examines the major challenges they face in a world where social media is a key source of communication.

Readers are provided with an in-depth and critical understanding of crisis communication and issues management through practical approaches, strategies and skills, which are supplemented by relevant theories based on evidence and experience. International perspectives have been included throughout to illustrate the impact of multinational companies on the digital world, including global media cycles and social media activism. Each chapter explores a different aspect of communications, including media, natural disasters and celebrity crises.

Written by authors with over six decades combined experience in the public relations field, *Crisis Communication in a Digital World* is an essential resource for those learning to apply communications and public relations to crisis situations.

Crisis Communication
in a Digital World

EDITED BY

MARK SHEEHAN AND DEIRDRE QUINN-ALLAN

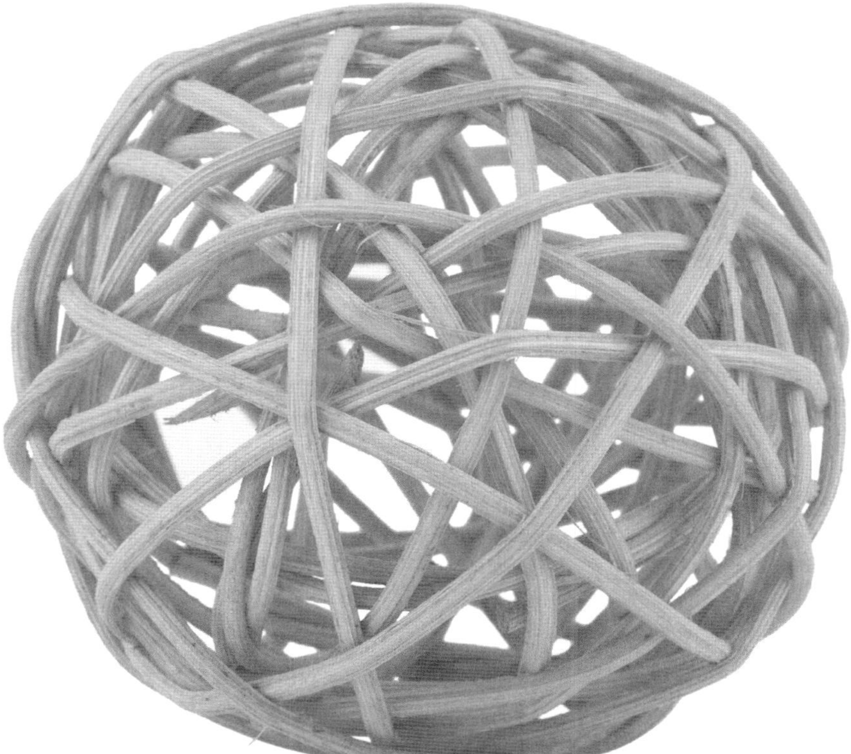

CAMBRIDGE
UNIVERSITY PRESS

CAMBRIDGE
UNIVERSITY PRESS

477 Williamstown Road, Port Melbourne, VIC 3207, Australia

Cambridge University Press is part of the University of Cambridge.

It furthers the University's mission by disseminating knowledge in the pursuit of education, learning and research at the highest international levels of excellence.

www.cambridge.org
Information on this title: www.cambridge.org/9781107678231

First published 2015

Cover designed by Zo Gay
Typeset by Integra Software Services Pvt. Ltd.
Printed in China by C & C Offset Printing Co. Ltd.

A catalogue record for this publication is available from the British Library

A Cataloguing-in-Publication entry is available from the catalogue of the National Library of Australia at www.nla.gov.au

ISBN 978-1-107-67823-1 Paperback

CONTENTS

About the editors and authors *page* x

Introduction 1

Mark Sheehan and Deirdre Quinn-Allan

Risk 2

Issues 3

Crisis 4

Assessing risk, recognising the issue and avoiding the crisis: Saving Australia's banks 5

1947–1949: Banking on victory 6

Case questions 8

Bibliography 8

PART 1: UNDERSTANDING CRISIS AND ISSUES MANAGEMENT 11

Chapter 1: Theorising and practising public relations crisis management 12

Steve Mackey

Introduction: When the crisis bells ring 12

Definitions and criticisms 13

Theory as models and procedures 15

Pre-crisis 15

Crisis response 19

Post-crisis 22

The overt protection of interests 23

The wide field of *apologia* theory 23

Conclusion 26

Case questions 27

Bibliography 27

PART 2: INDUSTRIAL DISASTERS 29

Chapter 2: Outrage management or consensus communication: What is the best way of doing risk communication? 30

Paul Adams

Introduction 30

Background 31

The Coode Island Community Consultative Committee 33

Communicating risk: Experts and the public 36

Conclusion 38

Case questions 38
Bibliography 39

Chapter 3: Confronting the reputation risks: New Zealand's biggest food safety scare 41
Chris Galloway

Introduction 41
The ripple effect of a crisis 42
Understanding the reputational risk 42
Reputation impacts: The ripples in the pond 44
Fonterra's perspective of the crisis 45
Media reaction to the crisis: The daily progression 46
The apology goes wrong 47
100% Pure? Damaging the national brand 48
In the end it was a false alarm . . . 49
Understanding and interpreting the crisis 49
In science we trust . . . too much? 50
Reputation: The ultimate loser in crisis 51
The stakeholder view 51
Conclusion 52
Case questions 53
Bibliography 53

PART 3: CORPORATE CRISIS 59

Chapter 4: Crisis communication: When sorry is the hardest word in elite sport 60
Hamish McLean and Maria Hopwood

Introduction 60
Case study: Into the inferno 61
Fans, connections and expectations 62
Personal transgressions forgiven only so far 64
A defence of attack 65
Confessing bad news 65
Previous reputation may not count 67
Controlling the message 67
Diverting attention 68
Conclusion 69
Case questions 69
Bibliography 70

Chapter 5: Corporate responses to a racially framed incident in Malaysia: The KFC i-City fight 73
Kiranjit Kaur

Introduction 73
Background 75
Case focus 76
Conclusion 78
Case questions 79
Bibliography 79

Chapter 6: Managing issues through cross-sector collaboration: Unilever and Greenpeace 80
Sharyn McDonald

Introduction 80
Cross-sector collaboration and issue management 81
Case background 84
Relationship portfolio 85
Conclusion 88
Case questions 88
Bibliography 89

PART 4: SOCIAL MEDIA AND CRISIS 93

Chapter 7: Media targets: When a spark in social media develops into a mainstream media firestorm 94
Kristy Hess and Lisa Waller

Introduction 94
Background 95
The changing nature of information subsidies 96
News values 97
Case focus 98
News values 99
Social media 100
Conclusion 104
Case questions 104
Bibliography 105

Chapter 8: Harnessing the power of slacktivism: The boom and bust cycle of issues management and crisis 107
Deirdre Quinn-Allan

Introduction 107
Background 108

Deforestation, consumers and supply chain slacktivism 110
Harnessing the power of slacktivism 111
Asia Pulp and Paper 112
Kony 12 114
Conclusion 116
Case questions 117
Bibliography 117

Chapter 9: Social media adoption and risk aversion: Australian not-for-profits 119
Emma Bennett

Introduction 119
Background 120
Case focus 120
Social media adoption and usage 121
The role of strategy development in risk aversion 126
Social media resources for NPOs 128
Conclusion 128
Case questions 129
Bibliography 129

PART 5: NATURAL DISASTERS 131

Chapter 10: Communicating during disasters: Insights from the 2013 Bundaberg flood 132
Amisha Mehta and Dominique A. Greer

Introduction 132
Background 133
What is risk communication during disasters? 134
Risk communication across the four phases of disasters 135
Risk communication in Bundaberg: Across the four phases 137
Risk, crisis and communication lessons learned 142
Conclusion 144
Case questions 144
Bibliography 145

Chapter 11: Government roles in emergency communication response 146
Jordi Xifra and Mark Sheehan

Introduction 146
Examining a crisis 146
Media coverage 148
Background of the crisis 148
Responsibility of government agencies 149

	Specific emergency plans	149
	Managing communication	151
	Social media: A critical tool	152
	Conclusion	155
	Case questions	156
	Bibliography	156
Chapter 12:	Post-crisis: Rebuilding a company, a reputation, a community *Mark Sheehan and Biagio Oppi*	158
	Introduction	158
	Physical or sudden crisis	159
	A crisis on three fronts	161
	The earthquakes: From one disaster to another	163
	Target publics	164
	'One Voice': Coordinated crisis communication	164
	Conclusion: Outcomes and recovery	166
	Case questions	167
	Bibliography	167
Appendix: Answers to case questions		169
Index		182

ABOUT THE EDITORS AND AUTHORS

Editors

Mark Sheehan is Course Director of undergraduate Public Relations in the School of Communication & Creative Arts (SCCA) at Deakin University, Australia. Since 2006, he has edited the *Asia Pacific Public Relations Journal*, and he has written widely on the history of PR in Australia, lobbying, crisis and risk communication. He is currently inaugural Chair of the PRIA National Education Advisory Committee. He was made a fellow of the PRIA in 2010 and is also a Senior Associate and Honorary Life Member of the Financial Services Institute of Australia. He worked as a PR practitioner in the publishing and the finance sectors before joining Deakin University in 1999.

Deirdre Quinn-Allan is Associate Head of School – Teaching and Learning in the School of Communication and Creative Arts at Deakin University, Australia. She has taught in the Public Relations discipline for 10 years in the area of marketing communication. Prior to joining Deakin, Deirdre worked in management, social marketing, PR and education and training roles in Australia and overseas. Her research interests include how organisations respond and adapt to external change drivers – particularly information communication technologies, and she has also written in the areas of social networking and user-generated content and their impact on PR and marketing communication practices and education.

Authors

Dr Paul Adams is a senior lecturer in Communication and coordinator of the Public Relations discipline at Victoria University, Australia. He has been a public relations educator for more than 20 years. He has research interests in risk communication, not-for-profit public relations and third sector public relations and has a long association with the environment movement. He has previously worked in public relations in non-government organisations.

Emma Bennett holds degrees in Public Relations and Communication from Deakin and RMIT Universities, Australia. Her professional experience focuses on social media community building and advocacy for the not-for-profit sector, including the development and implementation of strategies aiming to connect with and empower communities via social media. Emma provided social management and strategic direction for Multiple Sclerosis Australia national campaigns, including Kiss Goodbye to MS and MS Readathon. Her communication career includes copywriting for the health and community sectors and she currently works as social media consultant with community and NFP organisations.

Dr Chris Galloway is a senior lecturer in Public Relations at Massey University's Albany campus in Auckland, New Zealand. His research interests include issue, risk, and crisis communication. His work has been published in journals such as *Public Relations Inquiry, Public Relations Review, Prism*, and the *Asia Pacific Public Relations Journal*.

Dr Dominique A. Greer is a lecturer in Marketing at the Queensland University of Technology Business School. She has established an international research profile in consumer misbehaviour, services marketing, customer participation, and risk communication. From 2012 to 2014, Dominique led the Risk Communication stream of Project ResQu, a two-year $7.1 million collaborative research program between the Queensland Government, CSIRO, Boeing Australia, Insitu Pacific, and QUT. From 2014 to 2020, she will be a chief investigator in a seven-year $2.39 million Bushfire and Natural Hazard CRC research program investigating how to improve community compliance with instructional messages during natural hazards.

Dr Kristy Hess is a senior lecturer at Deakin University, Australia. She has worked as a journalist and coordinates the largest education/training program for practising journalists in regional Australia. Kristy is also the recipient of an Australian Office of Teaching and Learning (OLT) prize for teaching excellence in higher education. Her research interests focus on the role of the news media and its relationship to society, especially local media. She has also examined the intersection between journalism and public relations. Her academic work has been published in leading international journals such as *Communication Theory*, *Journalism Studies* and *Continuum*.

Maria Hopwood is a senior lecturer in Marketing at Northampton Business School at the University of Northampton, UK. Her research interest is sports public relations and marketing, meaning that her work bridges the disciplines of both public relations and sports management. Maria has previously taught at Leeds Metropolitan University (UK), Bond University (Queensland, Australia) and the University of Teesside (UK). She has gained extensive experience working with professional sports organisations in both Australia and the UK and has worked with UEFA as an academic consultant. A published author, Maria is a member of the editorial boards for the journals *Public Relations Review*, the *International Journal of Sport Communication* and the *International Journal of Sport Marketing and Sponsorship*.

Dr Kiranjit Kaur is an associate professor in Public Relations at Universiti Teknologi MARA, Malaysia. She is also a Fellow and Accredited member of the Institute of Public Relations Malaysia (IPRM); immediate past Chair of IPRM education committee; and she also serves as a Board member on the Malaysian Communication and Multimedia Content Forum Council; and chairs the Media Commission of the National Council of Women's Organizations, Malaysia. She has done research and published papers on public relations management, media ethics, new media technologies, and women in the media.

Dr Steve Mackey is a senior lecturer in Public Relations at Deakin University, Australia. He was formerly a journalist and then a regional government press officer in London. His 2001 PhD was titled 'Public relations and contemporary theory'. Steve's research highlights the relevance of modern rhetorical studies and Peircean semiotics to understanding public relations He teaches units in Public Affairs and Social Media Public Relations.

Dr Sharyn McDonald is a lecturer in Public Relations at Deakin University, Australia. With a strong interest in issue management, her research centers on cross-sector collaboration, social partnerships, and sustainable strategies for nonprofit organisations. Her PhD focused on cross-sector social partnerships and she continues to publish in the areas of collaboration and social responsibility. Sharyn has taught in a range of areas including management, entrepreneurship, communication and public relations and she currently lectures on the Master of Communication course at Deakin University.

Dr Hamish McLean lectures in Risk and Crisis Communication at Griffith University, Brisbane. He has 30 years' professional experience in journalism and PR. For more than a decade he operated a crisis and media consultancy with international clients in the health, aviation, law and allied sectors. His PhD is in media, crisis communication and disasters. Hamish's research interests are in social media and crisis communication, political communication during disasters and risk communication involving community resilience and disaster planning, response and recovery. Hamish has published internationally and is a sought-after commentator in the media on crisis communication.

Dr Amisha Mehta specialises in Risk and Crisis Management and Small Business Resilience at the QUT Business School, Australia. Amisha contributes to risk perception and crisis management research in unmanned aviation through Project ResQu, a $7.1 million collaborative research program funded by the Queensland State Government, Boeing Australia, and Insitu Pacific. As a chief investigator for the Bushfire and Natural Hazards CRC, Amisha works with government to deliver evidence-based risk and warning communication to increase community resilience. She is on the executive board at the QUT Centre for Emergency and Disaster Management and Public Relations Institute of Australia's National Education Committee.

Biagio Oppi is an Italian Public Relations professional, working in the field for nearly 15 years. He holds a bachelor degree in Communication Sciences and an executive PR masters degree from IULM University. Starting as journalist, he then focused on public relations and marketing, working in different industries: international relations, exhibitions, food and wine, healthcare, travel and motorsport. He is now Communication Manager of Gambro – part of Baxter International, a leading healthcare company – where he is responsible both for internal and external communication. Since 2013, he has been a member of the Board of Global Alliance for Public Relations and Communication Management.

Lisa Waller is a senior lecturer in Journalism at Deakin University, Australia. Her research centres on questions about how news shapes society, especially at the local level, but also in fields including the justice system and policymaking. She received her PhD from the University of Canberra in 2014.

Jordi Xifra is Professor at the Universitat Pompeu Fabra, Barcelona, Spain. His research focuses basically on the history of public relations, public relations sociology, public affairs and public diplomacy. He has also led a research group on think tanks' communication management. He has published more than 15 books on public relations and public affairs in Spain and South America, and his articles have been accepted for publication in *Public Relations Review*, *Journal of Public Relations Research*, and *American Behavioral Scientist*, among others. He is the co-editor of *Public Relations Inquiry* (Sage).

INTRODUCTION

Mark Sheehan and Deirdre Quinn-Allan

The analogy of the boiled frog has been recalled by scholars when dealing with the concept of risk, issues and crisis communication. A frog dropped into a saucepan of boiling water quickly jumps out. Placing a cold-blooded frog in a saucepan of cold water and slowly warming the water to boiling point sees the frog become accustomed to the heat and finally succumb. Many organisations react quickly (if often chaotically) to an emergency, but in a familiar environment where they view the potential risk as too remote to damage them, they tend to ignore it – and in some cases, succumb.

The tale is a useful illustration as we determine the differences and similarities of risk, issues and crisis communication and their interconnectivity and how they all come to be considered areas of practice in the profession of public relations (PR). This text seeks to examine these areas and assist the reader in discussing questions that can resolve the respective and combined challenges. This chapter will also discuss the synergies of these three areas and as you read through the case studies in the text you should ponder the existence of each element collectively and individually. They can co-exist and they can stand alone; while the evidence of one may be patently clear it is hoped that after your study of these cases you can observe the missing elements and ponder what might have been had a certain strategy been employed.

In the case studies presented, it is the intention of the editors and contributors to illustrate how the PR professional reacts to and learns from each situation and the role played in risk, issues and crisis communication. In that respect this is not a how-to book – it asks the reader to contemplate, consider and learn from the collective wisdom of the presented case studies. It does this by using the context of the digital world where the nature of each of the elements has changed as dramatically as the nature of communication itself. It also takes a deliberate international perspective including case studies from nations beyond Australia to ensure an understanding of the global impact of crisis. In each case study the crisis impact is featured – but the discussion of risk and issue management can also be observed. Readers will come to realise that recovery from crisis, if successful, can be viewed as an organisational strength and will actually build a corporate reputation.

The tools of risk and issues management can be seen at the forefront in crisis situations – sometimes used well and wisely; sometimes ignored until too late and the damage done. However the capacity to look at events through a lens of risk and issues management allows the PR practitioner a capacity to recover – it allows them to also consider the opportunities that can present in these critical events in an organisation's history.

Some may question the common denominator played by public relations in these settings. However scholars of risk communication and management, issues communication and management, and crisis communication and management (Palenchar, 2005; Galloway, 2012; Galloway & Kwanash-Aidoo, 2006, 2012; Regester & Larkin, 2002, 2008; Power & Hutter, 2005) have posited the connection's strong links – that although risk, issues and crisis are often linked with the noun *management*, it is just as viable to consider them as linked with the noun *communication* – and the management of communication falls squarely within the domain of public relations. Galloway (2012, p. 35) explained the connection when he wrote that 'For PR, forging a link between issue communication, risk communication and crisis communication matters, because some issues are 'risk issues' (Regester & Larkin, 2002) and it is in PR's clients' interests to use communication in their efforts to minimise risk and avert crises'. The role of communication is critical in the management of each element. Readers of this text will become aware that when the word *management* is used the author will be referring to an overall technical and organisational approach and that the communication aspect refers to the communication management subset of each risk, issue and crisis.

It is important to look at these three words in the PR context. They are commonly used words in everyday speech but as you will come to see their inclusion in the public relations lexicon requires a realignment from the reader; a new interpretation and new understanding. The chapters in this book will assist the reader in coming to grips with what the terms mean and how they apply in specific areas. Some chapters deal specifically with one concept – others will look at how events occurred through analysing two or three of these elements. The editors and contributors strongly believe that prospective practitioners should know how to apply these terms and the conditions under which they may occur and consequently gain a greater understanding by using definitive tools to analyse and review the circumstances.

The other common factor is the recognition that organisational decision-making is about developing and implementing internal and external responses for challenges. We will be examining how organisations from corporate, NFP and government sectors have anticipated for and succeeded and in some cases failed at planning for events. Yet, especially in times of natural disaster such as earthquakes and wildfires (see Part 5), it has not been possible to foresee the damage wreaked on the organisation and the community and environment in which it exists.

Risk

Risk is not the beginning, nor is a crisis the end point of the three areas – they are not linear. However as the public relations practitioner seeks to manage their responsibilities it is apparent that an assessment of challenges is required. The best-informed and most well-intentioned PR manager will attempt to identify the challenges that the organisation faces – yet many situations will not have been accounted for in that planning process.

Although we can give no date as to the invention of risk communication, Palenchar (2005, p. 253) has indicated that it came about when key publics realised that 'private sector and public-sector organizations failed to understand and exhibit appropriate levels of corporate responsibility by failing to achieve proper risk associated with their activities'. This could be from the time manufacturers realise that they had a responsibility to the end consumer to ensure their product was safe or when they came to realise that their processes in making these things were safe. Ultimately it means that 'corporate and institutional behaviour has come under increased scrutiny. People are less trusting' (Galloway & Kwanash-Aidoo, 2005, p. 3).

Harrison (2011) states that some people don't see risk as a PR matter, but more to do with operations concerning safety or security. However, as he identifies, risk is inherent in bad reputation, in controversial public issues, corporate crises, sponsorships turning bad, and so on. The management of risk must also involve the communication of risk or risks. Palenchar (2005) prescribes the topics of such a conversation as including the 'character, cause, degree, significance, uncertainty, control and overall perception of a risk' (p. 752). Fearn-Banks (2002) reinforces Harrison's approach of considering risk communication in all PR activities and seeing it as the 'ongoing program of informing and educating various publics' (p. 17) about negative and positive challenges that can affect an organisation.

It is of interest Harrison includes risk as part of the strategic development of a communication plan – the risk planning is undertaken when considering objectives for a PR plan or program. Galloway and Kwanash-Aidoo (2005) point to a process that involves 'the ability to integrate information from a variety of sources, to make sense of it, to assess possible approaches for the organisation to decide on' (p. 3).

Authors (Palenchar, 2005; Fearn-Banks, 2004) agree that risk communication and management cannot be conducted successfully unless there is a quality two-way relationship with the publics affected by the perceived risks. If this is present then recovery from a crisis can be achieved in a more appropriate timeframe and with little lasting damage to the organisation and its reputation.

Risk communication is a new practice in public relations but as more and more practitioners adopt the common techniques that underpin risk assessment for strategic planning it is becoming better understood. The blending of the 'risk issue' (Leiss, 2004, p. xvi) is a way of making the familiar new for practitioners. Just as issues management has come to be inextricably linked with crisis communication then it would seem logical that 'an altered perspective of PR's role in relation to risk would also see the profession complement its focus on crisis communication with a similar emphasis on risk communication as a crisis prevention strategy' (Galloway, 2012, p. 42).

Issues

While the establishment of risk and crisis in a communication context grew out of the management of crises and risks the provenance of issue management (sometimes called 'IM') and communication has been firmly placed in public relations. Galloway (2006) identifies it as a 'central concept' for both the public relations practitioners and academics. Dougall (2008) cites Heath and Casino's (1990) arguments of the public relations role, with its heavy dependence on communication and strategy in meeting and understanding issues. In fact, according to Jaques (2008), the very inception of IM can be traced to a specific time and place. On 15 April 1976, Howard Chase first defined and used the term 'issue management' (note the singular use of 'issue') as:

> the capacity to understand, mobilize, coordinate and direct all strategic and policy planning functions, and all public affairs/public relations skills, toward achievement of one objective: meaningful participation in creation of public policy that affects personal and institutional destiny.
>
> (Chase, 1982, p. 1)

In managing issues a PR practitioner 'anticipates the issues that are potential crises and ranks them in order of possible damage to the organisation' (Fearn-Banks, 2002, p. 20). We can see here that the tools of risk management become critical in categorising the issues. Chase himself saw IM's role in strategic planning as purely concerned with public policy and failed to recognise what Jaques has called 'the crucial interface with the practice of crisis management' (2008, p. 340) and points out validly that Chase did not see the growing complementarity between the emerging crisis management and IM which is now so widely accepted and taken as the norm. A retrospective opinion is given by Howard Chase's colleague, the author and practitioner Ray Ewing (1990), who agrees that companies were already using methods that predicated the rise of IM, and writes that 'Those of us in the corporate world developing foresight and planning techniques in the social-political arena which impacted the economic viability of our companies thought of it as an ad hoc process, not a planned and continuous process' (p. 19).

In technical terms, Howell (2009) notes that Heath (1977) indicates the four key functions in IM:

1. Anticipation of and analysis of issues.
2. Development of the organisational position on the issues.
3. Identification of the key publics and those whose support is needed for the public policy issues.
4. Identification of the desired behaviours of the key publics.

Howell (2009) refines this further by structuring IM into four key issues areas (identification, scanning, monitoring and analysis) although Heath and Palenchar (2009) more correctly discern more steps, in a different order (scanning, identifying, monitoring, analysing and priority setting). Every attempt should be made to identify these activities as you read the case studies in the text.

Crisis

No matter how well prepared an organisation is, the effect of a crisis may be extreme. It is critical to realise that the crisis is more than a disruption to daily activities – it is an event that threatens the very existence of the organisation. The case studies in this book reflect many of the major crisis types, and no two responses are the same. The modern manager is prepared to deal with disruptions – that is, problems that require solving either through immediate action or long-term policy changes. A crisis means that the main focus of business becomes survival.

Well-managed crisis communication helps to reduce stakeholder negativity. If a crisis is not the organisation's fault, but rather a natural disaster such as an earthquake, an organisation can still lose the confidence of the stakeholders if it appears to be confused or ill-prepared, or if its own reactions compound the crisis. The best crisis preparation will even go one better and suggest how the organisation might use a crisis communication to dispel a lingering rumour before a crisis expands, and to reaffirm commitment to the community and workforce; we can see this in practice in Chapter 12, 'Post-crisis: Rebuilding a company, a reputation, a community'.

As the reader proceeds through each chapter exploring the elements of risk, issues and crisis communication it is apparent how intertwined each element is – and although a crisis may occur it may better handled with better outcomes, but not avoided, because the risk and issue has been managed. Crisis is also covered in detail in Chapter 1, 'Theorising and practising public relations crisis management'.

Let us consider a case study. Unlike the other examples in this text, which all date from this century, this case comes from an earlier time. It indicates the presence of communication strategies which we now recognise as issues management.

Assessing risk, recognising the issue and avoiding the crisis: Saving Australia's banks*

Chase's identification of IM as a public policy role and Ewing's definition are reflected by the action undertaken by Australian banks in the post–Second World War period (Sheehan, 2011), led by Sir Leslie McConnan, Chief Manager (equivalent to a CEO) of the National Bank of Australiasia (now NAB), whose actions in 1944 reflect those of an organisation jumping from that boiling saucepan we discussed at the start of this chapter.

Australia's wartime Treasurer, Ben Chifley, had often stated that 'the best service to the community can be given only by a banking system ... entirely under national control' (Crisp, 1961, p. 172); in effect, the nationalisation of the banking system. It was Chifley, in late 1941, who became Australia, chief financial regulator as Treasurer.

In 1944, the government announced it would continue the wartime banking controls into the peace. In 1945, Chifley, now Prime Minister and Treasurer, introduced the *Banking Act* to give further control to the government.

In the post-war climate of the 'new order' society there was little sympathy for banks among Australians. It was only 15 years since the Great Depression, when the collapse of the banks had led

* This is an abridged version of a paper presented by Mark Sheehan: 'The 1947 bank nationalisation scheme: A prehistory of issues management?', *7th Australian Media Traditions Conference: Trends, Traditions & Transformations – Conference Abstracts*. Swinburne University of Technology, Melbourne, 1–11.

to extreme hardship and financial misfortune for many. To create a positive opinion climate for the banking industry was a major public relations undertaking in itself, but for the banks to include in their strategy the defeat of a popular government and its leader was a very bold initiative.

At the 1946 election, the banks had expected a change of government, which they expected would eliminate Chifley's banking legislation. However, Chifley was re-elected. The nine major banks had trodden carefully during the war, seeking not to antagonise the government, and had hoped for a conservative Liberal government win. McConnan, even during the war, had been boldly resolute in his opposition to further government control of banking. In late 1944, in response to Chifley's moves, McConnan's bank – the National Bank of Australasia – wrote to all its customers against the 'political control over industry and the individual' (Blainey, 1958, p. 357), a bold and unprecedented move in Australian banking. McConnan noted 'We are taking our courage in our hands, and *breaking the traditional banking silence* by making a plain statement to our constituents' (Blainey, 1958, p. 358, emphasis added). This communication was distributed by mail and hand, reprinted in newspapers and covered in opinion columns of the day 'Hundreds of thousands of circulars [McConnan's term for the material] were issued and the verbal fight was on in the press, Parliament and in the streets', yet many banks were 'fearful of departing from their long-standing tradition not to interfere in politics' (Kemp, 1964, p. 151).

Historian Ross McMullin (2000) notes that 'funds for this campaign were unlimited'. Others noted that it was 'the longest and most lavishly funded political campaign ever seen in Australia ... a campaign estimated to cost several hundred thousand pounds' (Goot, n.d.). The banks also realised that to change government they must change the public perception of Chifley and so 'the carefully crafted public image of Chif' as the old homespun Abe Lincoln philosopher' began to be blasted away by the most expensive publicity campaign in Australian history' (Day, 2001, p. 460).

The campaign to defeat the nationalisation of private banking and ultimately the Labor Government commenced in earnest after the 1946 election when all major banks decided to take courage in their hands.

Part of the legislation required all government bodies to bank with the government owned Commonwealth Bank. The Melbourne City Council decided to challenge this section (s. 48) in the High Court, which then declared the section invalid. The banks buoyed by this saw a way to weaken the government's position. But they were not prepared for Chifley's response to the High Court decision.

On 16 August 1947, Chifley 'dropped his bombshell' (Day, 2001, p. 457) and informed Australia of the decision that his government would nationalise the trading banks. Conservative author Charles Kemp (1964) observed that 'this entirely unexpected development hit the Australian community with the suddenness and force of an atomic explosion', and so the battle for the banks 'entered its final, climatic stage' (p. 155).

1947–1949: Banking on victory

When the banking bill was assented on 27 November 1947, the banks immediately challenged the legislation in the High Court 'while they simultaneously poured buckets of money into a public campaign of opposition to nationalisation' (Day, 2001, p. 464). Interestingly this time around the banks were leaving nothing to chance. Even though 'They already had the public on their side with a gallup [sic] poll in September 1947 reporting 65% opposition and 21% in favour'. Their action was necessary because despite their efforts three months later support for nationalisation had grown to 30% (Day, 2001, p. 464).

After the banks challenged the validity of the Act in the High Court and won, the government appealed to the Privy Council in the UK. In July 1949, the appeal was dismissed. The banks had won the argument in the court of law – now they must win in the court of public opinion and defeat the government to ensure nationalisation was dead and buried.

The outcome of the election was a foregone conclusion. A former banker in his memoirs wrote much later that: 'Ultimately we achieved our objective with the fall of the Chifley Government in December 1949 and the reaffirmation of the right of private trading banks to exist' (White & Clarke, 1995, p. 29). Chifley himself remarked on his defeat he had 'moved too fast on banking' and had 'incited a well-funded and popular campaign by the banks in communities across the country' (Day, 2001, p. 501).

Clearly, McConnan's experience with Chifley's membership of the 1936 Royal Commission on Banking lead him to anticipate and identify the likelihood of further regulation of banking under Chifley as Treasurer and then Prime Minister. When Labor ascended to power in 1941, McConnan would have monitored this issue, but would this have been reasonable given Australia's wartime footing? As Jaques (2000) has pointed out, no organisation can identify, track and respond to every issue, and certainly under wartime conditions that would not be a realistic goal. But McConnan, through his 'Circular' of 1944, met what Heath and Palenchar (2009) describe as the criteria for issue monitoring:

1. Journalists believe the issue is worth covering (difficult in wartime with censorship and war news competing).
2. Harm to operations (remember that McConnan was looking to after the war) and most critical.
3. The issue is associated with one group that has the potential of bringing it to the legislative agenda (it was the Labor Party's top policy priority for more than 20 years to nationalise banking [Day, 2001, p. 461]).

However, it can be argued that, with the end of the war, the banks expected that the wartime regulations would be relaxed, including the fixing of interest and exchange rates; control of all capital movements in to and out of Australia; details of all accounts of activities and the maintenance of compulsory deposits with the Central Bank (Salsbury, n.d.). The Allied victory of 1945 saw the banks, with the exception of McConnan's National Australasian Bank, still in that saucepan of water, and warming up nicely.

The extension of Chifley's regulations into peacetime, followed by his call in 1948 for nationalisation, finally led the issue to surface. However, McConnan's astute approach to issue management – and his ability to see the inherent risks for an entire industry – meant that the banks were prepared to meet their foe head-on and muster their considerable might in defeating them.

The failure of the Labor Government's bank nationalisation proposal was ultimately responsible for changing the face of the nation for a generation. Chifley's ambition to nationalise the private banks allowed the Liberal Party, then a new political force under Robert Menzies, to reshape conservative politics and sell a vastly different brand of political philosophy to the Australian people. McConnan may perhaps be given the posthumous title of 'Australia's First Issues Manager', a title that recognises his skill. His own actions during the campaign saw him 'absent from his desk for months at a time, travelling to lobby and organise, to galvanise his loyal troops of bank-workers and to make public appearances' (Merrett, n.d.). His well-developed issues analysis and priority setting capabilities, of understanding the public policy process, anticipating the social and political risks and understanding each advocates' objectives (Heath & Pelanchar, 2009) assured success from an early stage. To call the banking anti-nationalisation campaign a public relations campaign seems to sell short the strategic intent and value. McConnan's broader message of freedom created, as Heath and Pelanchar (2009) stipulate, a zone of meaning that Menzies and his Liberal Party, and the Australian public, embraced and understood.

CASE QUESTIONS

1. Identify the risks of nationalisation for Austraila's banks in the period following the Second World War.
2. How are McConnan's activities reflected in the quote from author and practitioner Ray Ewing?
3. Thinking about the bank nationalisation case, why did the banks continue their campaign when they had already been successful in the High Court?

The authors recognise the contribution of Dr Stephen Mackey, Deakin University, to this chapter.

BIBLIOGRAPHY

Blainey, G. (1958). *Gold and paper: A history of the National Bank of Australasia*. Georgian House: Melbourne.

Chase, W. H. (1982). 'Issue management conference: A special report'. *Corporate Public Issues and their Management*, 7(23), 1–2.

Crisp, L. F. (1961). *Ben Chifley*. Longmans: Melbourne.

Day, D. (2001). *Chifley*. Harper Collins: Sydney.

Dougall, E. (2008). *Issues management*, www.instituteforpr.org/topics/issues-management.

Ewing, R. P. (1990). Moving from micro to macro issues management, *Public Relations Review*. 16(1), Spring, 19–24.

Fearn-Banks, K. (2002). *Crisis communications: A casebook approach*. Mahwah, NJ: Lawrence Erlbaum Associates.

Galloway, C. (2012). Developing risk-literate public relations: threats and opportunities. *Asia Pacific Public Relations Journal*, 13(1), 20–44.

Galloway, C. & Kwanash-Aidoo, K. (2012). Victoria burning: Confronting the 2009 catastrophic bushfires in Australia. In G. Amiso & C. Pratt (eds), *Case studies in crisis communication: International perspectives on hits and misses* (pp. 279–89). Hoboken, NJ: Taylor & Francis.

Goot, M. (n.d.). Rubensohn, Solomon (Sim) (1904–1979). In *Australian dictionary of biography: Online edition*. Retrieved 7 May 2014 from http://adb.anu.edu.au/biography/rubensohn-solomon-sim-11579.

Heath, R. & Palenchar, M. (2009). *Strategic issues management: Organizations and public policy challenges*, 2nd edn. Thousand Oaks, CA: Sage.

Howell, G. (2009). Issues and crisis management. In M. Sheehan & R. Xavier, *Public Relations Campaigns*, South Melbourne: Oxford University Press.

Jaques, T. (2008). Howard Chase: The man who invented issue management. *Journal of Communication Management*, 12(4), 336–43.

Kemp, C. D. (1964). *Big business men: Four biographical essays*. Melbourne: IPA.

Leiss, W. (2004). *Mad cows and mother's milk: The perils of poor risk communication*. Montreal: McGill-Queen's University Press. Retrieved 21 May 2014 from http://site.ebrary.com/lib/deakin/docDetail.action?docID=10178234.

May, A. L. (1968). *The battle for the banks*. Sydney: Sydney University Press.

McMullin R. 2000, Joseph Benedict Chifley in M Grattan Australian Prime Ministers, New Holland Publishers, Sydney pp. 246–268

Merrett, D. (n.d.). McConnan, Sir Leslie (1887–1954). In *Australian dictionary of biography: Online edition*. Retrieved 7 May 2014 from http://adb.anu.edu.au/biography/mcconnan-sir-leslie-james-10916.

Palenchar, M. (2005). Risk communication. In R. Heath (ed.), *Encyclopaedia of public relations,* vol. 2. Thousand Oaks, CA: Sage.

Power, M. & Hutter, B. (eds) (2005). *Organizational encounters with risk: An introduction*. Cambridge: Cambridge University Press.

Regester, M. & Larkin, J. (2002). *Risk, issues and crisis management: A casebook of best practice*, 2nd edn. London: Kogan Page.

Salsbury, S. (n.d.). Gandon, Sydney John (1889–1959). In *Australian dictionary of biography: Online edition*. Retrieved 7 March 2011 from www.adb.online.anu.edu.au/biogs/A140276b.htm.

Sheehan, M. (2006). Super size me: A comparative analysis of responses to crisis by McDonald's American and McDonald's in Australia. In C. Galloway and K. Kwanash-Aidoo (eds), *Public relations issues and crisis management* (pp. 67–79). Thomson Social Science Press, Southbank Australia..

Sheehan, M. (2011). Learning from previous competition: The use of public relations techniques in averting an industry-wide crisis in the 1947 Australian bank nationalisation scheme, *International PR 2011 Conference – Competing identities: The state of play of PR in the 2010s*, Barcelona, Spain, 28/29 June 2011.

White, B. & Clarke, C. (1995). *Cheques and balances: Memoirs of a banker*. Ringwood, Vic.: Viking.

PART 1

UNDERSTANDING CRISIS **AND ISSUES MANAGEMENT**

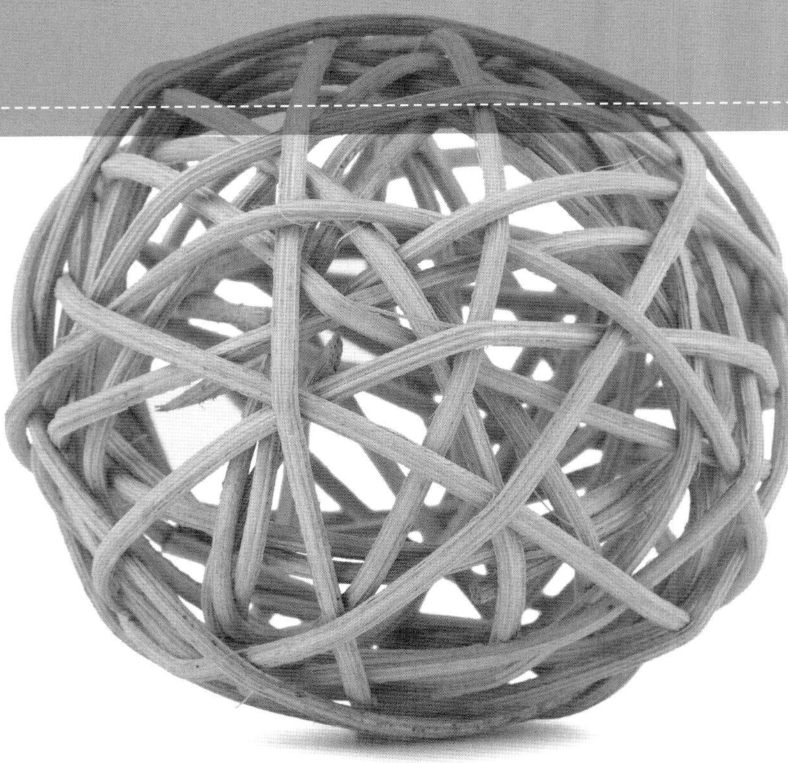

1

THEORISING AND PRACTISING PUBLIC RELATIONS CRISIS MANAGEMENT

Steve Mackey

Chapter objectives

This chapter aims to:

- explain how the true nature of public relations becomes explicit in the crisis situation
- outline procedures for managing public relations crises
- explore advanced theory in public relations crisis management.

Introduction: When the crisis bells ring

As the crisis bells ring, the organisation's best minds rush to the actual or virtual crisis war room. They scan what is already being said and pictured publicly and communicate swiftly with colleagues. If necessary the duty communicator makes a first, tentative response to an insistent inquirer: *'I'll get back to you as soon as I can.'* Suddenly someone with a high **Klout score** gets onto the story. Minutes later traditional and online news sources start to stream out a cacophony of increasingly worrying images and messages. Inside the organisation the **crisis communication** plan is set to be implemented and the first attempts at reassurance are being communicated. The anxious, adrenaline-fuelled race is on to try to maintain the faith, the confidence of vital employees, of essential investors, of government regulators, and of the customers and clients who are the enterprise's lifeblood.

Klout score: A numerical ranking of an individual's influence and engagement with other people through digital and social networks.

Crisis communication: A process that organisations employ to manage risk and instances of crisis. It is divided into three phases: pre-crisis period, crisis response, and post-crisis period.

This chapter examines public relations (PR) theories that provide a framework for analysing and understanding the high-pressure and high-stress PR field of crisis communication and management. First, this chapter examines the process of crisis communication. It is 'how to' theory which distils expert advice about how best to carry out crisis PR. This advice generally presumes an environment where there is no controversy about what PR is, or about its role in the relevant social, political and economic setting. Second, it discusses locating and understanding PR and crisis communication in a wider social context. The latter approach involves rhetorical and critical theories. A challenge for the reader is to compare case studies encountered in this book to both notions of PR theory. We need to start by establishing a clear view of what PR is.

Definitions and criticisms

Around the world, various national PR professional associations have slightly differing definitions of PR. It is generally billed as mutually beneficial and in the public interest. The Public Relations Institute of Australia currently defines it as:

> the deliberate, planned and sustained effort to establish and maintain mutual understanding between an organisation (or individual) and its (or their) publics. It is the key to effective communication in all sectors of business, government, academic and not-for-profit.
>
> (Public Relations Institute of Australia, 2013)

Critics, however, emphasise the self-interest that is involved in this activity (McGrath, 2009, p. 140; Korten, 1995, pp. 147–8; Burton, 2007, p. x; Hobsbawm, 2006, p. 11). Professor Robert Heath, a world-renowned expert in the field, acknowledges the controversy over interests in his introduction to the *The Sage Handbook of Public Relations* (2010). Commenting on this 49-chapter compilation of the views of more than 60 experts, he presents three relevant perspectives to this controversy:

> 1. Interest in 'self-interest' of an organisation is the driving and dysfunctional factor in theory building and research.
> 2. Those who focus on process argue that the symbolic critical interpretivists can only think about how argument can be made in defence of an organisation.
> 3. Others' propositional discourse, the paradigm of sharing ideas, offers a superior approach to the message/meaning/reflective management/collaboration paradigm.
>
> (Heath, 2010, p. 1)

Many of the contributors to Heath's (2010) handbook are clearly writing in the 'post-symmetrical-theory' idiom where the partisanship of PR work cannot be denied. That is they are critical of the James Grunig–inspired notion of symmetry in PR. Grunig's two-way symmetrical model is predicated on the notion that all parties within an organisational or public communication context ought to be regarded as equals in consensus building or in conflict resolution when dealing with matters pertaining to organisational mission or practice. In contrast, asymmetrical approaches to PR privilege the organisation above target publics and or stakeholders. The organisation employs PR to persuade target publics to support its goals or mission.

The notion of 'symmetry', or even-handedness, dominated PR theory for a generation after Grunig and Hunt (1984). That much-quoted textbook advocated the 'four models' approach to classifying PR activity:

1. Promotional work
2. Information work
3. Asymmetry
4. Symmetry

These models have been treated as a hierarchy with the notion of achieving a symmetrical – that is an even-handed, mutally agreeable relationship – which is seen as ideal practice. Critics suggest that symmetry is a very rare if ever attainable ideal which has the effect of distorting the correct understanding of PR (Moloney, 2006; McKie & Munshi, 2007; L'Etang & Pieczka, 2006). Smarting from this alleged theoretical misrepresentation, Grunig had already hit back in 2001 when he wrote:

> The misrepresentations of my idea cited in this chapter suggest that I have not always been successful in conveying the idea behind the term *symmetry* ... my original choice of a name for the model of public relations was *diachronic*, but when I learned that that term related more to time than to process, I dropped it in favour of the term *symmetry*. The basic idea was that public relations should go beyond the advocacy of self-interest without concern for the impact of an organisation's behaviour on others to a balance between self-interest and concern for the interests of others ... symmetrical public relations refers more to a process than to an outcome. That is why I used the term *moving equilibrium* [...] rather than *equilibrium*, *social harmony*, or *consensus*.
>
> (Grunig, 2001, pp. 27–8; italics in original)

The above seems to indicate that, in Grunig's mind, symmetry refers to the *intention* for the process to be even-handed to all parties, while he concedes that the *outcome* of the process may not be so. Despite Grunig's *mea culpa*, what might be argued to be a crude, overly benign interpretation of his thoughts has clouded this purportedly professional–academic subject for many years. Indeed, the view from before the *mea culpa* – with its simplistic application of the term 'symmetry' – is still presented in many textbooks and curricula. This chapter attempts to avoid this mistake by underlining the divide between, on the one hand, simple model/procedure conceptualisations which might be prey to mistaken symmetrical theory interpretation, and, on the other hand, more academic approaches which point towards more controversial rhetorical and critical notions. First, we will consider the conventional procedures, before posing what are essentially moral questions, such as:

- 'In whose interests are these "procedures" carried out?'
- 'Can, or rather, *should* public relations be considered an amoral – that is, a politically neutral – social technology?'
- 'Isn't it the case that when we apply wider intellectual, as opposed to constrained, instrumental conceptualisations, the desperate rawness of public relations crisis management betrays the reality that protection and projection of specific, often powerful interests is at the root of this whole field?'

Theory as models and procedures

Sequencing

It is common in crisis communication/crisis PR advice to separate out three chronological periods. The first is the pre-crisis period. This is limitless. In this period risk audits are carried out. Risks are calibrated in severity from inconsequential to needing costly remediation. Assessments are made of the potential effects on public perception of the different things that might go wrong. The lessons of previous problems are considered. Everything is done to minimise or prevent all conceivable future unfortunate incidents, but at the same time strategies to regain public confidence are created in case even the most watertight prevention strategies fail. Next, we turn to the crisis response. Here we consider the intense, acute, but hopefully short period when the crisis is at its height. The response period is when the organisation's full communication and managerial resources may have to be called in and dedicated on an hour-by-hour, or sometimes a minute-by-minute basis. Last, we have the post-crisis period, which involves an evaluation of the crisis PR effort, and an effort to repair image and identity, involving research, planning and execution (here, we use 'image' to refer to how the organisation appears, and 'identity' to refer to the organisation's human and organisational culture, including how it is administered and projected; the former is not always a faithful reflection of the latter). Repair to identity may involve significant changes to the way the organisation operates technically, managerially, or both.

Pre-crisis

Defining the type of crisis

An airline may have a sexual harassment crisis, an accountancy firm may have a fire, a power supply company may have a financial crisis, or a food producer may have industrial troubles. In other words, it is not always easy to identify what type of crisis may occur simply in terms of the industry or the endeavour in which the organisation is engaged. For this reason, in-house and external agency consultants need to anticipate the full gamut of the crisis types which may strike their client or employer. Otto Lerbinger (2012) is an authority on crisis categorisation. In commenting on a crisis typology offered by Coombs, of 'Natural disaster, malevolence, technical breakdowns, human breakdowns, challenges, megadamage, organisational misdeeds, workplace violence, rumours' (2012, pp. 17–18), Lerbinger explains his preference for three overarching categories of crisis:

- Crises of the physical world, for example, natural disasters such as bush fires and human-made technical disasters such as long-term utility outages.
- Crises of the 'human climate', including criminal actions and political and pressure group disruption. Industrial disputes would come into this category. Lerbinger associates an apparently increasingly difficult 'human climate' with ever-increasing, sometimes unrealistic consumer and individualist expectations.

- Crises attributable to management failure. Corruption is the most spectacular example of management failure, but mundane management incompetence is far more common. Incompetence is manifest in things like failure to meet workplace health and safety and anti-harassment standards, or failure to fulfil prudential requirements (pp. 18–22). Another fit for this category is what Lerbinger (1997) has called the 'smouldering crisis'. This is the 'crisis-in-waiting' caused by toxic employment or managerial culture where some individuals would rather see some of their colleagues, or even the whole organisation exposed as incompetent or fail. These people look forward to revelling in schadenfreude because they feel, perhaps accurately, that their clear-sighted warnings would be ignored, or would get them into trouble with bosses.

Imagining possible crisis events is a useful exercise and you may hit on one which is not in the textbooks but which nevertheless is the type that affects your organisation. However, it is important to understand that, when a crisis occurs, the reality of dealing with it is usually far from a textbook exercise. The writer of this chapter has been involved with PR work following deaths and on another occasion following a wide scale asbestos scare about the health of young children. Nor are financial, redundancy or industrial crises any less harrowing when they jeopardise families' economic well-being. This is why practitioners involved in crisis PR need considerable maturity and sensitivity. Their work may abut that of counsellors and human resources people as much as that of lawyers and executives. Crisis PR should not be thought of as a simple communication exercise.

Crisis risk auditing

One would hope that a PR risk auditor would not find they are compelled to report obvious dangers, instances of clear mismanagement or a possible smouldering crisis. Managers at many levels should already be working with employees and everyone associated with the organisation to guard against accidents, to improve communication, to ensure workplace propriety and to guarantee sound finances. As in a communication audit, a PR crisis risk audit starts from desk research, examining the internal and external factors that might indicate vulnerability. The internal audit focuses on such things as a review of company records and chats with employees. External review includes searches of specialist and general news media (which can also alert the analyst to the types of crises or controversies which have previously affected the industry). What relevant comments have external commentators, academics and professional associations made? Next, armed with this background information, the auditor speaks with departmental managers to determine how those in charge of risk see the situation. What do the chief safety officer, the chief finance officer and the head of human resources say?

The ensuing report should characterise and calibrate the intensity of the sorts of reputational damage which might be caused by the most likely risks if they got out of control. A gradation of the likelihood of risks would help decisions about what training is required, how resources should be allocated and the most suitable design of the crisis response plan. Where possible the audit might facilitate approximate dollar values on different intensities of reputational damage, particularly if it was able to compare examples from the same or other organisations in the past.

Ranking threats

Resources must always be allocated carefully. For this reason, the PR risk auditor's report should conclude with some sort of ranked list, indicating which damaging incidents are more likely and which are less likely to happen, and which damaging incidents would result in the worst and which the least troubling public perception difficulties. These variables, independent of each other, have led modellers to devise crisis graphs where probability of occurrence runs along one axis and potential degree of PR damage runs along the other (Macnamara, 2012; Fink & American Management Association, 1986). An incident with high probability but low damage potential is plotted in a quadrant not warranting much attention or resources for remediation. An incident that is very unlikely to happen, but that could cause major public concern if it did, shows up in the quadrant viewed for moderate attention and resource allocation. Risks located in the quadrant where the most likely incidents intersect with the highest potential relationship damage are flagged as needing the lion's share of attention and preparation. Working with senior managers and relevant industry insiders the crisis auditor brings their expertise and ingenuity to bear to decide where each identified risk should be located on this graph.

The crisis team

An organisation's chief executive is likely to be aware of his or her need to respond to any threat or tragedy, or conversely any fortunate windfall, that affects the thousands of employees, investors, customers, users or others who are affiliated to their organisation. He or she will also be familiar with the need for close legal, financial and human resources advice and in the age of social media, close communication advice. What the CEO *will* need, however, is advice on how these and other personnel and resources can best be organised in the compressed time scale of the crisis situation. How should regular managers work with internal communicators and agency staff who may be retained on contract for this purpose? In a severe and ongoing crisis, these top spokespeople may be advised to make only the most important announcements and responses. It may be best in a long-term crisis if the day-to-day public face of the organisation is a senior communicator, whose full-time role involves providing professional responses to a multitude of inquirers.

Training for crisis communication

All employees should know, or if necessary should be reminded, to contact their line managers immediately should any untoward circumstances occur, although they should of course call emergency services first if necessary. Line managers and security personnel should know how to alert senior executives and these seniors in turn should know to make the communications or PR department aware of serious matters irrespective of the hour. A well-planned crisis communication plan will include an up-to-date duty rota for 24-hour coverage. Once a crisis is apparent or declared senior members of the crisis communication team need to put the plan into action and respond quickly. They must decide whether they should monitor the crisis or make an immediate public comment. At this time the senior communication adviser should present a draft statement and suggestions for other communication actions. Even if the first draft needs correction, discussion of it will focus understanding about what is really going on and what can be said publicly without delay.

This is not a time to train anyone who might have to front TV cameras or produce media for a crisis website. Rather it is the time to take advantage of people's prior planning and training in these matters and suggest what should be communicated. The prior training should also have emphasised the organisational confidentiality which is vital at the time of crisis. Staff guidance on social media use should have already highlighted the potential legal or financial implications of unauthorised or ill-considered disclosure. Training should have made the point that for various reasons, including the privacy of the people affected, employees must refer questions about a tragic situation to the most senior levels of management.

Facilities needed

Mock crisis drills involving the potential main crisis players inside and outside the organisation should be held once or twice a year, depending on the degree of staff turnover, administrative changes and the perceived riskiness of operations. All relevant people should have an online and hard copy summary of how to act in a crisis, with an appendix of contacts. Communication specialists should be familiar with social media and should have an arrangement with a social media monitoring provider; they should also consider the cost, advisability and practicality or otherwise of buying potentially negative domain names such as www.ihatestarbucks.com (Norton, 2013, p. 163). However, some might say that buying up domain names smacks of corporate dirty tricks, which Chris Norton advises against elsewhere (Norton, 2013, p. 163). It is important to be wary of measures to manipulate search engine optimisation (SEO) with the intent of directing searches to the company website that might otherwise have gone to protest or lampooning websites. Instead, organisations should focus on using online facilities in a straightforward way, supplementing their efforts with an emergency website.

Most major progressive organisations already have a lively website with an online newsroom, which can act as the first port of call for crisis information. The website should be designed with SEO in mind, so that it ranks high in any search for that organisation and for the organisation's area of activity and industry. Consideration should be given to paid listing with the main search engine providers. The website may have already cultivated some of the audience which the organisation now urgently wants to reach through the use of blogs and Twitter feeds. There may be a link to a dedicated Facebook page. These social media should regularly carry interesting information and host engaging exchanges to maintain the attention of relevant journalists and other influencers. However, if the crisis develops into something more than the existing e-newsroom and Twitter streams can handle, prominent links to a dedicated emergency website should be posted and made active.

The emergency website is best placed on a '**dark site**' – a separated portion of the main website which has been kept disconnected or 'dark' for just this eventuality. The unseen dark site should be regularly updated with current, accurate background information which any journalist or blogger would want to know in a crisis. This would include brief summaries of the organisation's products and services, its finances, its leaders, its importance to the community or economy, its policies and social responsibility activities. It should prominently list crisis spokespeople and their contact information. Other pages would have spaces and layout where freshly produced crisis information including text, images and videos – perhaps a direct address from the CEO – could be posted and updated quickly. Initial video and text statements answering urgent questions would be made and posted in the immediate period before the website went live. If the crisis is appropriate to be photographed, newsworthy photos and videos made available on the emergency website may help to reduce intrusion by photographers and television crews elsewhere. Iconic, up-to-date pictures of organisational leaders, products or buildings could also be made available to prevent media using out-of-date or stock photography. Digital media publishing experts as well as technicians should be on hand to make sure that the website is constantly updated over the course of the crisis and that it runs smoothly. In an extreme crisis, the sheer volume of traffic is likely to be high and the organisation would need to ensure that the website can cope with the volume without crashing. In crisis communication terms, there is little worse than such a site going down because the organisation had not anticipated interest going viral. If something about the crisis is so shocking, unusual or interesting that it draws a worldwide audience, a low-capacity website may glitch at the precise time when it is absolutely vital to present the organisation's side of what is happening as widely as possible.

Dark site: A separated portion of an organisation's website which has been kept disconnected or dark. The dark site is regularly updated with content but will only be made live in the case of a crisis being declared.

Even in a significant crisis, journalists and independent bloggers will tend to do most of their communication by phone and online, but a corporate headquarters venue in a major city close to where the communication team is working should be made available for news conferences. Here just one or two very well-briefed leaders and experts – maybe the CEO and the police chief, or the CEO and the product specialist – can deliver the whole story or updates concisely and accurately to a range of media all at once. Major city news conferences that are easily accessible to the media may help the restoration of normality at the site of the crisis if the details of the story are easily available elsewhere.

Crisis response

1. Do everything to protect victims of any sort

Coombs writes that the central goals of crisis response are the prevention or minimisation of harm or damage to 'people, reputation, finance or the environment ... The number one priority in damage control is protecting people' (2009, p. 105). It is also about 'maintaining the organisation's operations; and reputation repair'. Coombs's set of priorities reminds us of the mutuality expressed in most PR definitions. The implication is that the primary purpose, the guiding principle, of any PR crisis response should not only be physical and emotional wellbeing but also protection of the legal, livelihood, environmental, financial and other interests of those affected. This priority, though it might have negative implications for an organisation's operations in the short term, may facilitate better reputation repair in the longer term.

2. Cooperate with authorities

Related to the priority of protecting people is the necessity of cooperating with authorities. This can mean cooperating with police in the case of extortion by food adulteration; with the emergency services at a time of natural or major technical disaster; or with legal and financial authorities if the crisis relates to accounting impropriety. If risk to lives, health or people's savings or livelihood are in jeopardy, there must be no reluctance to go to the authorities at the earliest instance despite instinctive feelings that internal disorder might be quietly kept in-house. Industries that are prone to serious danger, such as the petroleum and gas industries, must cooperate closely with emergency services in disaster planning and training.

3. Monitor the crisis

A Google search will reveal a plethora of free and paid for social media monitoring tools as well as a host of reviews about their utility or otherwise. Crisis day is not the day to familiarise oneself with these systems. If nobody in-house is across social media monitoring, there should already have been a good relationship set up with a commercial provider. Proper social media monitoring immediately tells crisis managers who is communicating most about this matter, what they are saying and to whom they are saying it. It is essential that the use of relevant names, including those of the brand, the organisation and its executives, is monitored. The sentiment and volume of messages sent by journalists and bloggers, in particular those using micro-blogging networks such as Twitter, must be watched carefully. A quick response may be needed to counteract an unfair or damaging comment seen to be gaining undue credence through widespread retweeting. Posts from aggrieved individuals, pressure groups, politicians and government departments should also be monitored.

4. Inform internal audiences

The CEO and senior managers do not want to hear bad news about their organisation from strangers before they have been informed or have processed the facts for themselves. And bad news – or, worse, inaccurate news – can spread very quickly via social media. When Malaysia Airways flight MH370 failed to arrive at its destination in March 2014, social media users filled the news vacuum with a range of reports, claiming variously that the plane had arrived safely in Vietnam and that it had made an emergency landing in China. As this crisis unfolded, the Malaysian government was criticised for lack of transparency in both how much it knew about the situation, and how it communicated in real time.

In times of crisis, employees should not be overlooked; they also need timely and accurate information. Maintaining employee morale and trust should be included in the crisis communication plan. Although employees are not part of the crisis communication team, they are front-line ambassadors for the organisation. Loyal people who feel respected will tend to respect organisational privacy when they chat on social media, at the school pickup, or in the pub. When informed people do gossip, they tend to get their facts right and counteract inaccurate rumours. For these reasons, the crisis team should remember to include internal communication when they tweet the address of the crisis website or post other information about the crisis.

5. Be first with the news

The crisis team should release the earliest and the most accurate facts, with the ambition of becoming the candid source of the story at all stages. Now, this may not work in Lerbinger's (2012) 'human climate' division, where people with different political views are never going to agree on the 'facts'. However, this will work in most other instances where people of goodwill take the reins of the organisation in its hour of need. Breaking the bad news yourself, as in the statement 'It was a $200 million deficit, not a $100 million deficit as we first thought', is the best policy. A proactive approach can help scotch a sensational 'exclusive' story and limit the scale and duration of the crisis. Newsbreaking, candidness and a reputation for accuracy will ensure that journalists, bloggers and political staff read the crisis website – these are the influencers the organisation needs to reach. Also, if forearmed with links to a useful, factually reliable website, the crisis team will get less backlash when they comment on relevant Facebook pages and with tweets to key influencers. Public relations people should, however, be wary of getting into online arguments; the mere allegation that you are a 'PR person' may be enough to ignite a social media campaign against you (Norton, 2013, p. 161).

Professional journalists and informed members of your target publics will understand that there are personal privacy and court-related legal constraints on some information disclosure. So do not feel bullied, or in some cases tempted to step over that line. If in doubt, it is wise to get legal or human resources department advice.

6. Consider news conferences

News conferences should only be called if it is important to impart a genuine new turn of events in a personal manner or to expose senior management or experts to detailed questioning which will help journalists and others to get a complex story correct. At a news conference dealing with a very complex situation, there should ideally be only one or two speakers, and certainly no more than three, since the more speakers there are, the greater the risk of contradicting each other. It is vital that each speaker knows his or her role and is totally aware of what the others will say, so that they cannot be played against each other by a hostile journalist aiming to emphasise culpability. Spokespeople must be fully briefed, so that there is no possibility that they will be caught out by a reasonable question that they cannot answer authentically and comprehensively. They must be substantial, unflappable personalities who can deal politely with questions that are irrational or mischievous or that nobody would be able to answer. In a democratic society, journalists are professionals who are the legitimate eyes and ears of millions of people. However irritating their questions, they must be treated politely. The one or two senior spokespeople must also be prepared to record or go live for particular news organisations at studio or other locations.

7. Record queries

Social media monitoring and attention to email, phone calls and hits on the crisis website will reveal who is querying the organisation, what they are asking, how often they ask and whether they appear to be satisfied with responses. Similar records should be kept of people who attend news conferences. These records should show which news organisations and individuals have received what briefing, along with their contact details, enabling the organisation to contact those who are already educated in the situation later on. The records are also useful for post-crisis analysis of the efficacy of the crisis communication operation when, for instance, the sentiment of media outcomes can be compared to what was said at briefings or in online interaction.

Post-crisis

1. Assess PR damage

During the crisis period, some affected publics of the organisation will have made their views and concerns known. They may contact the stricken organisation directly, or their opinions may emerge through social or traditional media coverage. These at times critical expressions will give organisational representatives a vivid picture of those who are (or who feel themselves to be) most involved with, most dependent on, or most aggrieved by what is happening. It is the job of PR professionals to keep these people informed and to do everything to maintain as good a relationship as possible during the course of the crisis. In the post-crisis period, these fleeting contacts, and records of interactions and media reports, can be recalled to help to re-establish good relationships.

2. Devise a recovery program

There is little difference between a post-crisis PR program and a regular program. The main distinctions are that, at the research stage what are likely to be the main problems will be well defined in many people's minds. Careful reflection by the team which handled the crisis as well as scrutiny of media records will tend to uncover target publics' views on salient matters and who the main opinion formers and spokespeople are. Experiences of what worked or did not work during the response period should guide the ways conciliatory, consultative and informative approaches could be designed.

3. Review of crisis response

Careful records of what the organisation said and how it behaved during a crisis can be a valuable resource for future operations. Record keeping during the crisis should not be so onerous that it impedes the efficiency of the response. However, at least one individual in any substantial crisis response team should be designated as the 'historian'. This person will keep a record of salient developments and responses. The record should be developed into a comprehensive report when things get back to normal, the latter part of which should be an analysis which concludes what worked and what could have been done better during the crisis response.

4. Review of crisis preparation

The post-crisis report should also draw from a wider organisational discussion about why the crisis happened in the first place and why it was not prevented by recommendations made in the pre-crisis period, particularly after the crisis audit and development of the crisis communication plan.

5. Possible strategic changes

For a major crisis, it is important that the above described record keeping and review are carried out professionally and with sufficient resources. This is because they may become the basis for strategic changes in the organisation involving its governance and operations. These changes may have implications for personnel.

The overt protection of interests

So far we have been discussing the outlines of procedures. We *have* been imagining a 'mechanics' of how crisis management PR might best be conceptualised as an efficient instrument. This approach is more easily aligned with what we have described as a misreading of Grunig's symmetrical theory of PR, a misreading that imagines that both the organisation and its publics are served equally by the PR project. When we look at more complex approaches to theorising this field, a less benign perspective emerges. This level of crisis management theory revolves about the Latin term ***apologia***, which means something quite different from the English word 'apology'.

Apologia: In the context of crisis communication, an *apologia* is not synonymous with an 'apology'. Rather, it is the corporate response to crisis in an effort to preserve and/or defend the organisation's reputation manifest in both crisis communication and strategy.

The wide field of *apologia* theory

The Oxford Dictionary of Foreign Words and Phrases gives *apologia* as: 'A written defence of one's own or someone else's opinions or conduct' (Speake, 1997, p. 20). Famous 19th-century churchman and later Cardinal John Henry Newman's *Apologia Pro Vita Sua* is attributed with launching this Latin word's contemporary currency (Martin, 1990). Marsh (2006) explains the relevance of *apologia* to crisis communication in this way:

> Ware and Linkugel (1973) define *apologia* as 'the speech of self-defense' (p. 273), and Hearit (1994) adds the caveat that it should not be confused with apology: 'An '*apologia*' is not an apology... but a defence that seeks to present a compelling counter description of organizational actions' (p. 115) ... Aristotle (1991, 1358b) contrasts *apologia* with *kategoria*, an accusation. Traditionally, an *apologia* would not exist without an instigating *kategoria*.
>
> (Marsh, 2006)

Marsh attributes the adoption of this Latin, but originally ancient Greek, concept to an emergence over the last two decades of an interest in rhetorical approaches to theorising PR. Timothy Coombs and his colleagues are among theorists developing what is meant by *apologia* in the PR context. They define corporate *apologia* as 'communicative effort to defend the corporation against reputation/character attacks', and extend their definition to include 'any crisis response strategies designed to protect' an organisation after a crisis, not just 'those communicative strategies found in traditional corporate apologia' (Coombs et al., 2010). Coombs (2009) charts developments in *apologia* studies over recent decades, which we turn to next.

Developments in *apologia* theory

Keith Hearit and Kasie Roberson (2009, pp. 545–55) parse established *apologia* theory into the following six divisions (their subsequent elaborations on this theory are beyond the scope of this present chapter). They list a menu of *apologia* actions from which an organisation may select depending on the circumstances:

- Counterattack/shifting the blame: Show that the cause of the problem lies with another organisation or individual. This may involve allegations that the fault lies elsewhere.
- Differentiation: Frame the crisis as so unusual that no organisation could have anticipated or responded to it in a way many stakeholders might allege it could.
- Transcendence: In the scheme of things the problem is really a minor detail. The bigger picture shows that the organisation is competent and reputable.
- Bolstering: Reminding publics of preceding accolades which the organisation had received before the crisis.
- Victimage: Explaining how the organisation is a scapegoat or is unfairly accused by vested interests, is being picked on by people or organisations with ulterior motives.
- Minimisation/misrepresentation: Show that a not very serious problem has been blown out of proportion and misrepresented as a crisis by opponents or inaccurate media.

Hearit and Roberson suggest that it is only if these denial strategies are found to be ethically or practically inappropriate that strategies of mortification (common apology), corrective action and sometimes compensation predominate in *apologia* activities. These authors make the point that corporations usually avoid out and out mortification under legal advice in case in subsequent proceedings the apology might be taken as an admission of guilt. Lerbinger (2012, p. 63), however, writes that apology in the normal sense is becoming more common and is a powerful and constructive form of conflict resolution in 'a situation of an ethical nature'. One wonders if this is the result of skilful media campaigns by increasingly sophisticated pressure groups and gifted individuals such as Erin Brockovich. Perhaps it is becoming harder for even lawyered-up corporations to ignore or bluff their way out of situations where they are culpable.

Impression management

Following Allen and Caillouet (1994), Coombs (2009, pp. 108–9) refers to a table of impression management strategies, including:

- claiming the unforseen events were accidental or unforeseeable
- saying the cause of the event was elsewhere beyond the organisation's control
- explaining the problem was exaggerated or distorted and not as made out
- arguing those harmed (financially, physically etc.) were responsible for their own difficulties
- blaming another organisation or individual for the situation
- making clear the legal muscle which could be directed towards complainants
- apology in the common sense
- trying to get positive approval from stakeholders irrespective of the crisis.

The last dot point in this schema involves displaying how the organisation is a socially responsible role model which holds values in line with those of stakeholders whose abilities and judgement it applauds.

Image restoration theory

Image restoration strategies are given by Coombs, following Benoit (1995):

- deny there is a crisis
- explain the crisis was caused by another individual or organisation – 'not us'
- restrict information on what caused the crisis
- foreground the accidental nature of the event
- insist the incident came despite the organisation trying to do the right thing
- remind stakeholders of the organisation's positive qualities
- downplay the scale of the crisis; it is insignificant compared to big crises
- it was a blot on an otherwise glowing canvas about the organisation
- challenge the credibility of those who claim that a crisis exists
- offer compensation to victims
- take corrective action; restore the situation; promise it won't happen again
- mortification: admit responsibility, ask forgiveness and express regret.

Situational crisis communication theory including attribution and narrative theory

Coombs associates himself with research using situational crisis communication theory (SCCT). After describing the above theories which are summarised here in dot points he says that SCCT shares many factors with those approaches. The difference appears to be how SCCT takes into account a more nuanced view about how stakeholders see the organisation's culpability:

> The stronger the attribution of organisational control for the crisis (crisis responsibility) the greater the reputational threat caused by the crisis... If crisis managers can lessen the organisation's connection to the crisis and/or have people view the crisis less negatively, the harmful effects of the crisis are reduced.
>
> (Coombs, 2009, p. 110)

Coombs explains that SCCT is based on attribution theory which holds that 'people will assign responsibility for negative, unexpected events' (p. 111). People will be affected by how the crisis appears, by what the history of this sort of event is, and by the prior reputation of the organisations involved. Coombs and colleagues (2010) have used this approach to weigh up emotions, including the anger of those harmed by crisis. They seem to conclude that, compared to the less intricate strategy choices in other *apologia* responses, an SCCT response can enable the crisis manager to more finely tune what they do. SCCT can help managers minimise reputational damage more precisely and more economically. For instance, it might be found that information about what is happening and information about how people can protect themselves from harm is the key factor. Alternatively, an expression of sympathy may be crucial. Do people who have reason to be cynical about the organisation need a more detailed explanation of how recurring problems will be fixed for once and for all? In response, Coombs suggests that crisis response decisions may be impacted by factors such as financial constraints, recognising that apology is 'a very expensive strategy because it opens the door to payments on lawsuits initiated by victims' (Coombs, 2009, p. 113).

Conclusion

The objective of this chapter has been two-fold. On the one hand, this chapter has discussed both the conceptualisation of crisis PR management at the procedural or model level as well as at the more scholarly level. On the other hand, it has provided evidence that a comparison of these two levels has the potential for a contribution to the critique of PR theory per se. The critical suggestion is that the model or procedural approach to conceptualising crisis PR, if considered on its own, may involve presumptions of a benign or neutral proto-profession, along the lines of what we have described as a misreading of Grunig's symmetry model. However, if *apologia* theories are included, a more complex understanding of PR emerges. This is an understanding which must take into account the sometimes desperate struggle by organisations to maintain favourable public opinion. This is a struggle which may involve ethical, legal and economic decisions which the organisation has to take at the highest levels when relationships with publics are brought into vivid relief at the time of crisis. What is usually a quiet and unseen activity (Cutlip, 1994) is called into the front line, where it may participate in or try to restrain even brutal recommendations. The recommendation to make clear 'the legal muscle which could be directed towards complainants' (Allen & Caillouet, 1994) was kinder than the reality, which Coombs (2009) describes as 'Intimidation: try to convey that the organisation is potent and dangerous, may include threats'. This is not to suggest that the largely useful and informative work of PR and other persuasive communication workers is undesirable or unacceptable. Rather, this chapter advocates more attention to scholarly research, which can bring a better critical understanding of the field. Rigorous theoretical debate about PR guards against simplistic assumptions, and enables ethics to come to the fore, which in the long run can only help to justify PR as a profession.

CASE QUESTIONS

1. Conduct an online search of the following crises, and categorise these crises according to Lerbinger's three crisis typologies:
   - Burger King: An employee posted a photograph online of someone standing on two containers of lettuce with the caption: 'This is the lettuce you eat at Burger King.'
   - Commonwealth Bank of Australia (CBA): Rogue financial planners at the CBA have been accused of lying and providing poor financial planning advice to the bank's customers putting profit and commission ahead of best interests of these clients.
   - Telstra Warrnambool Exchange Fire: In November 2012, a fire in Telstra's Warrnambool exchange left the Southwest region of Victoria without access to telecommunication services. More than 60 000 customers were affected, unable to make phone calls or use the internet. The worst-affected customers were without services for up to 20 days.
2. Why are a crisis audit and pre-crisis planning important?
3. Why should employees refrain from communicating with the media in times of organisational crisis?
4. Why might organisations avoid issuing an apology in time of crisis?

BIBLIOGRAPHY

Allen, M., & Caillouet, R. (1994). Legitimate endeavours: Impression management strategies used by an organisation in crisis. *Communication Monographs*, 61, 44–62.

Benoit, W. (1995). *Accounts, excuses and apologies: A theory of image restoration*. Albany, NY: State University of New York.

Burton, B. (2007). *Inside spin: The dark underbelly of the PR industry*. Crows Nest, NSW: Allen & Unwin.

Coombs, T. (2009). Conceptualising crisis communication. In R. Heath & D. O'Hair (eds), *Handbook of risk and crisis communication* (pp. 99–118). New York: Routledge.

Coombs, T., Frandsen, F., Holladay, S. & Johansen, W. (2010). Why a concern for apologia and crisis communication? *Corporate Communications: An International Journal*, 15(4), 337–49.

Cutlip, S. M. (1994). *The unseen power: Public relations, a history*. Hillsdale, NJ: Erlbaum Associates.

Fink, S. & American Management Association (1986). *Crisis management: Planning for the inevitable*. New York, NY: American Management Association.

Grunig, J. (2001). Two-way symmetrical public relations. In R. Heath (ed.), *Handbook of public relations* (pp. 11–30). Thousand Oaks, CA: Sage.

Grunig, J. E., & Hunt, T. (1984). *Managing public relations*. New York: Holt Rinehart and Winston.

Hearit, K., & Roberson, K. (2009). Denial, differentiation, and apology: On the use of apologia in crisis management. In R. Heath & D. O'Hair (eds), *Handbook of risk and crisis communication* (pp. 542–59). New York: Routledge.

Heath, R. L. (2010). *The Sage handbook of public relations* (2nd edn). Los Angeles, CA: Sage.

Henderson, D. (2013). Managing crisis communications in the digital era. Retrieved 5 December, 2013, from www.slideshare.net/newsstrategies/managing-crisis-communications-in-the-digital-era.

Hobsbawm, J. (2006). *Where the truth lies: Trust and morality in PR and journalism*. London: Atlantic.

Korten, D. C. (1995). *When corporations rule the world*. West Hartford, CT: Kumarian Press.

L'Etang, J. & Pieczka, M. (2006). *Public relations: Critical debates and contemporary practice*. Mahwah, NJ: Lawrence Erlbaum Associates.

Lerbinger, O. (1997). *The crisis manager: Facing risk and responsibility*. Mahwah, NJ: Erlbaum.

Lerbinger, O. (2012). *The crisis manager: Facing disasters, conflicts, and failures* (2nd edn). London: Routledge.

Macnamara, J. R. (2012). *Public relations: Theories, practices, critques*. Frenchs Forest, NSW: Pearson Australia.

Marsh, C. (2006). The syllogism of apologia: Rhetorical stasis theory and crisis communication. *Public Relations Review*, 32, 41–46.

Martin, B. (1990). *John Henry Newman: His life and work*. Homebush, NSW: St Paul Publications.

McGrath, C. (2009). *Interest groups and lobbying in the United States and comparative perspectives: Essays in ethics, institutional pluralism, regulation, and management*. Lewiston, NY: Edwin Mellen Press.

McKie, D. & Munshi, D. (2007). *Reconfiguring public relations: Ecology, equity and enterprise*. New York: Routledge.

Moloney, K. (2006). *Rethinking public relations: PR propaganda and democracy* (2nd edn). London; New York: Routledge.

Norton, C. (2013). Online crisis management. In R. Brown & S. Waddington (eds), *Share this too: More social media solutions for PR professionals*. Chichester, UK: John Wiley & Sons.

Public Relations Institute of Australia (2013). About public relations. Retrieved 10 November, 2013, from www.pria.com.au/aboutus/what-is-public-relations.

Speake, J. (1997). *Oxford dictionary of foreign words and phrases*. New York: Oxford University Press.

PART 2

INDUSTRIAL **DISASTERS**

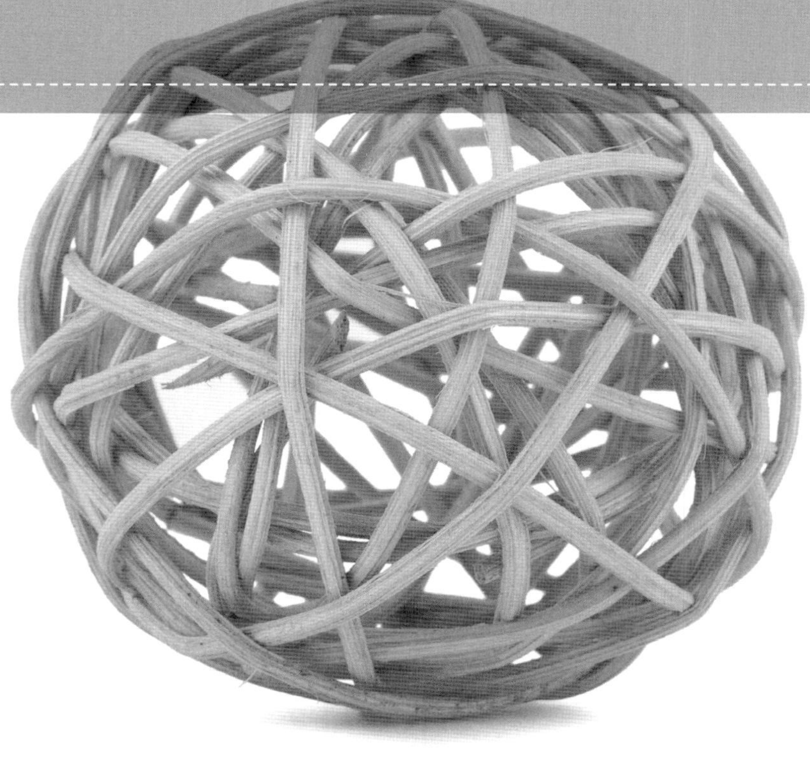

OUTRAGE MANAGEMENT OR CONSENSUS COMMUNICATION

WHAT IS THE BEST WAY OF DOING RISK COMMUNICATION?

Paul Adams

2

Chapter objectives

This chapter aims to:

- consider how the issues–risk–crisis communication cycle is a continuum and how a crisis can become a risk after recovery from a crisis
- look at the importance of different publics in risk communication and the concepts of expert publics, citizen experts and lay publics
- outline Peter Sandman's theories of risk communication, particularly in relation to the idea of outrage management and sharing of power
- investigate the difference between 'sharing power' and genuine negotiation in risk communication
- evaluate the benefits of consensus communication in risk communication over outrage management.

Introduction

Risk needs to be carefully considered because it is often a precursor to crisis: if risks are not effectively negotiated or dealt with, they become crises. This is particularly so with social and environmental risks such as climate change which may rapidly (if they have not already done so) escalate into crises. Sometimes crises can become risks again, as with a natural disaster such as a hurricane and especially if there has previously been a hurricane in the same area. This is also true for man-made disasters such as an explosion at a chemical facility, particularly if the facility subsequently remains close to residential areas and the public perceives that such a disaster could happen again. Risk communication may need to be carried out for many years. In this chapter, we look at risk communication after a major crisis and underline the importance of tailoring risk communication for different publics. We investigate the meaning of the terms 'lay public', 'citizen public' and 'expert public', and we consider Peter Sandman's theories on risk communication. We also look at consensus risk communication with a particular focus on the Coode Island Community Consultative Committee (henceforth CICCC), which was set up following the Coode Island fires and has more or less operated continuously since a large chemical fire engulfed the Terminals Chemical Storage Facility at Coode Island in Melbourne in 1991.

Background

On 21 August 1991, the City of Melbourne witnessed one of the biggest chemical fires in its history. The fire began at the Terminals bulk storage chemical facility, which is located in Melbourne's Docklands and is one of the largest facilities of its type in a metropolitan location in Australia. A huge plume of toxic black smoke spread across Melbourne. Footscray Primary School, less than a kilometre away, was immediately evacuated, as were the crews of five cargo ships berthed at Swanson Dock. The World Trade Centre office complex and the Spencer Street rail yards were evacuated as the smoke spread south and east. The fire lasted for two days and there were fears that city workers and residents might be badly affected by the toxic smoke. After more than 24 hours of fire, 12 of Coode Island's 44 chemical storage tanks had been damaged or destroyed, with about 10 million litres of chemicals burnt and more leaking. The then Kirner Labor Government announced a two-stage inquiry to be headed by former runner and future governor, John Landy, who released his first report that December. It found that Coode Island's storage systems failed international safety standards and that there had been about 400 breaches of regulations after years of poor scrutiny. It also recommended moving the hazardous chemical storage facility to West Point Wilson, near Geelong (Nancarrow 2007). However, a future Liberal Government would fail to honour this pledge and the failure to relocate the facility would mean that the continued perception of 'risk' that another accident might happen again would continue.

This perception of risk has also dogged Terminals' sister facility in Geelong. In 2012 the Geelong Chemical Action Network took legal action against Terminals because of concerns over expansion at the Geelong Facility. The group has also raised concerns about 'the potential for an explosion similar to [the] Coode Island fire in 1991' at Geelong (Fowles, 2012). While Colleen Hartland, the Greens Member for Metropolitan West in the Victorian State Parliament, has also continued to raise criticism about the location of the facility at Docklands in the heart of Melbourne, and the broken promise to relocate the facility and failure to create an adequate buffer zone between the facility and local residences (The Greens, 2014).

Issues, risks and crises have certain lifecycles. The classic issues–risk–crisis continuum is sometimes schematically outlined as follows.

ISSUES ANALYSIS

- Early identification of issues/emerging risks/problems before they become a crisis or risk.
- Scan of environment, research and consultation with potential issue publics.

- Identification of stage in cycle of issue and its progress to a full-blown risk.
- Consideration of what is at stake for the organisation.
- Identification of relevant publics.
- Depending on the issue, making publics aware that issues are likely to become risks.

RISK COMMUNICATION

- Identification of risks, publics and stakeholders.
- Establishment of goals, objectives and tactics.
- Consideration of the perception of the risk among relevant publics and development of strategies for communication.
- Development of a media strategy.
- Development of key messages, checking messages for accuracy, timing for release of messages and identification of channels of communication.
- Research, consultation and negotiation around involvement of 'risk' publics in risk assessment and risk communication processes.

CRISIS COMMUNICATION

- Last resort; what to do when an issue or risk has become a crisis.
- Assessment of potential long-term damage and possible responses.
- Setting of priority publics and channels of communications.
- Timing and immediate responses.
- Spokespeople, media responses messages and objectives.
- Development of strategies for reputation and image restoration.
- Recovery and risk communication once the crisis has ended.

In this formulation, the PR practitioner classically prevents issues from becoming risks by intervening early, scanning the environment and engaging with the relevant 'issue publics'. The practitioner will also carefully consider the life-cycle stage of the 'issue' and the type of intervention required. Following the crisis, there will be careful consideration of whether a crisis will remain a risk.

Risk communication is often defined as 'the interactive process of exchange of information and opinions among individuals, groups, and institutions, concerning a risk or potential risk' which could be to human health, the environment or risk to an organisation's reputation (Lundgren & McMakin, 2013, p. 377). Crisis communication might be thought of as 'risk communication in the face of extreme, sudden danger – an accident at an industrial plant, the impending break in an earthen dam, or the outbreak of a deadly disease' (Lundgren & McMakin, 2013, pp. 4–5). Much risk communication also focuses on the issue of **risk perception** or how to communicate to publics in circumstances where a risk maybe magnified by perception. Risk perception is often defined as an example of how people

Risk perception: an example of how 'people base their judgement of an activity or a technology not only on what they think about it but also on how they feel about it. If their feelings towards an activity are favourable, they are moved towards judging the risks as low and the benefits as high; if the feelings towards it are unfavourable, they tend to judge the opposite – high risk and low benefit.

> base their judgement of an activity or a technology not only on what they think about it but also on how they feel about it. If their feelings towards an activity are favourable, they are moved towards judging the risks as low and the benefits as high; if the feelings toward it are unfavourable, they tend to judge the opposite – high risk and low benefit.
>
> (Slovic 2013, p. 26).

However, also important in risk communication is the idea of different types of publics. Industry and corporations will often use **experts** to justify the risks of a particular hazard or product. Experts may work for government or industry and will have expert knowledge about a particular risk or field of study: doctors will have a good understanding of the threat of disease and chemical engineers an understanding of the threat of a chemical explosion. But expert publics may also form part of the general public and may be importantly influential on other publics and need to be carefully considered in any communication program. **Citizen experts** are publics who because of their commitment or interest in an issue, such as for example nuclear power or pollution issues, have self-educated themselves in order to speak as public experts in a discussion about the risk or debate about a risk. While the term 'lay public' is often used to identify people, including other scientists, who are non-expert in a particular field and therefore may be more likely to magnify the perception of risk beyond what is warranted on the evidence (Burns et al., 2003, p. 184). Care must be taken, however, to ensure that a different point of view about risk is not simply dismissed as risk over-magnification. Public concerns about risks and safety must be taken seriously and their validity accepted if based on sound factual information. Important to the notion of risk communication therefore is also the notion of 'consensus communication': 'Consensus communication is risk communication to inform and encourage groups to work together to reach a decision about how the risk will be managed (prevented or mitigated)' (Lundgren & McMakin, 2013, p.4). This is particularly important when expert points of view or public views may differ from industry and government.

Expert: A person who has expert knowledge about a particular risk or field of study.

Citizen expert: Someone who, because of their commitment or interest in an issue – for example, nuclear power or pollution issues – has self-educated themselves in order to participate in the discussion about the risk or debate.

The Coode Island Community Consultative Committee

Following the accident at Coode Island in 1991, Melbourne City Council, Maribyrnong Council and the chemical storage company Terminals established the Coode Island Community Consultative Committee, which has operated continuously to the present, with the following objectives:

- To maintain a forum of representatives from Terminals, the community and Government agencies, that monitors and responds to emergency, health, safety and the environment issues arising from the operation of the Coode Island facility.

- To promote a process of continuous improvement for Coode Island and encourage the operator to strive for the highest possible safety and environmental standards at all times.
- To provide information to the community about Coode Island, its operation, the hazards and risk it poses, emergency management procedures and any changes proposed to the facility. (CICCC, 2014a)

As well as monitoring health and safety, the aim of CICCC was also explicitly to communicate about the risks and hazards at the facility. Although the role of CICCC is only advisory and the committee is not able to make demands on Terminals to make changes to their operations, CICCC sees its role through discussion to 'encourage the operator' to improve safety at the facility.

The membership of the committee nominally includes:

- seven people nominated by the community
- a Combined Environment Groups representative
- representatives from Terminals Pty Ltd
- a Plastic and Chemicals Industries Association (PACIA) representative
- representatives of Maribyrnong and Melbourne City councils
- a trade union representative appointed by the ACTU
- an independent person appointed by the Cities of Maribyrnong and Melbourne, and subsequently confirmed by the Committee, as the chairperson. (CICCC, 2014a)

Although the CICCC was originally established by the two participating municipal councils, from the perspective of the chemical industry and Terminals the CICCC is also a member advisory committee covered by the Responsible Care program and part of a broader strategy of the chemical industry to develop 'networks and relationships with communities and their stakeholders'. The aim of the Australian Responsible Care Program is to 'improve the health, safety and environmental performance of operations, promoting sound product stewardship practices, and increasing community involvement and awareness of the industry' (PACIA 2011, p.13).

Peter Sandman is a corporate consultant and a well-known champion of the Responsible Care program in the USA, who has worked extensively in the areas of risk and crisis communication. His clients have included the chemical industry, nuclear industry, mining industry and US government and in Australia companies such as Rio Tinto, Western Mining, CSR and the Minerals Council of Australia. Sandman sees the main purpose of 'sharing control' through advisory committees as concerned with outrage reduction. A common problem confronting these committees is one of 'sustaining interest and attendance' (Sandman, 2012, p.40). Additionally, some panel members, having gained knowledge of the industry's challenges, become supporters. The possible problem with this formulation, however, is that not all publics are 'activist publics' and not all activist publics are the same.

Sandman's classic formula of 'risk equals hazard plus outrage' asserts that the real harm of risk is not the 'hazard' itself (i.e. the event or disaster) but the harm caused by the uncontrolled outrage of public, journalists and activists who may exacerbate the perception of risk by spreading unnecessary alarm. Sandman believes that through more effective engagement with these publics, companies can more effectively manage this outrage. Sandman believes that 'People do not listen very much to hazard data when they are experiencing high outrage' (2012, p. 78). Instead Sandman counsels various responses to the problem of risk communication.

• Find ways to ask permission.	Voluntary risks are more easily accepted than non-voluntary risks. Getting 'permission' from the public to have a hazardous facility located next to them maybe more important than proving the facility is technically safe.
• Do not compare risks you are imposing on people with natural risks.	Technological risks such as radiation from a microwave oven may seem more dangerous than sunburn because it is caused naturally.
• Make the risk more familiar: Explain the bad news.	Driving a car may seem less dangerous than travelling on something more unfamiliar like a horse.
• Acknowledge the ways in which the risk is memorable.	If a hazardous facility such as Terminals has previously had a large scale fire, this memory should be acknowledged as it will not go away.
• Legitimate the dread.	HIV and cancer maybe more dreaded than more dangerous illnesses such as high blood pressure but it is important to acknowledge the dread in order to progress risk communication about health issues.
• Take catastrophe more seriously.	Chronic risks such as regularly driving a car maybe less feared than catastrophic fears such as a plane crash but these fears should be acknowledged in effective risk communication.
• Increase the knowability: Remember that neon sign on the roof of the incinerator.	One of the central tenets of the Responsible Care program is 'Right to Know', that is if people are fully informed of all the dangers of a chemical facility, they are less likely to be outraged by it.
• Share the knife.	'Sharing control' with the public through Community Advisory Panels so as to reduce 'outrage' because public feels in 'control'.
• Share the benefits more fairly.	The public is more likely to accept a risk if they get a benefit from it such as a job or other benefit.
• Acknowledge the moral relevance of pollution.	Aim for zero pollution or zero risk as this is more morally defensible in the public mind than some risk even if it is safe.
• Build trust and don't demand too much trust.	Sandman believes that to build trust, you should not request it because if you request trust, you will create mistrust.
• And finally, respond to people openly, apologetically when you have screwed up, courteously even if they are discourteous, with attention to their values and compassion for their concerns (Sandman, 81).	Discourtesy creates 'outrage'.

Communicating risk: Experts and the public

In Sandman's mind, communicating about risk effectively and reducing risk perception or 'outrage' can be achieved by communicating about risk effectively in the way he outlines, and by establishing community advisory panels to monitor risk and involving communities in the discussion about risk: 'so the outrage can escape, not explode' (2012, p. 100).

While these strategies may have limited effects on some **lay publics**, a key problem with Sandman's risk communication, however, is that it does not involve any concession to the idea that publics might have a legitimate factual concern about a 'hazard' or risk. Rather, it is assumed normatively that the industry experts are always correct (i.e. the public is normally wrong about these issues).

Lay public: Publics who are non-expert in a particular field and therefore may be more likely to magnify the perception of risk beyond what is warranted from the technical data.

> I accept that the experts are right more often than they are wrong – or at least that when the experts and the public disagree about a technical issue, such as the size of a particular risk, the experts are more likely to be right . . . It is true that most laypeople know shockingly little about technical topics. It is true that this ignorance often extends to journalists, . . . It is true that environmental activists are in the business of nurturing and mobilizing the public's alarm, and that the media pay more attention to emotional charges of riskiness than to technical claims of safety . . . Ignorance can lead to enthusiasm as easily as to panic.
>
> (Sandman, 2012, pp. 4–5)

It is no doubt true that the public may not always have the technical skills to understand complex technical problems, and that journalists or that environmental activists are often 'outraged', but to assume that these publics are mostly 'wrong' is suggestive of a monolithic view of 'expert knowledge' without differing viewpoints that is always supportive of the corporate view of the world. It relegates, for example, the significant support of many experts for positions held by the environment movement about climate change and a range of other questions as simply 'alarmist' or irrational.

Looking at the 'community' membership of the Coode Island Consultative Committee, we find the substantial presence of experts among the community representatives and the environmental groups' representatives on this committee. Four of the community representatives clearly have strong expertise in the areas relevant to making educated judgements about the risks associated with Terminals Chemical Storage Facility, and the other representative has arguably related expertise.

The minutes of the Consultative Committee for 2013–2014 also show that a broad range of issues has been covered, where the community representatives and environmental representatives have been required to use this expertise. Topics have included:

- technical assessment of Greenhouse gas emissions released from the Terminals facility (CICCC, 2014d)

- discussion of a methodology for calculating safe separation distances between hazardous facilities and sensitive land uses (CICCC, 2014d)
- discussion about a data base, to be commenced to look for trends in leaks, with an independent third party to review inspection reports
- critical discussion about Terminal's maintenance management system (CICCC, 2013).

The topics covered show that the representatives of the committee have substantial factual knowledge of how Terminals works and are able to interrogate the information they receive from the company with expert knowledge. Terminals has shared technical and safety information with this committee, which the committee has expertly interpreted, and the problem of risk over-magnification is small.

As Tesh (1999, p.53) suggests, the issue may not be about the emotional reasoning of the public and risk magnification but the dilemma of what to do when expert knowledge differs. Risk communication guidelines 'define whatever information citizens bring to the table as mere values . . . [But] When citizens' organizations . . . submit to government agencies new information generated by their own consultants . . . The dilemma is what to do when experts disagree.'

In the case of CICCC, 'outrage management' of the community representatives would clearly be patronising and unnecessary. Certainly Terminals has used one of Sandman's principles and shared information with the CICC community representatives and provided a right to know. But risk communication as **consensus communication** has clearly yielded more useful outcomes by encouraging groups and individuals with different expert views to work together to reach a decision about how the risk will be managed. There is disagreement about the continued location of Terminals at Coode Island because most members of CICC 'still support relocation'. However as one community member of the committee has put it 'the vigorous debate of the committee over the years has resulted in numerous improvements to Terminals' Coode Island facility' (CICCC, 2007). There is thus consensus at least that the facility should be as safe as it can be if it is to remain at its current site in the heart of Melbourne.

Consensus communication: Risk communication to inform and encourage groups to work together to reach 'a decision about how the risk will be managed (prevented or mitigated)' (Lundgren & McMakin, 2013, p.4).

CICCC also sees its function as providing risk communication to the broader community by providing it with 'the assurance that there is [a] group of dedicated community representatives actively engaged in ensuring that the community's health, safety and environmental interests and concerns are being addressed at the Terminals facility' (CICCC, 2007) However, a survey conducted by Terminals in 1997, just before CICCC was formed, found that:

> a large percentage of the community (36%) did not know enough about Coode Island to form an opinion about the operational performance of the facility; 61% were also concerned about the Government's decision to allow the facility to stay at Coode Island. They expressed concerns about: the risk of explosions (51%); the facilities proximity to residential areas (31%); air pollution and emissions (26%); the risk of fires (24%); about the facility itself (13%); and transport hazards (2%).
>
> (CICCC, 2014e)

There has been no follow-up survey to see whether these opinions have changed. But legal action and continued comment in the media about the dangers of Coode Island would suggest that the perception of these risks has not abated. One US study of Responsible Care advisory committees found also that advisory committees did not reduce risk perception more broadly, stating that 'only 24% of the public living in the vicinity of chemical facilities . . . [believe] that the industry protects health and safety, and only 22% say that the industry is accessible and willing to talk to the public' (Prakash, 2000, p. 200).

Conclusion

Risk communication is thus an unfolding and pragmatic process that requires social solutions, groups working together to assess risk, continual improvement and further research. Broader forms of risk communication and involvement are required if risk communicators wish to engage publics over a longer period. With the increasing sophistication of publics, risk communicators should also expect that publics will be increasingly savvy about the technical issues and risks that affect them. Long lists of strategies such as those Sandman has developed may have their uses in risk communication situations where the purpose is to reduce alarm, but may be less useful where the purpose is to have a genuine dialogue about what constitutes an acceptable risk. Consensus approaches to risk communication which focus on what can be agreed upon and what can be achieved given different points of view may be of more value, particularly given the greater sophistication of publics involved in risk communication. The majority of CICCC members still want to see Terminals relocated from Coode Island. However, dialogue has at least gained some agreements about making the facility safer and reaching an agreeable level of risk in the short term given these circumstances. More research and work is required by CICC to engage the broader community.

CASE QUESTIONS

1. Can you give an example of a risk that has become a crisis, other than the Coode Island example? What risk communication was used and with which publics? How did those involved prevent a risk becoming a crisis?
2. Thinking of how risk perception can be magnified, can you think of a risk that is overly magnified in the public mind? What risk communication strategies would you put in place to reduce public alarm?
3. Can you think of some public authorities or corporations that have used Sandman's strategies for outrage reduction? What techniques were used? How successful were these techniques with the relevant publics?

4. What are some other examples of risk communication as consensus communication? How was risk communication used to inform and encourage groups to work together to reach a decision about how the risk would be managed, prevented or mitigated?
5. How would you develop a longitudinal risk communication program over a 20-year period? What would be important? Can you think of any examples of such programs?

BIBLIOGRAPHY

Burns, T., O'Connor, D., & Stocklmayer, S. (2003). Science communication: A contemporary definition. *Public Understanding of Science*, 12, 183–202.

Coode Island Community Consultative Committee (CICCC) (2013a). CICCC Meeting Summary, Adopted Minutes, 6 February. Retrieved 15 June 2014 from http://ciccc.org/community.htm#Survey.

Coode Island Community Consultative Committee (2013b). CICCC Meeting Summary, Adopted Minutes, 6 February. Retrieved 15 June 2014 from www.ciccc.org/minutes/AdoptedMinutes_2013_02_06.html.

Coode Island Community Consultative Committee (2014a). About the Committee. Retrieved 14 June 2014 from http://ciccc.org/about.htm.

Coode Island Community Consultative Committee (2014b). About the Committee. Retrieved 14 June 2014 from http://ciccc.org/about.htm.

Coode Island Community Consultative Committee (2014c). CICCC Meeting Summary, 4 February 2014. Retrieved 15 June 2014 from www.ciccc.org/updates/2014/February4.

Downing, M. et al. (2002). Community capacity building. WM02 Conference, 24–28 February, Tucson, AZ.

Fowles, S. (2012). Bitumen go-ahead, *Geelong Advertiser*, 5 January, p. 5.

Lindeman, N. (2013). Subjectivized knowledge and grassroots advocacy: An analysis of an environmental controversy in Northern California. *Journal of Business and Technical Communication*, 27(1), 62–90.

Lloyd-Smith, M. (2008). Information, power and environmental justice in Botany: The role of community information systems. *Journal of Environmental Management*, doi:10.1016/j.jenvman.2008.05.018.

Lundgren, E. & McMakin, R. (2013). *Risk communication: A handbook for communicating environmental, safety, and health risks*. NJ: John Wiley.

Lynn, F. et al. (2000). Chemical industry's community advisory panels: What has been their impact? *Environmental Science & Technology*, 34(10), 1881–6.

Nancarrow, K. (2007). Moments in time – August 1991: The Coode Island fire, *The Age*, 27 July.

Plastic and Chemical Industries Association (PACIA) (2011). Annual Report. Melbourne: PACIA.

Prakash, A. (2000). Responsible care: An assessment. *Business Society*, 39, 183–209.

Sandman, P. (2012). *Responding to community outrage: Strategies for effective risk communication*. American Industrial Hygiene Association.

Slovic, P. (2013). *The feeling of risk: New perspectives on risk perception*. Milton Park, UK: Taylor & Francis.

Tesh, S. (1999). Citizen experts in environmental risk. *Policy Sciences*, 32, 39–58.

The Greens (2014). Coode Island 20 year anniversary. Retrieved 14 June 2014 from http://vicmps.greens.org.au/content/coode-island-20-year-anniversary.

3 CONFRONTING THE REPUTATION RISKS

NEW ZEALAND'S BIGGEST FOOD SAFETY SCARE

Chris Galloway

Chapter objectives

This chapter aims to:

- explain what reputation risks may mean for the PR professional
- show how product recalls can trigger an organisational crisis
- explain how a reputation crisis can spread rapidly – from a company to an industry to a country
- demonstrate the long-lasting nature of crisis damage and the difficulty of rebuilding stakeholder relationships, by examining the case of the world's largest dairy company, Fonterra.

Introduction

Risk management may be defined as organisational effort to manage environmental uncertainty issues and crises for their potential impact on the organisation's goal attainment. When uncertainty and adverse events collide to produce crisis, how well the organisation handles the crisis will impact on its long-term reputation with stakeholders. This chapter examines the 2013 crisis faced by global milk processor and dairy exporter Fonterra. A crisis of consumer confidence and reputation damage quickly ensued following reports that **botulism**-causing bacteria had been found in some of its products during routine food safety tests.

Botulism: Potentially fatal poisoning caused by the presence of micro-organisms, normally in processed food products.

Potential for crisis is ever present for an organisation such as Fonterra. When people think they have reason to worry about food safety, the result can be a crisis of confidence not only in a product but also in its supplier, the industry of which it is a part, and even the country of origin. While companies such as Fonterra seek scientific clarification through routine product testing what they do immediately following adverse test results is important. The timing, as much as their reactions, warnings and apologies, can create havoc among stakeholders. This case study illustrates how quickly a crisis can spread and how the number of stakeholders and critics increase exponentially to fill the uncertainty created by a communication vacuum.

The ripple effect of a crisis

In 2013, 'the biggest food safety scare in New Zealand's history' occurred (Dean, Astin & Nowell, 2013, p. 5). It was not only consumer trust in New Zealand dairy products that wavered because of a potential contamination threat, but also the reputation of Fonterra, the world's largest dairy exporter, was tarnished. Like the ripples in a pond the crisis kept spreading in concentric circles to include the country's dairy sector and New Zealand's reputation itself as a trusted supplier of safe, high-quality food. The outcomes of the crisis were significant and included precautionary **product recalls**, and costly compensation claims. Fonterra was also charged with overlooking 'explosive reputational risk' (Hodder, Trainor & Heida, 2013, p. 6) and has faced questions not only about operational procedures but also about Fonterra's governance and the regulatory oversight of the entire industry.

Product recall: A manufacturer chooses or is instructed to withdraw its product from the market because of inherent defects that can cause harm to the consuming public.

Compensation demands followed an announcement on 3 August that some **whey** (a milk by-product) Fonterra supplied to French food giant Danone and seven other companies could have been contaminated. It was thought that the contamination involved a toxic micro-organism that causes botulism, a rare and sometimes fatal illness. Several countries which had received potentially affected product, especially infant formula, quickly imposed import restrictions and initiated precautionary recalls. Danone demanded 'full compensation' for losses reportedly as high as NZ$326 million from a precautionary product recall and brand damage (Adams, 2013, 3 October). Product recalls are not only prompted by risks, real or perceived, but also carry organisational risk as 'recalls of contaminated food that receive extensive media coverage result in drastic and lasting declines in consumption which in some cases threaten the survival of the companies and sectors concerned' (Gauthier, 2011, p. 270).

Whey: A by-product of the manufacture of cheese used as a supplement in variety of products.

Frustratingly for Fonterra, within weeks the tests which purportedly showed potential risk were proven to have returned 'false positives' (Hodder, Trainor & Heida, 2013, p. 4). There never was any health danger, and Fonterra chief executive Theo Spierings claimed that the chances of a genuine food safety risk had only ever been 'one in millions' (Meadows, 2013). However, a widely held perception of a serious food safety risk, especially to vulnerable infants, had already created significant domestic and international commercial damage before it was known that the bacteria concerned were linked to food spoilage, not botulism (Rutherford, 2013).

Understanding the reputational risk

Corporate, industry and national reputations were very much on the line. Reputation is 'anticipated corporate conduct' based on meeting stakeholder expectations (Helm & Gray, 2009). Although the nation of New Zealand is not a corporation, the idea of 'NZ Inc.' – the country's entrepreneurs and exporters working together in coordinated ways – is widely used in discussion about how New Zealand government agencies and businesspeople should operate. The term connotes not only a united front (Sharples, 2012) but also 'New Zealandness' (DNA, n.d.). Reputation risk – regarded as 'one of the most elusive risks' because it is hard to measure and to understand the ways in which it is formed – is 'any risk that can potentially damage the standing or estimate of an organization in the eyes of third parties' (de Fontnouvelle & Perry, 2005, p. 4). It is influenced by 'negative publicity regarding an institution's business practices, whether true or not' (Board of Governors of the Federal Reserve System, 2004, in de Fontnouvelle & Perry, 2005, p. 4).

Some of the negative reportage about the supposed contamination revisited Fonterra's earlier food contamination crises: one in 2008, via a jointly owned Chinese company, Sanlu, where melamine contamination led to deaths, and another earlier in 2013, arising from traces of the agricultural chemical DCD being found in milk. This history led some commentators to suggest that, in effect, Fonterra was a serial offender. The problems went beyond the company itself. A feature of this crisis was not only the possible health threat from the contaminated product but also the interlinked nature of the reputation risk, drawing in not only Fonterra but also the wider dairy sector and 'New Zealandness' as articulated in the country's strongly promoted 'clean and green' image. It was not possible to ring-fence Fonterra's dilemmas from this reputation 'spill' and its anticipated economic impacts. Tainting of a whole industry by the actions of one company is not unknown: for example, according to Larkin (2003, p. viii) Monsanto's failed efforts to introduce technology for genetically modifying crops to Europe 'wrecked an entire industry as well as its own brand'.

The harm from the botulism scare was particularly felt in China, a NZ$2 billion–a-year market for Fonterra (Fox, 2013b). China imposed import curbs which affected not only New Zealand exporters but also Australian dairy producers (Adams & Theunissen, 2013). The New Zealand dollar fell (Walters, 2013, 5 August) along with the reputation of the country's dairy industry for safe and quality food, which has allowed it to attract premium prices for those perceived attributes. New Zealand exports of infant formula alone are estimated at NZ$1billion a year and growing (Dean, Astin & Nowell, 2013, p. 5). It is accepted that the country's 'prosperity depends heavily on the continued success of the dairy sector' (Deane, 2013, p. 5), which generates nearly a third of all export receipts or about NZ$13.4 billion annually. This is more than the fishing, forestry and mining sectors combined (Deane, 2013) and Fonterra is by far the largest player in its sector.

The Fonterra incident not only put a question mark over the dairy industry's practices but also was seen as undermining the integrity of the long-running '100% Pure New Zealand' branding used to promote both foods and tourism. One British newspaper labelled this promotional claim 'pure manure' (Field, 2013) while the state-owned Chinese news agency described it as a 'festering sore' (Rutherford & Watkins, 2013). Fonterra did not seem fully aware of these intangible threats: a post-crisis independent report commissioned by its board found that the company failed to recognise and respond effectively to 'explosive reputation risk' (Hodder, Trainor & Heida, 2013, p. 6.). As commentators, including government ministers, had their say, there seemed to be a consensus that the company's approach to the crisis fell short; that it was less than might be expected of a company in a special position in its own industry and in New Zealand as a whole. As the crisis developed, there appeared to be a gulf between the company's performance and stakeholders' expectations.

This was significant beyond the company itself because Fonterra is considered a 'poster child' for New Zealand exporting (Key, in Young, 2013, para. 20) with a *de facto* 'national champion' (Hodder, Trainor & Heida, 2013, p. 12) status. As the country's only Fortune 500 company, Fonterra was seen as carrying an exceptional responsibility given 'the significance of New Zealand's global reputation as a leader in food production and food quality' (Hodder, Trainor & Heida, 2013, p. 16). Yet in the wake of the crisis-that-wasn't, there was an identifiable and 'significant sense of concern that Fonterra had damaged New Zealand's interests' (Hodder, Trainor & Heida, 2013, p. 18). One agribusiness academic even suggested that a farmer-owned cooperative structure was not suited to the complex operation Fonterra had become, and proposed it should be broken up (Williams, 2013, 8 August).

Reputation impacts: The ripples in the pond

The crisis, therefore, damaged more than immediate relationships with stakeholders, who included business customers, consumers, regulators, shareholders and both New Zealand and international media. There were also 'serious effects on New Zealand's economy and reputation' (Dean et al., 2013, p. 13). It is the reputation impacts that this chapter explores, as these appear to be under-researched in the literature on food safety crises. In such a crisis, overlaid with lay people's sense of risk, fear and anger, it can be difficult to address the reputation risk issues, given that sales effects can be quantified but it is much harder to measure reputation. As one commentator noted, 'One of the things with infant formula is it's a very emotional sort of thing' (Walters, 2013, 6 August, para. 9). New Zealand's prime minister, John Key, confirmed the importance of the reputational aspect of the crisis. Commenting that he would head to China if required to reassure New Zealand's biggest export market, he said that 'In the end our reputation is everything and if that's what was required, I'd do it' (Rutherford & Watkins, 2013, para. 5).

Of course, many (though not all) crises have to do with real harm. People die, get sick or wounded. The physical environment may suffer, too. Yet a crisis that concerns a threatened harm that never materialises is unusual, even more so when it is scientifically proven that there never was a risk, notwithstanding fears about the anticipated danger. When Fonterra announced on 3 August 2013 that a potentially dangerous bacterium had been found in 38 tonnes of whey supplied to business customers, who then used it in products sold to consumers in several countries, there was an international furore. By 28 August, when overseas testing of the whey in question had proved that there was no risk, substantial reputational damage had been done. Consumers, regulators and mass media both within and outside New Zealand questioned the country's reputation as a safe country of origin for food, initiated product recalls, and in some cases imposed wider bans on Fonterra products. This posed a threat to the whole country, as the finance minister Bill English made clear. He said the public now understood the potential risk Fonterra posed to the wider economy: 'Fonterra's been a very successful entity, on behalf of New Zealand, but I think everyone now understands that when they loom so large in the economy, there's risks to the whole economy when things go wrong' (Rutherford & Watkins, 2013).

Bill English's view was supported by a former deputy prime minister, Wyatt Creech (co-founder of a smaller dairy company and a director of a cheese company), who reportedly said putting the entire dairy industry into the hands of one group was taking a huge risk (NBR, 11 August, a). The faux crisis, therefore, opened up questions extending far beyond the immediate suspected cause. Even though no illness was reported, Greenwood and Elliott's (2009, p. 192) observation is pertinent: where deaths and mass illness result from contaminated food, legitimacy is threatened not only in a legal sense 'but also by creating an opportunity in which wider concerns about business practices or policy can be raised' (Knight & Roper, 2009). Questions are raised about at what point in the 'food chain' problems arose and who was to blame: 'In this sense, crises are about much more than the presence of "objective" circumstances that indicate something may be wrong – they are fundamentally about the "social relations of definition" (Beck, 1992) through which meanings about putative problem conditions arise' (Greenwood & Elliott, 2009, p. 192).

Fonterra's perspective of the crisis

Debate about these social relations of definition was intensified because of Fonterra's scale. In a country that exports more dairy products than any other, no exporter is larger than Fonterra. The company employs 16 000 staff around the world, and its milk suppliers produce 22 million litres a year, 19 million of them in New Zealand. This output is the basis of more than two million dairy-based food ingredients, specialty ingredients and consumer products, exported to 140 countries (Fonterra.com, *Company overview*). The company asserts on its website that the 'world-renowned quality of New Zealand dairy is . . . a key point of differentiation for all Fonterra products, especially given the sensitivity of consumers towards the health and safety of dairy products'. It was this point of difference that was compromised when the company issued a media statement titled 'Fonterra advises of quality issue'. Distributed in the early hours of a Saturday morning, the statement said Fonterra had informed eight of its wholesale customers that whey protein concentrate (known as WPC80) supplied to them could have been contaminated. The concentrate is used as an ingredient in various food products including some produced for babies and infants, such as infant formula. Fonterra said a micro-organism associated with botulism, a highly toxic (Stuff.co.nz, 2013, 3 August) but very rare condition in New Zealand, could be present in the WPC80 and downstream food products. The micro-organism, *Clostridium botulinum*, is so rarely seen that tests would not normally be carried out to determine whether it is present.

Fonterra's announcement led quickly to an international commotion, with damning publicity, product bans on imports and sales in several countries, especially China, and precautionary recalls by manufacturers. As Gauthier notes, 'food safety is ubiquitous in the print media, but coverage tends to cluster around crisis situations . . . without connection to a larger food safety agenda' (2011, p. 271). China was particularly important because in 2012 it took almost a quarter of New Zealand's milk powder, and dairy products accounted for almost 40 per cent of New Zealand's export trade with the People's Republic (J. Gray, 2013). While the media coverage remained intense and occasionally virulent – particularly in China – through much of August, it diminished after it was revealed on 28 August 2013 that the tests thought to have shown the presence of the botulism micro-organism had returned 'false positives' and 'consumers of products containing the relevant batches of WPC80 were never in fact in danger from *C. botulinum*' (Hodder, Trainor & Heida, 2013, p. 4). Meanwhile, both the company and the government launched inquiries. The government even sent officials to Fonterra offices in both New Zealand and Australia (Watkins, 2013) to double-check its claims about the whereabouts of contaminated product (Rutherford, Day & Field, 2013). One customer for the whey concentrate, French food giant Danone, stated it wanted 'full compensation' for damages caused by precautionary product recalls (Adams, 2013, October).

Media reaction to the crisis: The daily progression

This section draws on some of the media coverage of the crisis, treating it in chronological order, to provide a fuller picture of developments and responses to them. Later sections discuss the analysis of the company's handling of events developed by an independent inquiry commissioned by the Fonterra board and the reputation risk dimensions of what became known popularly as the 'botulism botch-up' (Adams, 2013, 20 November, para.1). In Fonterra's initial media release on 3 August, the chief executive, Theo Spierings, affirmed that food safety was its number one priority. Mr Spierings said the company was working closely with New Zealand's regulatory authority, the Ministry for Primary Industries, to keep New Zealand and offshore regulators informed (Fonterra, 2013, 3 August).

The potential issue had first been identified in March 2013 in product manufactured in May 2012 (Rutherford, Colishaw & Kidd, 2013) but gave no immediate cause for alarm, according to Mr Speirings:

> We found the clostridium level was up, but you can't start reacting on that basis because you have no idea what you are seeing. There are 191 strains (of clostridium) of which only a very limited number produce toxic strains. We have to go by the rules of microbiology.
>
> (Smellie, 2013, para. 3)

However, the time taken in the quest for scientific certainty and the associated delays in reporting created the perception that the company was too slow off the mark to communicate to stakeholders, especially infant formula consumers. Fonterra was roundly criticised not only by consumers and competitors but also by senior government ministers, including the prime minister – who said he was 'staggered' (Agence France-Presse, 2013, para. 6) over delays in notification (Smellie, 2013).

A Fonterra spokesperson, Gary Romano, head of New Zealand milk products, attributed the problem to 'a dirty pipe' (Wade & Theunissen, 2013, para. 3) although a professor of food microbiology questioned this explanation, saying that it would be very unusual for a dirty pipe to harbour the botulism organism (NBR, 2013, 5 August). When later his chief executive blamed a lax 'she'll be right attitude' (Adams, 2013, 16 October) and human error for a 'sanitation issue, which should not happen' (Bridgeman, 2013, para. 3), that did not impress the prime minister, who said the role of the company and the [government] regulator was to eliminate or rectify any human error before it became a problem (Young, 2013). The heart of the matter, he suggested, was overseas commodity buyers' continued faith in New Zealand's food safety systems. The trade minister, Tim Groser, described the situation as 'very serious' (Adams & Theunissen, 2013), saying he hoped the country could get away with nothing more than 'a bloody nose' (McBeth, 2013). The prime minister, John Key, said the trade implications were worrying (Manning et al., 2013). Meanwhile, the company initially refused to comment on why it took so long to make its risk issues public. Gary Romano said that Fonterra was doing everything possible to protect human health and that issues of timetables would be given clarity at 'a future date'. In a television interview, he was unable to state clearly which brands of infant formula could be implicated. On 6 August, Mr Romano was asked whether there had been much damage to Fonterra's brand. 'Ultimately the answer to that is yes', he said (Bridgeman, 2013, para. 6). Mr Romano later resigned and two senior managers were placed on leave while the company conducted its own investigation (NBR, 2013, 19 August).

The apology goes wrong

It was not until two days after its early morning disclosure of a potentially serious problem that Fonterra apologised: at a media briefing in Beijing on 5 August, Mr Spierings said, 'We really regret the distress and anxiety which this issue could have caused' (Aljazeera.com, 2013). He blamed the problem on a pipe in a factory in New Zealand that was seldom used, so a normal cleaning was insufficient to sanitise it (Aljazeera.com, 2013). He was not reported as commenting on why, if this were the case, special cleaning measures were not taken. He noted that 'Parents have the right to know that infant nutrition and other dairy products are harmless and safe' (NBR, 2013, 6 August). A further apology followed three days later in New Zealand, where Mr Spierings described as 'unfortunate' the fact that 'some statements were made that were not correct', having been made before the company had all the answers. However, he said, 'if there is a food safety issue, we decide to disclose immediately ... we go out, whether we have all the information or not' (Deane, 2013, para.10).

Once the news of possible contamination broke, overseas markets responded quickly with product bans of varying scope, with Russia imposing a temporary block on all New Zealand dairy product imports despite not being one of the countries which imported the suspect product (Rutherford et al., 2013). Other countries that received potentially affected product included Sri Lanka, Malaysia, Saudi Arabia, Thailand, Vietnam and Australia. New Zealand exporters said the

Fonterra debacle was affecting them all and damaging the country's reputation for food safety around the world (Johnston et al., 2013).

The government eventually allocated NZ$2 million to help smaller dairy companies deal with their flow-on reputation issues. The situation was exacerbated by the fact that it was not the first time that Fonterra had had highly visible problems with food contamination. A senior executive of the Chinese infant formula processing company, Yashili, William Zhao, was reported as saying that 'From a marketing perspective, New Zealand's reputation for its clean environment is seen by Chinese people as being synonymous with good quality, naturally produced food' (Gardner & Leaman, 2013). But against the background of the earlier issues to do with melamine and the discovery of traces of the agrichemical DCD in milk, a counsillor at the Chinese embassy in New Zealand, Zhang Fan, said the company had run out of chances with Chinese consumers. 'Three times and you are out', he said (NBR, 2013, 11 August).

100% Pure? Damaging the national brand

China's state-owned news agency Xinhua reported that

> For a long time, New Zealand has marketed its products overseas as being '100 per cent pure' and this has been especially true of its dairy products. However, Fonterra has had a series of problems, and this is beginning to shake the confidence of some Chinese consumers in its '100 per cent pure' milk powder'.
>
> (Dougan, 2013, para. 8)

In an editorial, Xinhua criticised Fonterra's failure to tell the public and authorities sooner (Watkins & Fox, 2013). It commented that 'New Zealand's quality-control problems were no longer looking like one-offs, but systemic' (Watkins, 2013).

Although the ANZ Bank expressed the view that the product bans would eventually be lifted, it argued that 'of greater import to New Zealand is the question of how much lasting damage has been done to our reputation for clean, safe food, and our trustworthiness when it comes to revealing issues promptly. Trust needs to be rebuilt' (Gray, J., 2013, para. 20).

The bank's chief economist, Cameron Bagrie, noted that while 'the reputational hit' was hard to quantify, three quality issues in five years were 'not pretty'. He noted that when it came to infant formula, there was 'zero tolerance of food safety scares' (Fallow, 2013, para. 7). Fonterra's communications had also come under fire from exporters, who claimed poor performance in this area was further damaging New Zealand's reputation (Johnston et al., 2013). The company blamed 'procedural issues' for communication delays (Manning et al., 2013, 5 August). Fonterra did later apologise for creating 'unnecessary confusion' over which products were affected but did not say why it took so long to tell the public (or the NZX stock exchange) about the potential health risk (Read et al., 2013). Ironically, the crisis broke the day after a new corporate communications director, Kerry Underhill, started in his job and in the midst of moves by the company to take more direct control of its communications strategy, having used a PR consultancy to both supply seconded staff to work inside the company and to handle implementation outside it (Drinnan, 2013).

In the end it was a false alarm . . .

On 28 August, the alarm was shown to be false when the Ministry for Primary Industries announced that 195 tests in the United States and New Zealand showed the bacteria found in the Fonterra whey concentrate were not capable of producing botulism-causing toxins. The testing used the original samples analysed by state-owned AgResearch, after which the precautionary recalls had been issued. On 29 August, Theo Spierings said that he was 'not there to judge the mistakes of others', but that Fonterra had questions about the false positive (Rutherford, 2013) A few days later, AgResearch distributed a news release denying that it confirmed the presence of botulism-causing bacteria in the material Fonterra gave it to test. AgResearch said it had 'reported that the research had potentially detected *C. botulinum* and recommended that further testing be conducted'. It had reviewed its own tests 'and remains confident in the work its experts carried out and reported to Fonterra' (AgResearch, 2013).

While farmer spokespersons welcomed the outcome of the new laboratory processes, questions remained not only about the safety of New Zealand dairy products but also about the regulatory framework governing their production and export. Early in the crisis, China's Xinhua news agency had commented that

> While it's true the government isn't responsible for the contamination of Fonterra produce, it should be held accountable for the fact that nothing was done to identify the problem before it was dispatched to export markets and domestic customers.
>
> (Hosking, 2013)

A subsequent government report on New Zealand's dairy food safety regulatory system found that the Fonterra incident was not due to a failure of the system, which is 'considered among the best in the world', but it also found that improvements were possible (Dean et al., 2013, p. 5).

Understanding and interpreting the crisis

There are some lessons to be learned and implications to be considered from what has been called the 'botulism botch-up'. One commentator (B. Gray, 2013, paras 4–5) reports a study which showed that

> Imported milk brands that were perceived to have close business relationships [as Fonterra did, via a jointly owned company] to the guilty domestic brand implicated in the Chinese melamine scandal in 2008 were more likely to be considered by consumers to be guilty by association than more distant

> brands. If one extrapolates this finding to a wider country context, then guilt by association could influence overseas consumers' perceptions of New Zealand's clean and green image...
>
> If the situation stabilises, the threat is neutralised and the guilty firm appears to take corrective action, then consumers might forgive a transgression and resume buying the affected brand. This implies that the severe dent to New Zealand's clean-and-green image might also recover, but is likely to take a long time.

The financial cost for Fonterra remains high, while the reputational damage to the dairy sector and to New Zealand's standing as a safe country of origin for foods is much harder to assess. At a media briefing on the company's annual results, Mr Spierings said a NZ$14 million loss provision had been made for the botulism scare. He commented that 'No contingent liability can be reliably quantified in regards to potential market access, customer claims or reputational consequences' (Williams, 2013, 25 September, para. 4). Mr Spierings also disclosed that Fonterra was working with the American consulting firm McKinsey to develop a strategy for rebuilding the company's reputation.

A key reputation issue was perceived delays in communicating to stakeholders. Media commentators slammed the delays, with especially acerbic comments being published in New Zealand on 5 and 6 August. Referring to the fact that Fonterra had been criticised for communication delays in two earlier food contamination scares, Fox (2013a) commented that

> being kept in the dark too long for a third time on a food safety issue is simply not good enough. Nor is it acceptable to refuse to answer – or take days to respond to – basic questions.

The chief administration officer of the New Zealand Infant Formula Manufacturers Association, Chris Coleridge, said 'there wasn't full and frank disclosure of the full facts at the earliest possible time so parents could make a decision what to do regarding the safety of their infant' (Manning et al., 2013, para. 36). Corporate communication experts were reported as describing the company's communications team as clumsy and its communications to government, customers and consumers as ham-fisted (Bond, 2013) despite reports the company was spending more than NZ$5 million a year on PR (NBR 2013, 29 November).

In science we trust . . . too much?

An important issue was that of the science involved in first indicating the potential existence of a problem and then in proving one did not, in fact, exist. Theo Spierings said that when the company found possible contamination there was nothing it could do but order more tests as one has to go by the rules of microbiology. However, media commentator Matthew Hooton noted that in a scientific sense, Fonterra was right. In the food business – especially dairy, given milk's high levels of bacteria, safety scares happen and they happen often (Hooton, 2013).

In a contrasting (and early) view, *National Business Review* editor Neil Gibson (2013) said it was 'far from proven' that Fonterra's pursuit of science, as opposed to a media and political strategy, was at fault. Nevertheless, despite Fonterra's declared commitments to food quality and consumer safety, its reputation took a serious hit, one not alleviated by the detail of scientific testing. Rather, consumers simply wanted to know what formula they could safely feed their infants and when the company initially could not tell them because of difficulty tracing the potentially affected product, they became outraged.

Reputation: The ultimate loser in crisis

According to Helm & Gary (2009), perceived corporate reputation may be defined as anticipated corporate conduct. On this basis, 'meeting divergent stakeholder expectations is crucial to gaining a favourable corporate reputation' (p. 67). They note that stakeholders' perceptions of the *motivations* behind companies' CSR, product/service, communication and other reputation-building activities, are likely to be as important influences as the tangible and intangible *outputs* (i.e. economic and social benefits) that organisations produce. In this case, the company's motivations were somewhat problematic, according to the independent inquiry, which identified 'a perception . . . of self-centredness – that Fonterra is focussed on its own immediate interests and insufficiently concerned with the interests of, or relationships with, others' (Hodder, Trainor & Heida, 2013, p. 8).

This perceived neglect called for 'serious remedial attention', the inquiry team found. To this degree, Fonterra's reputation was tarnished because there was a gap between stakeholder expectations, as articulated in media reports, and the company's past and prospective performance. The taint did not appear to be mitigated significantly by apologies in China and New Zealand, nor did it shield the company from intensified regulatory scrutiny. Greenberg and Elliott (2009, p. 191) argue that corporate apology can not only protect a company's identity and help repair damaged trust relations but it can also 'serve a strategic role of helping to mitigate the potential for political intervention'. However, given the wider significance of Fonterra's role in New Zealand's economy, even though Fonterra issued apologies, averting political intervention was not feasible.

The stakeholder view

Greenberg and Elliott (2009, p. 192) note that crises are important to the extent that their harmfulness can be translated into grievances which operate rhetorically as claims on an organisation's actions, resources or plans that may impinge upon and interfere with organisational autonomy, although

> The potential for grievances to encroach upon corporate decision-making tends to vary . . . depending on the relative strength and clout of different stakeholders. In most cases, the grievances of top investors will exercise greater influence than those of ordinary consumers, although

> consumer concerns can intensify to such a point that they become consonant with the concerns of the more powerful stakeholders.

This is what appeared to occur in the Fonterra case: both consumers and powerful stakeholders such as the government formed a consensus that Fonterra's approach fell short of their normative expectations. Lehmann (1985, cited in Greenberg and Elliott, 2009) distinguishes between cognitive and normative expectations. Cognitive expectations are based upon scientific reasoning, 'in which expectations can be legitimately changed or dropped if the reality turns out to be different than what was initially anticipated. Such thinking is more about finding solutions and improving performance than finding fault (Knight & Roper, 2009, in Greenwood & Elliott, 2009, p. 193). On the other hand, 'when we say that harms disrupt or contravene expectations, we are talking not in cognitive but normative terms, because harms are assumed to be illegitimate...' (Knight & Roper, 2009, in Greenwood & Elliott, 2009, p. 193). In the case of infant formula, consumer stakeholders expected zero risk, just as the New Zealand prime minister expected zero tolerance for human error in regulatory and production systems – although zero risk does not exist (FAO, 1998).

Conclusion

Corporations deal with their own harm-doing by putting 'the spin' on action and generating 'accounts' which 'explain an offense to an audience by justifying it, excusing it, refusing to accept responsibility for it, or conceding to having committed it' (Folkes & Whang, 2003, in Greenwood & Elliott, 2009, p. 196). Fonterra's account of what had happened initially lacked clarity, consistency and arguably credibility; nor did it contain an apology. As the independent report to the board noted, 'The persistent adjustments to the estimates of affected product were corrosive of credibility with Ministers and officials' (Hodder, Trainor & Heida, 2013, p. 8).

In a devastating critique, the inquiry commented that

> In the first few days after the WPC80 issue became public, Fonterra did not seem to make it clear the recall was precautionary, it did not say sorry, and it was inconsistent in its tone – sometimes quite alarming, at other times seeking to minimise ... There is a significant body of ... knowledge on how to promote strong relationships and communicate during usual times, and in times of risk and crisis, so as to maximise trust and credibility. Fonterra's communications style and substance did not consistently demonstrate the characteristics of that knowledge.
>
> (Hodder, Trainor & Heida, 2013, p. 23).

The inquiry recommended that Fonterra's crisis management arrangements be revised to be 'best in class' 'recognising that FQS [food quality safety] reputational risks are likely to affect every market in which Fonterra has a presence (and differently)' (Hodder, Trainor & Heida, 2013, p. 10). Risk management protocols should emphasise early escalation to senior management of potential reputational risks, especially those related to food quality and safety, the inquiry said. Of the inquiry's 33 recommendations to the board, 18 related to crisis management and crisis communication, corporate communication, government relations and stakeholder relations and engagement (Hodder, Trainor & Heida, 2013, pp. 10–11). The inquiry team suggested the company should 'develop a communications style and approach which better reflect Fonterra's values and aspirations as well as best practice risk communications to enhance trust in Fonterra' (Hodder, Trainor & Heida, 2013, p. 11). The board, it said, should recognise 'the paramount importance of Fonterra's reputation, and the need to achieve and sustain a reputation second to none for the quality and safety of its food ingredients and products' (Hodder, Trainor & Heida, 2013, p. 12). The inquiry identified that

> In circumstances involving global reputational risk, and notwithstanding the high calibre of its people and most of what it does, Fonterra fell short of the expectations of excellence associated with a leading global nutritional products company.
>
> (Hodder, Trainor & Heida, 2013, p. 21)

The Fonterra case illustrates how negative reputation 'spill' can spread fast and internationally, with costly consequences. It shows how even a high-performing global company can be caught by reputation risks – inherently to do with potential harm – which become actual commercial damage. 'Predictable surprises' (Bazerman & Watkins, 2008) such as this one may be productive in the long run if the company, and the government, respond effectively to the various post-crisis recommendations of the inquiries they commissioned. However, as Gray (2013) has suggested, it may be a long time before the reputation ripples subside.

CASE QUESTIONS

1. What is meant by the definition of reputation as 'anticipated corporate conduct' based on meeting stakeholder expectations (Helm & Gray, 2009)?
2. Why is reputation difficult to measure?
3. Risk management is generally discussed in the context of a single organisation. Why was the crisis and damage to Fonterra's reputation a matter of national interest and allied to New Zealand's reputation?
4. Although Fonterra's initial testing identified the presence of potentially dangerous bacteria which produce the botulism toxin, subsequent testing in overseas laboratories found there was no contamination and therefore no risk. Review the case and list the reasons attributed to Fonterra for their failure to manage the crisis. What could they have done differently?

BIBLIOGRAPHY

Adams, C. (2013, 7 August). Fonterra on notice in China. *New Zealand Herald*. Retrieved from www.nzherald.co.nz/business/news/article.cfm?c_id=3&objectid=10909114.

Adams, C. (2013, 3 October). Danone seeks full compensation from Fonterra. *New Zealand Herald*. Retrieved from www.nzherald.co.nz/business/news/article.cfm?c_id=3&objectid=11134155.

Adams, C. (2013, 16 October). Spierings blames 'she'll be right' attitude for Fonterra botulism scare. *New Zealand Herald*. Retrieved from www.nzherald.co.nz/business/news/article.cfm?c_id=3&objectid=11141061.

Adams, C. (2013, 20 November), Nutricia: Botulism botch-up may cost jobs. *New Zealand Herald*. Retrieved from www.nzherald.co.nz/business/news/article.cfm?c_id=3&objectid=11160239.

Adams, C. & Theunissen, M. (2013). Botulism scare big news in China. *New Zealand Herald*, 4 August. Retrieved from www.nzherald.co.nz/nz/news/article.cfm?c_id=1&objectid=10908095.

Agence France-Presse (2013, 5 August). New Zealand PM accuses milk scare firm of 'staggering' delay. Inquirer. Retrieved from http://newsinfo.inquirer.net/458983/new-zealand-pm-accuses-milk-scare-firm-of-staggering-delay.

AgResearch (2013, 5 September). AgResearch statement regarding Clostridium botulinum research undertaken for Fonterra. AgResearch website. Retrieved from www.agresearch.co.nz/news/pages/news-item.aspx?News-id=13-09-05-1.

Aljazeera.com (2013, 5 August). Fonterra apologises for tainted milk scare. Retrieved from www.aljazeera.com/news/asia-pacific/2013/08/20138585941904184.html.

Bazerman, M. H. & Watkins, M. D. (2008). *Predictable surprises: The disasters you should have seen coming and how to prevent them*. Boston: Harvard Business School Press.

Bond, G. (2013, 7 August). Fonterra crisis: What the PR experts say about bungled response. *National Business Review*. Retrieved from www.nbr.co.nz/article/fonterra-crisis-what-pr-experts-say-about-bungled-response-gb-p-143973.

Bridgeman, D. (2013, 6 August). 'Human errors in life happen': Fonterra. *National Business Review*. Retrieved from www.nbr.co.nz/article/human-errors-life-happen-fonterra-db-p-143891.

de Fontnouvelle, P. & Perry, J. (2005). Measuring reputational risk: The market reaction to operational loss announcements. Working Paper, Federal Reserve Bank of Boston.

Dean, M. R., Astin, A. & Nowell, T. (2013, 3 December). Report on New Zealand's dairy food safety regulatory system: Government inquiry into the whey protein concentrate contamination incident. Wellington: Department of Internal Affairs. Retrieved 4 December 2013 from www.dia.govt.nz/Government-Inquiry-into-Whey-Protein-Concentrate-Contamination-Incident.

Deane, S. (2013, 8 August). Fonterra head says 'Sorry, NZ'. *New Zealand Herald*. Retrieved from www.nzherald.co.nz/business/news/article.cfm?c_id=3&objectid=10909661.

DNA (n.d.). Case study: NZ Inc branding for export success. www.idealog.co.nz. Retrieved from www.idealog.co.nz/businessplan/creating-the-perfect-storm.

Dougan, P. (2013, 5 August). Fonterra milk scare: Global reaction. *New Zealand Herald*. Retrieved from www.nzherald.co.nz/nz/news/article.cfm?c_id=1&objectid=10908530.

Drinnan, J. (2013, 7 August). Crisis hits in midst of PR shakeup. *New Zealand Herald*. Retrieved from www.nzherald.co.nz/business/news/article.cfm?c_id=3&objectid=10909109.

Fallow, B. (2013, 6 August). Economic fallout awaited. *New Zealand Herald*. Retrieved from www.nzherald.co.nz/business/news/article.cfm?c_id=3&objectid=10908610.

FAO (Food and Agriculture Organization) of the United Nations (1998). Food Quality and Safety Systems – A Training Manual on Food Hygiene and the Hazard Analysis and Critical Control Point (HACCP) System. Retrieved from www.fao.org/docrep/w8088e/w8088e07.htm.

Field, M. (2013, 9 August). NZ's 100% Pure claim rubbished by UK press. Stuff.co.nz. Retrieved from www.stuff.co.nz/environment/9023731/NZs-100-Pure-claim-rubbished-by-UK-press.

Fonterra (2013, 3 August). Media release: Fonterra advises of quality issue. Retrieved from www.fonterra.com/global/en/hub±sites/news±and±media/media±releases/media±release±-±fonterra±advises±of±quality±issue/media±release±-±fonterra±advises±of±quality±issue.

Fox, A. (2013, 6 August a). Is dairy giant too big for its gumboots? Stuff.co.nz. Retrieved from www.stuff.co.nz/waikato-times/business/9005163/Is-dairy-giant-too-big-for-its-gumboots.

Fox, A. (2013, 6 August b). Export hit from botulism scare eases. Stuff.co.nz. Retrieved from www.stuff.co.nz/business/farming/9005003/Export-hit-from-botulism-scare-eases.

Gardner, C. & Leaman, A. (2013, 5 August). Parents' anger over dairy scare. Stuff.co.nz. Retrieved from www.stuff.co.nz/business/farming/dairy/9001720/Parents-anger-over-dairy-scare.

Gauthier, E. (2011). Foodborne microbial risks in the press: The framing of listeriosis in Canadian newspapers. *Public Understanding of Science*, *20*(2), 270–86.

Gibson, N. (2013, 8 August). Editor's insight: When science falls victim to 'food scares' – Fonterra Affair. *National Business Review*. Retrieved from www.nbr.co.nz/opinion/editors-insight-when-science-falls-victim-food-scares.

Gray, B. (2013, 9 August). Fonterra crisis dents NZs '100% Pure' image. The Conversation. Retrieved from http://theconversation.com/fonterra-crisis-dents-nzs-100-pure-image-16845.

Gray, J. (2013, 5 August). Milk scare: Fonterra fund shares plunge. *New Zealand Herald*. Retrieved from www.nzherald.co.nz/business/news/article.cfm?c_id=3&objectid=10908410.

Greenberg, J. & Elliott, C. (2009). A cold cut crisis: Listeriosis, Maple Leaf Foods, and the politics of apology. *Canadian Journal of Communication*, 34(2), 189–204.

Helm, S. & Gray, B. (2009). Corporate reputation as anticipated corporate conduct: Introduction to the AMJ special issue (Editorial). Australasian Marketing Journal, *17*.

Hodder, J., Trainor, G. & Heida, J. (2013, 23 October). Report of WPC80 Independent Inquiry for Fonterra Board. Auckland: Fonterra. Retrieved 24 October 2013 from http://wpc80-inde-report.fonterra.com/executive-summary.

Hooton, M. (2013, 9 August). Fonterra inquiry must include company culture. *National Business Review*. Retrieved from www.nbr.co.nz/article/fonterra-inquiry-must-include-company-culture-ck-144184.

Hosking, R. (2013, 8 August). Damaging downside as Chinese hammer clean green NZ. *National Business Review*. Retrieved from www.nbr.co.nz/article/chinese-reaction-could-yet-be-highly-damaging-rh-p-143935.

Johnston, K., Rutherford, H., Cowlishaw, S. & Leaman, A. (2013, 4 August). Fonterra boss reassures over botulism scare. Stuff.co.nz. Retrieved from www.stuff.co.nz/business/farming/dairy/9000131/Fonterra-boss-reassures-over-botulism-scare.

Larkin, J. (2003). *Strategic reputation risk management*. Basingstoke, UK: Palgrave Macmillan.

Manning, B., Trevett, C., Adams, C. & Wade, A. (2013, 5 August). Milk scare angers parents. *New Zealand Herald*. Retrieved from www.nzherald.co.nz/nz/news/article.cfm?c_id=1&objectid=10908265.

Meadows, R. (2013, 8 August). Botulism risk was only ever 'one in millions'. *Stuff.co.nz*. Retrieved from www.stuff.co.nz/business/farming/dairy/9015228/Botulism-risk-was-only-ever-one-in-millions.

McBeth, P. (2013, 5 August). Fonterra to come under microscope once dust settles in food scare, Key says. *National Business Review*. Retrieved from www.nbr.co.nz/article/fonterra-come-under-microscope-once-dust-settles-food-scare-key-says-bd-143886.

National Business Review (NBR) (2013, 5 August). Fonterra's 'dirty pipe' story sounds wrong: Massey prof. *National Business Review*. Retrieved from www.nbr.co.nz/article/aut-prof-outlines-real-and-justified-botulism-concern-ck-143872.

National Business Review (NBR) (2013, 6 August). Spierings 'regrets stress and anxiety' caused by whey contamination. *National Business Review*. Retrieved from www.nbr.co.nz/article/fonterras-spierings-%E2%80%98regrets-stress-and-anxiety-caused-whey-contamination-bd-143882.

National Business Review (NBR) (2013, 11 August a). Fonterra too big for its gumboots: Ex National minister. *National Business Review*. Retrieved from www.nbr.co.nz/article/fonterra-too-big-its-gumboots-ex-national-minister-ck-144211.

National Business Review (NBR) (2013, 11 August b). Fonterra has run out of chances: China diplomat. *National Business Review*. Retrieved from www.nbr.co.nz/article/fonterra-has-run-out-chances-chinese-diplomat-ck-144209.

National Business Review (NBR) (2013, 16 August). Senior Fonterra managers 'placed on leave'. National Business Review. Retrieved from www.nbr.co.nz/article/senior-fonterra-managers-placed-leave-dw-144534.

National Business Review (NBR) (2013, 29 November). Fonterra's $5m PR spend, homeowners 'underinsured', strong economy might boost equities and Foss plays Colombo. *National Business Review*. Retrieved from www.nbr.co.nz/article/fonterras-5m-pr-spend-homeowners-underinsured-strong-economy-paper-pointerc.

New Zealand Herald (2013, 6 August). Editorial: Reassurance on milk purity vital for NZ to get right. *New Zealand Herald*. Retrieved from www.nzherald.co.nz/business/news/article.cfm?c_id=3&objectid=10908628.

Radio New Zealand News (2013, 9 December, 3.15 p.m.). Fonterra hopes Danone will seek a commercial solution to its compensation claim. Retrieved from www.radionz.co.nz/news/rural/230279/fonterra-hopes-danone-will-seek-a-commercial-solution-to-its-compensation-claim.

Read, E., Rutherford, H., Watkins, T. & Small, V. (2013, 7 August). Fonterra to face multiple inquiries. Stuff.co.nz. Retrieved from www.stuff.co.nz/waikato-times/business/9010145/Fonterra-to-face-multiple-inquiries.

Rutherford, H. (2013, 29 August). Fonterra had problems before false alarm. Stuff.co.nz. Retrieved from www.stuff.co.nz/national/politics/9103094/Fonterra-had-problems-before-false-alarm.

Rutherford, H., Colishaw, S., & Kidd, R. (2013, 5 August). Threat to dairy exports widens. Stuff.co.nz. Retrieved from www.stuff.co.nz/southland-times/business/9002631/Threat-to-dairy-exports-widens.

Rutherford, H., Day, S. & Field, M. (2013, 6 August). Fonterra systems get full scrutiny. Stuff.co.nz. Retrieved from www.stuff.co.nz/business/farming/9005126/Fonterra-systems-get-full-scrutiny.

Rutherford, H. & Watkins, T. (2013, 6 August). Economy safe from Fonterra fallout: English. Retrieved from www.stuff.co.nz/waikato-times/news/9007826/Economy-safe-from-Fonterra-fallout-English.

Sharples, P. (2012, 16 February). Māori contribution to NZ Inc. Retrieved from www.beehive.govt.nz/speech/%E2%80%9Cm%C4%81ori-contribution-nz-inc%E2%80%9D.

Smellie, P. (2013, 5 August). Fonterra could not have given formula warnings in March, says Spierings. *National Business Review*. Retrieved from www.nbr.co.nz/article/fonterra-could-not-have-given-formula-warnings-march-says-spierings-ck-143890.

Stuff.co.nz (2013, 3 August). Botulism: What you need to know. Retrieved from www.stuff.co.nz/national/8999213/Botulism-What-you-need-to-know.

Stuff.co.nz (2013, 5 August). Scope of dairy contamination unclear. Retrieved from www.stuff.co.nz/business/farming/dairy/9001765/Scope–of-dairy-contamination-unclear.

Wade, A., & Theunissen, M. (2013, 3 August). Fonterra botulism scare caused by dirty pipe. New Zealand Herald. Retrieved from www.nzherald.co.nz/business/news/article.cfm?c_id=3&objectid=10907604.

Walters, L. (2013, 5 August). Fonterra storm hits kiwi dollar. Stuff.co.nz. Retrieved from www.stuff.co.nz/business/industries/9002722/Fonterra-storm-hits-kiwi-dollar.

Walters, L. (2013, 6 August). Firms could sue for brand damage. Stuff.co.nz. www.stuff.co.nz/business/farming/dairy/9008014/Firms-could-sue-for-brand-damage.

Watkins, T. (2013, 6 August). Local and global frustration at Fonterra. Stuff.co.nz. Retrieved from www.stuff.co.nz/waikato-times/business/9006519/Local-and-global-frustration-at-Fonterra.

Williams, D. (2013, 8 August). It's time to break up Fonterra, academic says. *National Business Review*. Retrieved from www.nbr.co.nz/article/its-time-break-fonterra-academic-says-dw-p-144068.

Williams, D. (2013, 25 September). Fonterra sets aside millions for botulism scare. *National Business Review*. Retrieved from www.nbr.co.nz/article/fonterra-sets-aside-millions-botulism-scare-dw-p-146312.

Young, A. (2013, 12 August). Govt eyes new Fonterra inquiry. *New Zealand Herald*. Retrieved from www.nzherald.co.nz/business/news/article.cfm?c_id=3&objectid=10911220.

PART 3

CORPORATE **CRISIS**

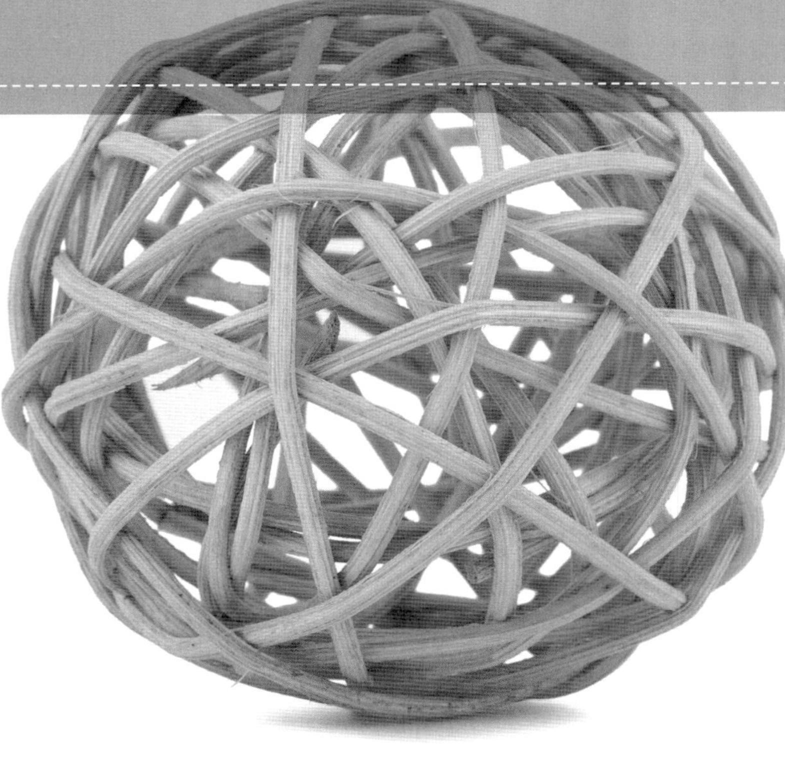

4

CRISIS COMMUNICATION

WHEN SORRY IS THE HARDEST WORD IN ELITE SPORT

Hamish McLean and Maria Hopwood

Chapter objectives

This chapter aims to:

- explore how and why social media builds relationships between elite athletes and their fans
- examine how sport fans reacted on social media to confessions of wrongdoing by an elite athlete following long periods of denial
- consider the benefits and risks of traditional or social media platforms to control the confession message and safe-guard reputational image
- examine the role of social media during a high profile fall from grace by a world-renowned elite athlete
- consider the implications in terms of sports crisis communication management.

Introduction

Fans: People who have a strong interest in or admiration for a particular sport, team or athlete. Fan is the abbreviation of the word 'fanatic' which is used to refer to people who display an obsessive interest and enthusiasm in something.

Social media platforms breathe life into crises (McLean, 2014), and the world of the elite athletes, who often enjoy a privileged existence beyond the reach of their **fans**, is no exception. Sport inherently is a breeding ground for crises, particularly of a reputational nature. Fueled by social media, transgressions – or wrong-doings – by elite athletes spread like wildfire worldwide. This can range from in-game competitions (Brown & Billings, 2013) to 'the conscious and emotional decision' to engage in doping (Overbye et al., 2013). Summers and Morgan (2008, p. 176) observe that the 'constant demand and supply of information, competition and excitement breeds heroes, villains, celebrities and superstars', where a 'sporting celebrity is subjected to scrutiny and the increasingly high expectations of fans'. This is not surprising, given Dimeo's observation that 'Sport is fundamentally about winning, hierarchy, elitism and losers get nothing' (2007, cited in Lopez, 2010, p. 134).

It is in this arguably toxic environment that the 'market value' of an **elite athlete** is measured by their 'public reputation' (Brazeal, 2008), which Hopwood (2007) found is pinned on healthy relationships with stakeholders, such as fellow athletes, team managers, coaches and, importantly, fans. Our chapter examines the intriguing – and still evolving – case of professional elite cyclist Lance Armstrong's fall from grace, when in January 2013 he confessed to an audience of millions on the US-based *Oprah Winfrey Show* that he had a lengthy history of doping, despite years of denial. Perhaps this quote from blogger Richard Finger, of Forbes.com, puts the case study of this chapter into context:

> In his Inferno, Dante would have consigned Lance to the eighth circle specifically reserved for frauds. How can you trust words from a man when the foundation of his career was built on a decade and a half of consistent perjury?

Our case study on Armstrong, a devotee of micro-blogging platform Twitter, provides you with an insight into the world of elite sport and the powerful dynamics of social media to champion heroes and demonise those who fall from grace by their own hand. Although Armstrong used popular social media platforms, such as Twitter, extensively he chose **traditional media** in which to 'come clean' on his involvement in 'doping'. We found that Armstrong's choice of Oprah Winfrey to host his 'confession' on her national US television program in fact alienated many of his legion of fans on social media, where reaction ranged from disbelief to shock (News.com.au, 2013). The reason may be the bonding power of social media, as you may have experienced, in this case to build personal bridges between an elite athlete and their fans, who can be forgiving of transgressions but that extends only so far. A second point is that Armstrong's failure to apologise without reservation during his 'confession', and subsequently ignoring the issue on social media, intensified fan outrage. Almost one-third of the 1.5 million social media posts in the days following the confession 'think of him differently' while 24 per cent 'think his career is over' (Polipulse, 2011). Ironically, it was social media that finally pushed Armstrong to confess. Choking back tears, Armstrong told Winfrey he had made the decision to come clean after his son defended him on the social media site Instagram against accusations of doping (Bacon, 2013). Even this display of emotion failed to convince some fans of his sincerity, with one tweeting: 'Lance Armstrong's tears have tested positive for narcissism' (Yadav, 2013).

Elite athlete: An individual who excels in their chosen sport, consistently performing at the highest level and often, though not exclusively, on a professional basis.

Traditional media: The pre-technological methods of disseminating information involving only one way communication such as print (e.g. newspapers, magazines) and broadcast (e.g. television, radio) media.

Case study: Into the inferno

On two nights in January 2013, Lance Armstrong, world-renowned cyclist, cancer survivor, Livestrong Foundation founder, Olympic Bronze medalist and winner of an unprecedented seven Tour de France titles, finally admitted to US chat show host Oprah Winfrey and a television audience of 4.3 million what many had long suspected – he had used banned performance enhancing drugs (PEDs) throughout his professional cycling career. In a statement released within an hour of the interview's broadcast, Travis Tygart, CEO of the United States Anti-Doping Agency (USADA), the organisation with whom Armstrong had been battling for many years against persistent allegations of doping, said: 'Tonight, Lance Armstrong finally acknowledged that his cycling career was built on a powerful combination of doping and deceit' (USADA, 17 January 2013). Armstrong was undoubtedly a global sporting icon but an individual who, as his career and image grew, divided opinion. Until 1994, the year that he began working with Dr Michele Ferrari, who was known, even in those days, to dope cyclists (Roberts & Epstein, 2011), Armstrong achieved moderate, but not outstanding success in his sport. In 1995, his winning streak began and he rose to seventh place in the world rankings and joined the French team Cofidis. In 1996, aged just 25, Armstrong was diagnosed with testicular cancer which swiftly spread throughout his body. He was not expected to recover. However, following aggressive treatment, by early 1997 he was in full remission. Just a year later, in 1998, he got back on his bike and made his post-cancer fully supported comeback:

> Sponsored by Nike, the US Postal Service (USPS), Discovery Channel, RadioShack, Anheuser-Busch, Oakley, Nissan, Trek-Bicycle Corp, Johnson Health Tech, SRAM Corporation, FRS, Easton-Bell Sports, Honey Stinger and 24-Hour Fitness Gyms, Lance built a team strong in cycle technology, sports gear, nutrition and capital.
>
> (Young, 2013, p. 1)

In 1999, against seemingly unbelievable odds, Armstrong won the first of seven consecutive Tour de France races and became a living legend. He acknowledged this during his opening speech to the World Cancer Congress in Montreal in August 2012. This appearance followed his announcement the previous week that he would no longer challenge USADA's drug charges against him and USADA throwing out his competitive victories dating from1998. These included all seven Tour wins: 'My name is Lance Armstrong. I am a cancer survivor. I'm a father of five. And yes, I won the Tour de France seven times' (Associated Press, 2012). Armstrong's inspirational and iconic status was further enhanced by his links with the Livestrong Foundation of which he is acknowledged as 'Our Founder' on the organisation's website (Livestrong Foundation, 2013). 'He and Livestrong were indivisible; he was not merely a rider, he was a cancer survivor. He credited his fitness and willpower with his "beating" cancer, which appeared to convey greater cult status' (Young 2013, p. 1). Armstrong helped to create and promote for himself an image of the invincible sporting hero. What the millions of fans around the world did not see, or perhaps did not want to see, was that underneath it all, Armstrong was a cheat who used his power unethically (Young 2013, p. 8).

Fans, connections and expectations

At this time Armstrong arguably understood the power of a devoted fan base and the benefits of **social media** interaction. This is not surprising considering fans, the lifeblood of sport, are bonded by intellect and emotion in sport (Gantz, 2012) and, through social media, have the ability to engage with other fans across the road, or across the world in many ways, from discussion to simple fun. Gantz explains: 'These forums can break news as well as serve as a bullhorn expressing and galvanizing fan pleasure or disgust' (2012, p. 184).

Social media: Websites and applications, such as Twitter and Facebook, which enable users to create and share content or to participate in social networking.

Social identity theory is a useful way to examine how identity is drawn from association with groups. Osborne and Coombs (2013) explain that fans associate their identity with the on-and-off-field performances of elite athletes and teams. This bond can manifest into a 'religion' (Garratt, 2010), and in the extreme become 'so intense that some fans are willing to engage in hostile and criminal acts towards opposing teams and players (Sanderson & Emmons 2014). In a nutshell, powered by social media, fans can become a valuable support base for elite athletes.

Social identity theory: A theory developed by social psychologist Henri Tajfel in 1979, which proposed that the groups people belong to give them a sense of belonging to the social world and an important sense of pride and self-esteem. Social identity theory is highly relevant to the concept of fans in sport.

Armstrong's use of Twitter was undoubtedly strategic. Due to his multi-dimensional image – elite cyclist, cancer survivor, humanitarian, living legend – Armstrong managed to develop distinctive character traits and personalities which appealed to varied publics, thereby creating a number of different fan bases. As Hambrick et al. (2013, p. 2) note: 'Twitter and other social media channels function as a mechanism to alternate between a variety of identity positions that may "make sense" to fans. . .'

Among the plethora of social media platforms, Hambrick et al. (2010, p. 454) have found that Twitter is popular because it allows athletes, within the confines of 140-character messages, to connect directly and immediately to fans, 'instead of having their messages filtered through the public relations departments of sports organisations and mainstream media outlets. Online social networks have created a significant shift in the sports communications paradigm'.

Fans also use Twitter to connect with athletes, other fans and the traditional media. Athletes have extended this symmetrical communication to encompass off-field personal activities, such as social events and pointing fans to personal pictures, blogs and other internet content. Social media is therefore creating a personal world between athletes and their fans. Hambrick et al. (2010, p. 463) explain that 'this interactivity element adds another dimension to fan perceptions regarding athletes as fans watch them engage in personal exchanges'. Needless to say, athletes who conducted extensive interactivity with fans enjoyed higher numbers of followers on Twitter. This unique window into the life of an elite athlete strengthens the personal bond with fans. This engagement drives loyalty towards the athlete or team (Hambrick et al., 2010). Fans are drawn to learn more intimate details about the athlete, cementing a bond that may be difficult to break in a crisis. This changes the relationship dynamics when fans 'are no longer observers, they are participants' (Kishner & Crescenti, 2010, p. 25). Social media platforms, such as Twitter, become valuable tools in uniting fans who then seek to defend the reputation of the athlete or team (Brown & Billings 2013).

For example, when exploring social media support for troubled Boston Red Sox pitcher Curt Schilling, Sanderson (2010) found that 'communicating directly to fans via blogs seems to be a strategy to quickly mobilise support networks that bolster the athlete during a personal crisis'. In our case example, Armstrong's use of social media is interesting in that he implemented different strategies and tactics at different times during the crisis. Hambrick et al. (2013) have observed that he maintained image repair strategies on Twitter both before and after the USADA investigation, but during and following the Oprah Winfrey interview, he chose not to mention it on Twitter. Our review of Armstrong's Twitter feed after the broadcast finds no reference to the confession. Armstrong's usually engaging Twitter activity was silent for almost a month after the broadcast. It returned to life with a mix of social and sport comments and a constant stream of tweets in relation to his high profile in the charity work for cancer. It seems the 'confession' remained strictly off-topic. Interestingly, we found that in the days following the broadcast, social media posts on the confession reached around 1.5 million (Polipulse, 2013).

Given the power of social media to maintain the support of fans, and Armstrong's already strong following, you may agree it presents a missed opportunity for Armstrong not to have utilised Twitter for a period of questions and answers. Had he done so, this would have allowed fans an on-going personal and exclusive insight into his confession and an opportunity for him to understand and address their concerns. In other words, Twitter would have provided Armstrong with a real-time awareness of, and engagement with, fans. Sanderson (2010) observes that elite athletes can counter negative media coverage by engendering their fan base to support 'their actions and views' with direct dialogue on social media platforms. Thus,

> In such circumstances, it seems plausible that communicative exchanges between professional athletes and fans via blogs would empower professional athletes to be more open in their disclosures about such events, which may translate to fans expressing support for the athlete's openness.
>
> (Sanderson, 2010, p. 189)

Instead, for reasons only known to himself, Armstrong opted to continue to tweet about his personal life, but now without the promotional messages, which disappeared together with his sponsors. Although Armstrong's professional landscape was changing for the worse, it seems he assumed his Twitter fan base would remain supportive without the further need to communicate specifically about the 'confession'.

Personal transgressions forgiven only so far

We now explore the question of how tolerant fans are of transgressions. Summers and Morgan (2008) suggest that although fans idolise their sporting heroes, the impact of bad behaviour depends on several factors, such as the athlete's profile and whether or not the misdeed was related to sport. For example, a transgression in the personal lives of elite athletes may attract more pity than outrage, but fans would be more incensed if the wrongdoing involved their athletic ability (Summers & Morgan, 2008). Transgressions in the personal lives of athletes seem 'almost expected and certainly not always the fault of the celebrity' (Summers & Morgan, 2008, p. 181).

For example, Australian Olympic swimmer Stephanie Rice lost a valuable sponsorship deal after posting a homophobic tweet in which she ridiculed a South African rugby team as 'faggots' (Byrnes,

2010). Rice made an emotional public apology on national television after critics labeled her a 'homophobic idiot'. Summers and Morgan (2008, p. 180) observe that

> we really do expect a lot from our sporting celebrities and we are largely intolerant of their mistakes . . . the fact that these people are paid to play sport removes any obligation to treat them with the same degree of humanity that we would impart to our fellow workmates or colleagues.

Rice unreservedly and nationally apologised for her 'transgression', but as we will see in our case study, Armstrong did not.

A defence of attack

Social media comments can frame a crisis, much like that of the traditional media. In their examination of the role of fans in a sport-related crisis, Brown and Billings (2013) discovered that fans using social media often adopted the strategy of 'attacking the accuser', while reminding each other of past achievements and proud moments of the athletes. However, in our case example, it was Armstrong who took on the role of 'attacking the accuser'. For more than a decade, Armstrong strenuously denied any involvement in doping, and verbally attacked and sued anyone who suggested that he did. From his first Tour de France victory in 1999 – ironically hailed as 'The Tour of Renewal' as it was intended to bring the event out of the shadows of doping accusations – until he finally gave up his fight with USADA in August 2012, Armstrong, as leader of the US Postal Service cycling team, was involved with what Tygart described as 'the most sophisticated, professionalized and successful doping program that the sport has ever seen . . . A program organized by individuals who thought they were above the rules and who still play a major and active role in sport today' (USADA, 10 October 2012).

Confessing bad news

We now explore the reasons why Armstrong decided to 'confess' on national television. Crisis response and reputation repair strategies have been the subject of extensive scholarly attention (for example, Benoit, 1995; Coombs, 2012; Ulmer, Sellnow & Seeger, 2011). In the business world how stakeholders react and attribute blame depends on the source of the crisis and who is responsible (McDonald, Sparks & Glendon, 2010; Coombs, 2012). The worst position is for an organisation to have caused a crisis that could have been prevented. This attracts high levels of blame by stakeholders. In these circumstances, McDonald, Sparks and Glendon (2010) suggest that 'confession' is one of the most successful strategies to reduce negative reaction. At the end of the day, Armstrong adopted this approach in tandem with a strategy of 'stealing thunder'; that is, he chose to attempt to tell his own bad news. This strategy was first used in the law courts, where defendants would reveal their own damaging information which in turn had less negative impact on a jury than had it been revealed by the prosecution. This self-disclosure allows the defence to produce information damaging to its case in the best light, and builds on the credibility of its case (Williams et al., 1993). In the context of crisis communication, Wigley (2011) has found that 'stealing thunder' considerably reduces news coverage overall and increases the percentage of positive stories. Wigley points to commodity theory to explain how 'stealing thunder' works: if a source is upfront and forthcoming by freely providing information to a reporter, the information is considered plentiful and therefore of little value. However, Wigley adds, if a source withholds information by stonewalling or remaining silent, the information is perceived as scarce or secret and will rise in value (2011, p. 51). In other words, 'stealing thunder' turns what could be described as fresh news into old news, thereby reducing its news value. For example, Wigley asserts, stealing thunder produces more positive articles, and moves media forward into the frame of 'what comes next' for the individual involved. Coombs (2012) points out that stakeholders expect organisations that have caused a crisis to make some form of amends, such as a full apology and compensation – or both. Coombs (2012, p. 155) sets out four approaches to responding to a crisis: denial, diminishment, rebuilding and bolstering.

1. Denial: This involves attacking the accuser, such as threatening legal action, denial that the crisis exists or scapegoating by blaming others outside the organisation.
2. Diminishment: This includes excusing the crisis by minimizing responsibility or justifying by minimizing the impact of the crisis.
3. Rebuilding: This includes offering compensation or gifts and apology by accepting responsibility.
4. Bolstering: This involves reminding stakeholders of past achievements, ingratiation (where stakeholders are praised) or victimage (where the organisation is too a victim of the crisis).

In the worst-case scenario, a preventable crisis caused by an organisation, the postures of rebuilding and bolstering would need to be adopted. Interestingly, until the televised 'confession', Armstrong maintained Coombs's denial posture. On the Oprah Winfrey program, he changed posture to that of diminishment and rebuilding, though he still did not make a full, unreserved apology. He maintained throughout that the fault is with the sport of cycling rather than him as an individual. This has led to claims of arrogance, particularly when he aligned himself with former President Clinton's rehabilitation, stating that Clinton was a 'hero of mine' that he wanted to copy him in becoming 'president of the world' and publicly stating that: 'I'm like Bill Clinton and people will forgive me' (Daniel Bates, Mail Online, 12 March 2013). The closest Armstrong came to a full unreserved apology during the interviews was to acknowledge anger:

> I see the anger in the people and betrayal and it is all there. Those people who supported me believed what I was saying. They have every right to feel betrayed. It's my fault. I will spend the rest of my life to earn back the trust and apologise to the rest of the people.
>
> (quoted in Yadav, 2013)

Previous reputation may not count

Into the 'confession communication mix' is Armstrong's reputation as a charity leader with his founding of the Livestrong Foundation, something that he continued to bring to the fore in his Twitter activity following the 'confession'. Although Coombs (2012, p. 162) observes that organisations with a positive reputation 'can experience stakeholders ignoring bad news about the organization because they are unlikely to believe that a good organization did anything bad', there is little doubt that not even Armstrong's charity role would keep fans onside. The extent and depth of the transgression in this case, coupled with the lack of social media interaction on the confession we argue compounded negative social media reaction. In fact, 18 per cent of people posting on social media after the confession believe Armstrong's transgressions made 'the good things he did irrelevant' (Polipulse, 2011).

Controlling the message

So, why did Lance Armstrong choose the traditional media outlet of the *Oprah Winfrey Show* rather than Twitter as his preferred 'confession' communication channel? The answer can be found in van der Meer and Verhoeven's (2013) observation that a crisis initially conveyed on Twitter results in the public making assumptions with increased anxiety and alarm, presumably given the limited detail in a tweet. Traditional media has the opposite effect; as van der Meer and Verhoeven (2013, p. 231) observe, 'the news media have a soothing effect on public panic and speculation and therefore have the potential to prevent crisis escalation'. Thus, more time on the Winfrey talk show allowed more time to frame and deliver the confession and 'steal the thunder' as previously discussed. There is a second reason. It is evident that Armstrong is an individual who is very accustomed to being in control and controlling, and this is reflected in his choice of media channels for his *mea culpa*. As a televised interviewee, confessing all to his friend Oprah Winfrey, Armstrong could both craft his message and his image. However, we argue that also communicating to the world through Twitter would allow him to engage on a more 'personal' level with his supporters. Of course, the downside to this approach is that his followers on Twitter could ask questions of him in a very public forum. As William Fotheringham observes, Armstrong maintained control of the message, giving access in return for more friendly coverage (*The Guardian*, 12 November 2013).

It is suggested that by his use of Winfrey's show as his confessional platform, Armstrong felt that he could control his message. Arguably the fundamental principles of crisis PR are these: knowing your audience; crafting the message accordingly; communicating a credible message through appropriate communication channels with the ultimate objective of getting the audience onside; apologising for a transgression and making amends. However, Armstrong's communication behaviour since August 2012 suggests that he feels that such rules do not apply to him. As recently as 7 November 2013, he was sniping with Tyler Hamilton (a former cycling team mate) on Twitter (@lancearmstrong @Ty_Hamilton Twitter exchange, 7 November 2013).

Diverting attention

Research for this chapter also found that Armstrong engaged in another form of diversion – to that of painting himself as a victim of the sport. There is extensive evidence of Armstrong implementing this strategy in both the Winfrey interview in January 2013 and in the interview he gave to the BBC World Service Newshour on 11 November 2013. In answer to Oprah's question 'You said to me earlier you don't think it was possible to win without doping?', Armstrong is accusatory:

> Not in that generation, and I'm not here to talk about others in that generation. It's been well-documented. I didn't invent the culture, but I didn't try to stop the culture . . . and the sport is now paying the price because of that. So I am sorry for that. I didn't have access to anything else that nobody else did.
>
> (BBC Sport, 2013)

In his interview on 11 November, Armstrong, during his protestations about unfair treatment and inconsistencies in punishment said, 'The playing field at the time was level, the judge has been anything but level . . . there will always be some form of performance enhancement – has been since the Ancient Greeks' (BBC World Service Newshour, 2013). Broadening this claim, Armstrong made reference to other sports being involved with doping in an interview with the French newspaper *Le Monde*, in which he stated that he did not invent doping; that it did not end with him. He continued:

> The whole story has still not been told . . . (USADA) did not paint a faithful picture of cycling from the end of the 1980s to today. It succeeded perfectly in destroying one man's life but did not benefit cycling at all.
>
> (ESPN.com News, 2013)

This approach is not uncommon. Bruce and Tini (2008) note that in an Australian rugby league crisis, the club concerned opted for a reputation protection strategy of 'diversion', where attention on criticism of the team's management was clouded by refocusing on players and fans as 'innocent victims'. This tactic of diversion, argue Bruce and Tini (2008, p. 112), allows the organisation to 'connect with their fans and to limit the overall damage to the sport and team, because the aspects of the organisation with which fans most relate – the players and on-field performance – could be divorced from the scandal'. Hence, the team's public statements stressed the players 'had the right to feel proud' and quoted fans as 'being concerned for the players' (2008, p. 112). Bruce and Tini (2008, p. 113) explain that:

> by protecting the players and coach, with whom fans have the strongest emotional connection, and sacrificing the management team, the organisation ensured that the relationship with at least one key stakeholder group would continue. Indeed, the increased spectator numbers the following year may reflect the strength of this relationship as fans turned out to demonstrate their support for the players and, incidentally, contributed to the rebuilding of the organisation.

Conclusion

As stated previously, Armstrong strongly divides opinion and therefore analysis of his 'confessions' and his media strategy will reflect this. In these days of open access communication, a polarity of viewpoints is to be expected. Nonetheless, from a crisis PR perspective, you will see that it seems more important that individuals and organisations who are mindful of their image and reputation, together with their relationship management strategies, give closer consideration to how and when they communicate with their publics. From the perspective of the celebrity sports personality – into which category Lance Armstrong undoubtedly positions himself – this is even more critical. 'Armstrong has been a strong proponent of Twitter since its inception, and social media analysts have attributed much of Twitter's growth to early adopters in the sports world such as Armstrong' (Fisher, 2009, cited in Hambrick et al., 2013). Though he currently has almost four mililon Twitter followers, he is losing followers at the rate of 133 per day (http://twittercounter.com/lancearmstrong), which suggests that his communication strategies may be backfiring. Armstrong continues to be a focus of social media attention. For example, the now-infamous '*Back in Austin and just layin' around...*' tweet he posted on 10 November 2012, just days after he had resigned from the Chair of the Livestrong Foundation, has received 11 992 20 views and 782 comments, both for and against the cyclist. The tweet shows him relaxing on a couch surrounded by the yellow jerseys from the seven Tour de France wins that had earlier in the year been expunged from the records. Comments posted include:

> venmex: a year ago – cheat, cheat, cheat, cheat, cheat, cheat, cheat. That's seven right?
>
> jdusvet: Lance is the man. And those drugs don't work unless the man is already a beast. Lance was a beast without them, but to stay on top, you have to level the playing field. He wasn't the only one, and they all knew it.
>
> (http:/www.mobli.com/media/show/id/22700756?referer=tw17, viewed November 2013)

Despite this, Armstrong has maintained somewhat of a strategic approach to his image repair efforts. For example, to coincide with the World Anti-Doping Agency Conference in Johannesburg, he offered to give 100 per cent transparency in return for the overturning of his lifetime ban from competitive cycling (BBC World Service, 11 November 2013). Yet what Armstrong consistently fails to do is unreservedly apologise for his transgressions. Instead he continues to adopt the role of the victim, which arguably continues to alienate his publics and further diminish his credibility in the eyes of both the cycling and wider sporting community. Armstrong and his transgressions will undoubtedly continue to have repercussions not only within the sport of cycling, but more generally within the context of crisis communications.

CASE QUESTIONS

1. Why is it important that elite athletes value the relationship with their social media fan base?
2. What are the ramifications for an athlete who confesses to wrongdoing but fails to apologise without reservation?

3. Describe one benefit and one risk of the social media micro-blogging platform Twitter in a crisis.
4. Armstrong adopted the strategy of 'stealing thunder' to confess on the *Oprah Winfrey Show*. Why is 'stealing thunder' considered a useful strategy to reduce reputational damage?

BIBLIOGRAPHY

Armstrong, L. (2011). Back in Austin, just layin' around. *Mobli*. Retrieved 17 November 2013 from www.mobli.com/media/show/id/22700756?referer=tw.

Associated Press (2012). Lance Armstrong says he's champ. *ESPN*. Retrieved 4 November 2013 from http://espn.go.com/olympics/cycling/story/_/id/8315779/lance-armstrong-introduces-7-time-tour-de-france-champ.

Bacon, E. (2013). The Lance Armstrong confession concludes: Part two. *Cycling Weekly*. Retrieved 18 November from www.cyclingweekly.co.uk/news/latest/536498/the-lance-armstrong-confession-concludes-part-two.html.

Bates, D. (2013). Lance Armstrong: I'm like Bill Clinton and people will forgive me. Mail Online. Retrieved 16 October 2013 from www.dailymail.co.uk/news/article-2292248/Lance-Armstrong-Im-like-Bill-Clinton-people-forgive-me.html.

BBC Sport (2013). Lance Armstrong and Oprah Winfrey interview transcript. BBC Sport. Retrieved 1 November 2013 from www.bbc.co.uk/sport/0/cycling/21065539?print=true.

BBC World Service (2013). Lance Armstrong's interview. *BBC World Service Newshour*, 11 November 2013. Retrieved 11 November 2013 from www.bbc.co.uk/news/world-24900159.

Benoit, W. L. (1995). *Accounts, excuses and apologies: A theory of image restoration*, Albany: State University of New York Press.

Brazeal, L. (2008). The image repair strategies of Terrell Owens. *Public Relations Review*, 34, 145–50.

Brown, N. & Billings, A. (2013). Sports fans as crisis communicators on social media websites. *Public Relations Review*, 39, 74–81.

Bruce, T. & Tini, T. (2008). Unique crisis response strategies in sports public relations: Rugby league and the case for diversion. *Public Relations Review*, 34, 108–15.

Byrnes, H. (2010, 8 September). Shattered Stephanie Rice says sorry over homophobic tweet. *The Telegraph*. Retrieved 12 October 2013 from www.dailytelegraph.com.au/shattered-stephanie-rice-says-sorry-over-homophobic-tweet/story-e6freuy9-1225915930831.

Coombs, W. T. (2012). *Ongoing crisis commuication: Planning, managing and responding*. Thousand Oaks, CA: Sage.

ESPN.com News Services (2013). Lance: Can't win Tour without doping. Retrieved 14 November 2013 from http://espn.go.com/sports/endurance/story/_/id/9432050/lance-armstrong-says-the-record-tour-de-france-winner.

Finger, R. (2013). Lance and Oprah sittin' in a tree. Forbes.com. Retrieved 14 November 2013 from www.forbes.com/sites/richardfinger/2013/01/18/lance-and-oprah-sittin-in-a-tree.

Fotheringham, W. (2013, 12 November). Lance Armstrong's media offensive is rightfully doomed to failure. *The Guardian: Talking Sport*. Retrieved 13 November from www.theguardian.com/sport/blog/2013/nov/12/lance-armstrong-media-offensive-doomed?INTCMP=ILCNETTXT3487.

Gantz, W. (2012). Reflections on Communication and Sport: On fanship and social relationships. *Communication & Sport*, 1(2), 176–87.

Garratt, D., (2010). Sporting citizenship: The rebirth of religion?, *Pedagogy, Culture & Society*, 18(2), 123–43.

Hambrick, M., Frederick, E. & Sanderson, J. (2013). From yellow to blue: Exploring Lance Armstrong's image repair strategies across traditional and social media. *Communication & Sport*, 4 October 2013. Retrieved 5 October 2013. doi:10.1177/2167479513506982.

Hambrick, M., Simmons, J., Greenhalgh, G. & Greenwell, T. C. (2010). Understanding professional athletes' use of Twitter: A content analysis of athlete tweets, *International Journal of Sports Communication*, 3, pp. 454–71.

Hopwood, M. (2007). The sport integrated marketing communications mix. In J. Beech & S. Chadwick (eds), *The Marketing of Sport*, Harlow, UK: Pearson Education.

Kishner, I., & Crescenti, B. (2010). The Rise of Social Media, *The Entertainment and Sports Lawyer*, 27(4), 24–6.

Lance Armstrong's Twitter counter. Retrieved 14 November 2013 from http://twittercounter.com/lancearmstrong.

Livestrong Foundation (2013). Our founder. Retrieved 14 November 2013 from www.livestrong.org/Our-Founder.

Lopez, B. (2010). Doping as technology: A re-reading of the history of performance-enhancing substance use. *Institute for Culture and Society Occasional Paper Series*, 1(4), 1–17.

McDonald, L., Sparks, B. & Glendon, A. (2010). Stakeholder reactions to company crisis communication and causes, *Public Relations Review*, no 36, pp. 263–71.

McLean, H. (2014). Crisis and Issues Management. In J. Johnston & M. Sheehan (eds) *Public Relations Theory and Practice*, Crows Nest, NSW: Allen & Unwin.

News.com.au (2013). Social media reacts to Lance Armstrong confession. Retrieved 15 November 2013 from www.news.com.au/world/social-media-reacts-to-lance-armstrongs-confession/story-fndir2ev-1226554364547.

Osborne, A. & Coombs, D. (2013). Performative sport fandom: An approach to retheorizing sport fans. *Sport in Society: Cultures, Commerce, Media, Politics*, 16(5), 672–81.

Overbye, M., Knudsen, M. & Pfister, G. (2013). To dope or not to dope: Elite athletes' perceptions of doping deterrents and incentives, *Performance Enhancement & Health*. Retrieved 1 October 2013 from http://dx.doi.org/10.1016/j.peh.2013.07.001.

Polipulse (2013). America reacts to Armstrong confession. Retrieved 15 November 2013 from http://polipulse.com/america-reacts-armstrong-confession.

Roberts, S., & Epstein, D. (2011). The case against Lance Armstrong. *Sports Illustrated Vault*. Retrieved 1 November 2013 from http://sportsillustrated.cnn.com/vault/article/magazine/MAG1180944/index.htm.

Sanderson, J. (2010). The nation stands behind you. *Communication Quarterly*, 58(2), 186–206.

Sanderson, J. and Emmons, B. (2014). Extending and withholding forgiveness to Josh Hamilton: Exploring forgiveness within parasocial interaction. *Communication & Sport*, 2(1), 24–47.

Summers, J. & Morgan, M. (2008). More than just the media: Considering the role of public relations in the creation of sporting celebrity and the management of fan expectations. *Public Relations Review*, 34, pp. 176–82.

Ulmer, R., Sellnow, T. & Seeger, M. (2011). *Effective crisis communication: Moving from crisis to opportunity*, 2nd edn, Thousand Oaks, CA: Sage.

United States Anti-Doping Agency (USADA) (2012, 10 October). Statement from USADA CEO Travis T. Tygart regarding the US Postal Service Pro Cycling Team doping conspiracy. Retrieved 4 November 2013 from http://cyclinginvestigation.usada.org.

United States Anti-Doping Agency (USADA) (2013, 17 January). Statement from USADA CEO Travis T. Tygart regarding Lance Armstrong interview. USADA. Retrieved 4 November 2013 from www.usada.org/media/statement11713.

van der Meer, T., and Verhoeven, P. (2013). Public framing organizational crisis situations: Social media versus news media. *Public Relations Review*, 39, 229–31.

Wigley, S. (2011). Telling your own bad news: Eliot Spitzer and a testing of stealing thunder strategy, *Public Relations Review*, 37, 50–6.

Williams, K. D., Bourgeois, M. J., & Croyle, R. T. (1993). The effects of stealing thunder in criminal and civil trials, *Law and Human Behavior*, 17(6), 597–609.

Yadav, A. (2013). Fans and sportspersons react to Armstrong admitting drug abuse. Retrieved 19 November 2013 from www.merinews.com/article/fans-and-sportspersons-react-to-armstrong-admitting-drug-abuse/15880593.shtml.

Young, S. (2013). Lance Armstrong: Everybody's doing it – A case study about a leader's ethics and use of power. Retrieved on 1 November 2013 from https://www.researchgate.net/publication/245024505_Young_-_Lance_Armstrong_2013_v1-4.

5 CORPORATE RESPONSES TO A RACIALLY FRAMED INCIDENT IN MALAYSIA

THE KFC I-CITY FIGHT

Kiranjit Kaur

Chapter objectives

This chapter aims to:

- demonstrate the importance of planning a response to a **racially framed incident** online
- outline key communication principles and practices for corporate response to a social media crisis.

Introduction

Social media provide corporations with a powerful tool to engage with customers and promote their goods or services. It has become a norm to have social media network accounts such as Facebook, Twitter, Wikipedia, forums and blogs to communicate with their customers directly on promotions, queries or even for friendly banter. Speed in communication is of utmost importance and prior approval from top management is seldom sought to post a response, thereby increasing the imminent risk of misstatements. While it is important to entrust this task of dealing with internet users to experienced staff, often organisations recruit young staff who have little understanding of the organisation for this purpose. This is partly because the latter are more internet savvy and partly because they are better able to establish a youthful style of communication with the increasing number of young customers active on the social media.

Nevertheless, the cyber-world is unpredictable and, no matter how good a brand is, there will be someone hating it and waiting to go viral with that hate. An organisation cannot afford to underestimate the wrath of angry netizens and must deal with online complaints promptly, just as they would acknowledge other complaints instead of ignoring or deleting them. There must also be a contingency plan to manage social media disasters, especially, with a rise in social network postings stoking religious and racial tension.

Malaysia is a multi-ethnic nation in which cultural, racial and religious variety is part of its modern social fabric. Organisations operating in the country are well-advised to incorporate that variety prudently into their business strategy. This poses a considerable challenge to organisations whose employee and client base stretches across communities and needs to be prudent in the way tensions are managed that might arise between sub-groups. This chapter describes such a challenge by focusing on the outbreak of violence in a Kentucky Fried Chicken (KFC) outlet in i-City, a theme park in Shah Alam, Selangor, Malaysia; an incident that became framed in racial (anti-Malay and anti-Chinese) terms.

Racially framed incident: Refers to stereotyping a conflict in terms of race.

There are two related points of note to put the case discussed in this chapter into perspective. The first is the socio-cultural mosaic in the country. Malaysia has a population of about 28.3 million with diverse racial, cultural and religious groups. The three main racial groups comprise the Bumiputeras, or Malays, and Indigenous people (67.4 per cent), Chinese (24.6 per cent) and Indians (7.3 per cent) (Malaysian Department of Statistics, cited in Kanyakumari, 2014, 26 February). In Malaysia, race and religion are generally bound together. The Malays are Muslims; the Chinese are mostly Buddhists, Taoists, or Christians; and the Indians are primarily Hindus with a small number of Sikhs, Muslims, and Christians. With such diverse beliefs and practices, Malaysia's racial stability is sometimes tested and racial and religious tolerance has become a constant clarion call by the country's political and social leaders. While these communities have a generally tolerant relationship, the years since Malaysia's independence in 1957 have seen a few clashes arising from racial and religious conflicts.

The second is the breadth of use of social media by Malaysians, especially among the youth. Broadband penetration rate in Malaysian households is at 67.2 (ETP, 2013). In addition, 90 per cent of Malaysian internet users have access to social media sites. According to comScore (a leading internet technology company that measures what the people do as they navigate the digital world), social networks accounted for one third of the time spent online by Malaysians. Malaysians prefer to surf the internet and 51 per cent have an active YouTube profile. Facebook was at the top of the social network list at 46.6 per cent or 13 389 520 subscribers with more than nine million of those older than 21 years. Malaysians are considered as 'very friendly 'online as they have the highest average number of friends on social networks in the world. Malaysian Facebook users have an average of 233 friends which is nearly 80 per cent higher than the global yardstick. Facebook was also listed as the second most watched video content site at more than four million video viewers after YouTube at nine million unique visitors (Kemp, 2012; Muniandy & Muniandy, 2013).

In addition, today's youth prefer to get their news from social media irrespective of whether the reports were from unverified sources. A survey by pollster Umcedel shortly after the 13th Malaysian general election in May 2013, showed 96 per cent of youths – or close to half of Malaysia's 13 million registered voters – relied on social media for information pertaining to the polls (www.themalaysianinsider.com/malaysia/article/mainstream-media-suffering-as-more-malaysians-turn-to-social-media-for-news, 30 November 2013). The internet in Malaysia is uncensored, with minimal social media regulations, although specific laws apply, such as in the case of defamatory remarks and criminal activity.

In such an environment, an occasional conflict or crisis involving a clash between members of different racial and religious groups results in allegations of racial sentiments being circulated by netizens on the internet. The incident becomes framed along racial lines and goes viral on social media. For an organisation having to deal with and manage a social media crisis that has the potential of damaging its reputation, it becomes a double task to contain the racial innuendos as well. Such was the situation in the case of a KFC branch in i-City.

Background

The fast-food restaurant Kentucky Fried Chicken was marred by an isolated incident in 2012. A counter staff member hit a customer, which then snowballed into a debacle for the brand putting KFC in a negative spotlight. There were 835 026 views of the punching incident in seven days on YouTube and negative sentiment rose significantly within a matter of days. (Information is sourced from the advertising agency submission to the 2013 Media Specialist Award for best media campaign.)

The assault that occurred on a busy day at the KFC i-City outlet involved a Malay male employee and a Malaysian Chinese male customer, Danny Ng, and it became a heated topic on Malaysian social media. Another customer recorded the incident at the fast-food restaurant when she heard an angry argument between the staff member and a few disgruntled customers who were telling off the staff for not informing them earlier that the restaurant had run out of chicken although they had known the customers were waiting to order for almost an hour. According to a witness, the server shouted back rudely '*Ayam sudah habis, apa you mahu lagi?*' ('The chicken has finished, what else do you want?') at the customers. This incident occurred at the end of a busy day during the holidays, a time when i-City, a technology park comprising corporate, leisure and residential components, including several family attractions is very busy.

When Ng found out that somebody had posted a video clip of the incident on Facebook, he lodged a police report for assault. Ng explained he had visited i-City on 6 February 2012 with his wife and sister to redeem vouchers worth RM132, which were expiring the following day, and they included a meal at KFC as well as admission to the Ferris wheel, snow house and outdoor rides. They went to the restaurant at 10.15 p.m. and, after queuing for about 45 minutes, Ng heard customers ahead of him complaining that there was no more chicken. He said a worker then uttered derogatory remarks, which prompted him to ask for the manager, who refused to attend to him. Because of his dissatisfaction, Ng tried to photograph the workers and take down their names, at which point a group of the workers rushed out from the kitchen and one of them ran towards him and grabbed his neck and punched him on the back of his head (Ho, 2012).

Both parties were alleged by onlookers to have uttered racist comments at each other, though Ng later denied having done so. There were varying public reactions on social networking sites towards the video clip, with many criticising KFC, Ng and the employee and sometimes framed their comments with derogatory racist slurs. This led to police threats to take action under Section 323 of the Penal Code against individuals disturbing the peace and harmony in the multi-ethnic society. The unexpected involvement of netizens on this issue led to even the victim urging the public not to fan racial sentiments over the incident, which he said was merely poor customer service.

An additional complaint among the netizens was that KFC was slow in showing closure to the issue. They had mentioned in the press that they had suspended three employees pending investigation but were criticised for not being seen to actively prevent the issue from being turned into a political mud-slinging contest and one with racial connotations around the issue (Lee, 2012; Ho, 2012).

The KFC management later apologised to Ng. Several traditional and online media carried the formal apology made by the fast-food chain deputy president to the customer, Danny Ng, on 17 February 2012 with almost a similar headline: 'KFC apologises to assault victim at i-City outlet' (Malaysiakini, 18 February 2012).

Case focus

Problem

The punching incident went viral on Facebook, Twitter, and YouTube, and it was also picked up by online news portals and traditional print and electronic media, which gave it wide coverage over a number of weeks. A number of online posts contained negative racial sentiments, either anti-Chinese or anti-Malay sentiments depending on viewer support for either the customer (a Chinese man) or the KFC employee (a Malay man), respectively. The Malay and Chinese media were also deemed to be slanted in their news coverage favouring the emotional interests of their respective ethnic-based audiences.

Ng was accused by netizens of provoking the incident with **'racial' comments**, which he denied. In addition, as is the case sometimes in Malaysia, incidents take on not only a racial but also a political turn and Perkasa, a Malay rights political group, was also accused of inciting racial conflict over this incident by demanding a meeting with the KFC i-City management, since a Malay employee and Chinese customer were involved. The story carried on news portals fuelled online postings for and against their interference. Moderate individuals responded to such statements by stating that this incident was not about politics or race, but an employee–customer relationship issue compounded with a criminal case of assault.

Racial comment: Any remark suggesting a slur or an attack on the basis of ethnicity.

Stories ran with headlines like the following and which were in turn shared by netizens. '*Stop fanning racial flames, says man attacked in KFC outlet*' (9 February 2012); or '*Gaduh di KFC pun boleh jadi isu perkauman?*' ('Even a fight can become a racial issue?') (9 February 2012). A popular and active e-community site of a middle-income residential area of Subang Jaya in the Klang Valley also asked for views from among its reader base on USJ e-community.com.my (www.usj.com.my/bulletin/upload/showthread.php?34388-KFC-Staff-Beats-Customer) to illustrate the different parties taking up the issue, partly because of the perceived racial sentiments.

Netizens also seemed disappointed with the KFC management, which was deemed to be 'slow' in managing the incident especially as some thought race sensitivity was being exploited. KFC was probably caught unawares as the incident was a minor one and not perhaps viewed to require involvement by senior personnel. Standard assurances and platitudes on KFC's Facebook page were not acceptable to the netizens, who threatened to call for a total boycott of its outlets. There was even a suggestion that the issue be taken up with KFC International if the local franchisee was not interested in resolving the issue.

Solution: KFC response to crisis

KFC launched a *'KFC finds love again'* campaign soon after the punching incident at KFC i-City, which had evolved into a social media crisis. KFC had to respond quickly to the crisis to reinstate consumers' confidence in the brand. They identified four different audiences to communicate with simultaneously and strategically, that is, strangers, onlookers, activists and propagators.

- First, *strangers* were identified as people who were unaware of the incident and needed to be diverted from being influenced.
- Second, *onlookers* were those people who just observed and so there was a need for constructive effort to neutralise the situation.
- Third, *activists* were people who were emotionally attached and so the corporation had to dilute the one-off incident by showing closure.
- Fourth, *propagators* were people who shared posts on the incident and efforts had to be made to stop them from sharing posts and comments.

KFC used a three-pronged strategy – contain, co-create and convince – to manage the crisis and messages were customised for each audience segment. They also focused on the crisis impact across the general population rather than the racial framing of the incident by the specific different ethnic groups.

Contain

The first strategy was to *contain*; that is, to control the outbreak of the negative sentiments on the internet. They dealt with *search* as their first line of defence by posting several messages online through Google, Yahoo and Bing search engines and the like. This included a ruse to deflect the strangers, by posting information to promote KFC outlets, menus, latest offers and other promos. Second, to convert the onlookers who were eagerly following the latest updates, they provided latest updates on how the incident was being managed. Third, to convince the activists who thought KFC was not doing enough, they showed they were taking action through posting an official apology, their press conference outcome, and pointing out the legal action being taken against the employee. And fourth, to stop propagators who were further spreading the incident, they explained their actions through the KFC i-City Facebook page that was especially set up for the purpose, through YouTube, and through the KFC incident forum. Premium search advertisements were bought and placed on top to push the negatives down.

Co-create

The second strategy was to *co-create*. Plans were made to bring back the joy of KFC via sharing the 'So good moments' campaign. Once the online conversation was intercepted with search, KFC built positive advocacy through Facebook to gather 'so good moments' by posting pictures and statements of customers enjoying their meal experiences in KFC with family and friends, with the theme of '*Gathering is so good*' at KFC parties and childhood moments. Consumers became the engine of content creation as they shared their 'so good moments' under 29 life experience buckets.

Convince

The third strategy was to *convince*. After intercepting negative online conversation with positive advocacy and 'so good moments' postings, KFC went about restaging its server image in a massive way. KFC recruited 10 popular radio DJs from popular radio stations including *mix.fm*, as well as Chinese DJs from the Chinese station *My FM*, and Malay DJs from the Malay station *ERA FM*, to host part of their shows in designated KFC outlets nationwide as well as to temporarily become their part-time new frontliners, serving and interacting with customers for a period of five weeks. These moments were posted on Facebook and YouTube. They turned the point-of-sale to point-of-endorsement.

All these efforts brought about the outcome of *strangers* not discovering negative content and viewing KFC business as usual; *onlookers* viewing updates KFC wanted them to; *activists* pleased with KFC apology and actions; and *propagators* starting to share positive stories that KFC had wanted them to do.

The 'KFC finds love again' campaign also resulted in neutralizing 5.5 million searches online; KFC social community leaping from 320 000 to 720 000 fans within a month; and positive brand conversation improving from 31 per cent to 77 per cent. Over time, there were also an increase in sales records of 19.8 per cent, in transactions of 15.4 per cent, and twice as many visit shares. (Information is sourced from the advertising agency submission to the 2013 Media Specialist Award for best media campaign.)

Conclusion

KFC Malaysia won several awards, including the Global KFC awards for best crisis management and for the '*KFC finds love again*' campaign. In addition, Universal McCann, the advertising agency for the KFC Malaysia brand, received the Grand Prix Malaysian Media Award 2013 for the management of this case. The Malaysian Media Awards, organised by the Media Specialists Association (MSA), is the media industry's prestigious award designed to recognise excellent work and achievements within the media fraternity in Malaysia. Some of the lessons to be learnt from this case include the need for a speedy response from a senior official in both real and cyber time, especially in a digital world.

CASE QUESTIONS

1. What key issues did KFC need to consider in this situation?
2. What makes a company in a multi-ethnic society vulnerable from a communications standpoint?
3. In what ways could KFC have managed the situation in a risk management context?
4. Would you have resolved the case differently from KFC Malaysia's approach? What recommendations would you suggest?

BIBLIOGRAPHY

Economic Transformation Programme (ETP) (2013). Epp7: Ensuring broadband for all. Retrieved 6 December 2014 from http:etp.pemandu.gov.my.

Gaduh Di KFC Pun Boleh Jadi Isu Perkauman? (2012, 9 February). Retrieved 1 February 2014 from www.mykmu.net/?p=16627.

Ho, S. (2012, 10 February). Assault not a racial issue, says man in KFC attack. The Star Online. Retrieved 15 January 2014 from www.thestar.com.my/News/Nation/2012/02/10/Assault-not-a-racial-issue-says-man-in-KFC-attack.

Kanyakumari, D. (2014, 26 February). Malaysia's population to number 30 million on Thursday, *Star Online*. Retrieved 6 December 2014 from www.the staronline.com.my/News/Nation/2014/02/06/Malaysia-30-mil-population/.

Kemp, S. (2012). We are social: Social, digital and mobile in Malaysia. Retrieved 15 January 2014 from http://wearesocial.net/blog/2012/01/social-digital-mobile-malaysia.

KFC fist fight: Perkasa jumps into the barrel. (2012, 11 February). Malaysiakini. Retrieved 1 February 2014 from www.malaysiakini.com/news/188820.

KFC apologises to assault victim at i-City outlet. (2012, 18 February). Malaysiakini. Retrieved 1 February 2014 from www.malaysiakini.com/news/189562.

Lee, P. (2012, 10 February). Expert: Loss of control caused KFC incident. Free Malaysia Today. Retrieved 15 January 2014 from www.freemalaysiatoday.com/category/nation/2012/02/10/expert-loss-of-control-caused-kfc-incident.

Muniandy, L. & Muniandy, B. (2013). The impact of social media in social and political aspects in Malaysia: An overview, *International Journal of Humanities and Social Science*, 3(11), 71.

Stop fanning racial flames, says man attacked in KFC outlet. (2012, 9 February). *Malaysian Insider.* Retrieved 1 February 2014 from www.themalaysianinsider.com/malaysia/article/stop-fanning-racial-flames-says-man-attacked-in-kfc-outlet.

6

MANAGING ISSUES THROUGH CROSS-SECTOR COLLABORATION

UNILEVER AND GREENPEACE

Sharyn McDonald

Chapter objectives

This chapter aims to:

- examine how proactive strategies towards issue management can avert crisis
- consider how cross-sector collaboration can lead to sustainable solutions.

Introduction

Proactive issue management, where organisations identify key stakeholders, and consider themselves as part of a solution can avert crisis and reap the reputational advantages as change makers. Stakeholders are defined by McIntosh et al. (1998) as individuals or groups that may have an impact on an organisation or who may be impacted upon. From this definition it is clear to see that no one channel or message will appeal to all. As such, effective dialogue must occur with a range of stakeholders, including internal and external stakeholders. All have specific wants and needs which ultimately may change over time.

Private sector/business/corporates/for-profit organisations (FPO): An organisation that seeks to generate a profit through the sale of goods and/or services.

Corporate social responsibility (CSR): 'The social responsibility of business encompasses the economic, legal, ethical, and discretionary expectations that society has of organizations at a given point in time' (Carroll, 1979).

Growing stakeholder expectations are being acknowledged by many private sector organisations, or **for-profit organisations (FPOs)**. In the past, it was accepted that the role of a FPO was to meet demand while generating a profit thus meeting economic requirements. Added to this was the need to work within the laws governing their operation, thus meeting the legal requirements. However, over time, stakeholders have demanded more; FPOs are increasingly expected to demonstrate their contribution to society. Many FPOs fulfil such obligations through strategic **corporate social responsibility (CSR)** initiatives.

While some FPOs simply react to the negative impact they have on communities and the environment as and when necessary, others adopt a more proactive approach. The later may be considered strategic for they are aware of issues that need attention and can structure their CSR initiatives accordingly. Some address their CSR responsibilities alone using in-house expertise, while others have forged relationships with members of the **not-for-profit sector** to enact their CSR agenda (Husted, 2003). Emerging are best practice exemplars of resultant **cross-sector collaboration**.

Not-for-profit sector *or* **organisations (NPOs), non-governmental organisations (NGOs), civil society:** Groups that are neither business nor represent government that seek to address societal issues.

Cross-sector collaboration: Where organisations from different sectors exchange dialogue and/or resources in an effort to resolve issues.

This chapter focuses on global manufacturing giant, Unilever, which has reached the pinnacle of cross-sector collaboration with a range of different not-for-profit organisations (NPOs). Of particular interest is their dynamic relationship with Greenpeace. Over time, both organisations have adapted their strategies and tactics to meet stakeholder expectations and solicit change. Focusing on the very successful 2008 campaign led by Greenpeace, this chapter demonstrates the importance of being proactive, of reacting to crisis in a timely manner, and of being willing to embrace responsibility. United, both organisations have positively altered the fate of Indonesia's forests while demonstrating the influence of cross-sector collaboration.

Cross-sector collaboration and issue management

Seminal articles on CSR date back to the 1970s (Carroll, 1979). Over time, CSR has grown from an 'add on' activity that few FPOs engaged in, to become an integrated approach to business activities. The tide has turned, and it is reasonable to expect that FPOs will assume responsibility and repair, restore and support any impact they may have on the environment and the communities in which they operate. While there are still some FPOs which do not invest in society, or which choose to only fulfil basic stakeholder expectations, others are leading the field and have taken CSR to new heights. These organisations are proactive and strategic in the manner in which they deal with social and environmental issues. As a result, they are generating positive changes both locally and globally. As such, social investment initiatives not only fulfil an organisation's CSR agenda but have become models of best practice towards resolving societal problems.

Speculation surrounds who should be responsible for the management of issues, particularly those that fall outside the scope of business activities. Overall, there is growing recognition that the public (government) sector has insufficient resources to resolve all of the problems society faces and as such they are reliant on the support of other sectors to fill this void (Austin, 2000a, 2000b; Googins & Rochlin, 2000; Waddock, 1988).

It would be unreasonable to assume that any one sector should be responsible for resolving society's ills, yet there is mounting pressure on the private sector to take the lead. Realising that FPOs do not have the expertise, knowledge and skills to address broader societal issues, they have turned to the not-for-profit sector to fill this void. Resultant cross-sector collaboration sees organisations work together with the FPOs injecting much needed financial resources into initiatives guided by the skills and expertise of NPOs. The result is an 'everybody wins' situation for the private and not-for-profit sector partners and the communities they serve.

Cross-sector collaboration has become an important tactic for some NPOs; together they are exploring new ways of addressing their missions (Murphy & Bendell, 1999; Rondinelli et al., 2006). Organisations from the not-for-profit, private and public sectors may link or share resources and skills to help each other resolve a problem or search for a solution that alone they would be unable to achieve (Bryson, Crosby & Middleton Stone, 2006; Gray, 1989).

While entering into relationships with the private sector has become an acceptable, viable option (Austin 2000a), not all NPOs wish to collaborate with businesses. Collaboration represents a shift in thinking from the not-for-profit sector, particularly those that traditionally employed adversarial tactics. An NPO's organisational strategy may provide an indication of their willingness to collaborate. Elkington and Fennell (1998) classified NPOs according to their organisational strategy, which reflects their operational practices or tactics, their level of influence on other stakeholder opinions, and their representation of public opinion. They referred to this as **typology** (Elkington & Fennell, 1998); the style an NPO adopts depends on its ideology, skills, campaign success or behaviour, and responsiveness to business.

Typology: The tactics NPOs use to create awareness.

A spectrum of NPO typologies can be visualised, ranging from adversarial through to collaborative. Adversarial NPOs adopt a confrontational approach with many regarding collaboration with the private sector as a risk to their values and reputation. Adversarial tactics include confrontational activities such as media campaigns and boycotts which are used to force change among organisations that are deemed to be impacting society and/or the environment. In their fight for marine protection, The Sea Shepherd Conservation Society is an example of an NPO that utilised adversarial tactics. Organisations employing such tactics are labelled as 'polarisers' (Elkington & Fennell, 1998) or 'protesters' (Åhlström & Sjöström, 2005).

While confrontation and campaigns that single out organisations may be the preferred tactics of a polariser, others will adapt their range of tactics to suit the situation as it unfolds. There are times when dialogue can work just as effectively. While this may not be considered a truly collaborative approach, periodic exchanges of formal or informal communication (Elkington & Fennell, 1998) ensures that private sector organisations are aware that their activities are being watched and noted.

The other end of the spectrum contains NPOs that are willing to collaborate with the private sector; however, there are differences as to how they will engage. Bendell supported the notion that there is a growing trend towards more collaborative styles of behaviour (2000). Here, NPOs choose to promote, facilitate and produce change through negotiated agreements, consultation and providing alternatives. NPOs that employ such tactics are labelled 'integrators' by Elkington and Fennell (1998: 58), which is the hardest strategy for NPOs to adopt, but the one to which they most aspire, mixing their skills as integrators: 'trust, openness, and willingness to understand the other's perspective' with the credibility they convey as discriminators; seeking 'interesting projects requiring a sophisticated and intelligent approach'.

Cross-sector collaboration takes many forms. Once a decision to collaborate has been made, the type of activity and degree of collaborative commitment needs consideration. When grouped according to the amount of engagement that exists between partnering organisations, there are three general classifications of cross-sector collaborations that have been summarised by Austin (2000a; 2000b): 1) philanthropic, 2) transactional and 3) integrative. Contributions from several authors investigating cross-sector collaboration have provided further expansion of Austin's (2000a, 2000b) three general classifications. Table 6.1 provides a synthesis of activities relevant to each type of relationship, noting the subtle differences and associated benefits for participating sectors.

Not-for-profit acceptance of private sector involvement can be considered a positive turning point for innovative solutions towards issue management. The realisation that the private sector can help NPOs achieve solutions towards their social and environmental objectives, Heap (2000)

Table 6.1 Types of not-for-profit and business collaboration

Collaboration	Type of relationship	Activities	Commitment	Business benefit	Not-for-profit benefit
Philanthropic	Corporate philanthropy	Charitable donations, in-kind contributions or gifts from the business to the NPO.	Lowest ↓	Tax write-off, public relations, business rationale, alignment, brand recognition, reputation/image, reach new target market.	Finance, application towards NPO cause/goal.
	Corporate foundation	Grants or charitable donations through separate NPO entity created by a business.		Reputation/image, reach new target market/increase awareness.	Finance, application towards NPO cause/goal.
Transactional	Licensing agreements	Business uses NPO name for a fee or royalty.		Increased revenues through increased sales, reputation/image.	Finance, increase awareness, application towards NPO cause/goal.
	Commercial sponsorship	Business exchanges cash or in-kind contributions for NPO promotion of product or service.		Reputation/image, reach new target market/increase awareness, advertising, increased revenues through increased sales.	Finance, application towards NPO cause/goal.

(continued)

Collaboration	Type of relationship	Activities	Commitment	Business benefit	Not-for-profit benefit
	Socio-sponsorship	Business resources meet social needs and receive compensation rewards.		Reputation/ image, reach new target market/ increase awareness, social responsibility, compensation rewards.	Finance, application towards NPO cause/goal.
	Cause-related marketing (or transaction-based promotions)	Percentage of revenue generated from business sales is donated to a publicised NPO cause.		Increased revenues through increased sales, reputation/ image, and increased goodwill.	Finance, increase awareness/ expo, application towards NPO cause/goal.
Integrative	Partnership approach	Cross-sector collaboration to solve social problem of mutual concern. Aim to create new value together.		Reputation/ image, changes to administrative system, social relations, physical infrastructure. Innovation opportunities.	High NPO control, application towards NPO cause/goal, changes to administrative system, social relations, and physical infrastructure. Innovation opportunities.
	Social partnerships				
	Alliances				
	Joint ventures		Highest		

Source: Adapted from Austin, 2000a, 2000b; Elkington & Fennell, 1998; Hartman & Stafford, 1997; Kanter, 1994; Samu & Wymer, 2001; Seitanidi, 2006; Seitanidi & Ryan, 2007; Waddock & Post, 1995; Wymer & Samu, 2003, cited in McDonald, 2010:15.

believed, has contributed to an increase in the number of cross-sector collaborations. This is supported by Milne, Iyer and Gooding-Williams (1996: 203) who suggested that environmental organisations in particular 'are abandoning the "us versus them" mentality with regard to business by allying themselves with businesses to better pursue mutual goals'. In describing the benefits of adopting an inclusive strategy, Lyons (2007) believed NPOs that partner with private sector organisations can create faster, necessary and far-reaching changes.

Case background

Unilever is a global consumer goods company that owns and manufactures a range of products including food, beverages and toiletries. Included in its portfolio are well-known brands such as

Dove™ hygiene products, Flora™ margarine, and the Omo cleaning range (Unilever, 2013a). Unilever globally employs 171 000 people, sells products in over 190 countries, and estimates that two billion consumers use a Unilever product on any given day (Unilever, 2011).

Evident throughout its history, Unilever prides itself on its underlying values. It began in the late 19th century with products that sought to improve the health and hygiene of their employees and continues today with the ethos 'that success means acting with 'the highest standards of corporate behaviour towards our employees, consumers and the societies and world in which we live' (Unilever, 2013b). Its social and environmental investment which includes philanthropy, innovative campaigns and sustainable practice are recognised globally. Sustainable brands have been acquired, such as Ben and Jerry's ice-cream, and positive initiatives have been generated within the organisation, such as the Omo *'Dirt is good'* campaign. This case will focus on the collaborative activities that Unilever has undertaken.

Relationship portfolio

A portfolio of relationships exists between Unilever, NPOs and/or government departments. Some of the issues being addressed are localised to one town, region or country, while others span borders and are considered global relationships. The relationships Unilever has with communities, government departments and NPOs span the collaborative spectrum arranged in Table 6.1, yet those with the highest profile tend to be those addressing broader issues on an integrative level. Table 6.2 presents a selection of some of the relationships between Unilever and NPOs or government agencies that tackle broader issues and thus are classified as integrative (Table 6.1).

The partnerships listed in Table 6.2 provide evidence of Unilever's strategic approach to issue management. It is unlikely that stakeholders linked to the issues identified in Table 6.2 would single out Unilever as responsible for the overall improvement in these diverse areas, yet in each example Unilever has taken a proactive leadership role, assumed responsibility to help present a solution, and helped establish and maintain momentum for each cause.

Unilever's leadership role became pivotal in the quest for sustainable palm oil. As one of the largest buyers of palm oil (Unilever, 2013g), Unilever relies on suppliers in Malaysia and Indonesia to source this ingredient. Conscious of the devastating effects associated with deforestation, Unilever developed 'Good Agricultural Practice Guidelines for Palm Oil', which led to its representation as founding member of the Roundtable on Sustainable Palm Oil (RSPO) in 2004 (Unilever, 2013h). The RSPO was composed of representatives from industry and the NPO, WWF. RSPO is a not-for-profit association that brings together stakeholders from seven sectors of the palm oil industry, namely oil palm producers, palm oil processors or traders, consumer goods manufacturers, retailers, banks and investors, environmental and social NGOs, to develop and implement global standards for sustainable palm oil. The RSPO currently has more than 500 members, representing more than 40 per cent of all palm oil produced in the world. Working to increase the amount of certified sustainable palm oil

Table 6.2 Unilever partnership initiatives

Partner	Initiative
United States Agency for International Development (USAID)'s Maternal and Child Health Integrated Program (MCHIP)	'Handwashing to reduce newborn mortality': 'The partnership aims to improve handwashing practices among birth attendants and family members in developing countries, reducing the risk of newborn deaths caused by infection.'[1]
FDI World Dental Federation	'[T]he two organisations drive nationwide campaigns globally and widely promote educational material on the importance of tooth-brushing to schools and dentists.'[2]
World Wide Fund for Nature (WWF)	'Marine Stewardship Council (MSC)': '[T]o establish a global standard for sustainable fisheries management.'[3]
Learning Links	'Reading for life': Volunteer support helps improve children's reading, self-esteem and motivation.[4]
Butterfly Foundation	'The Dove BodyThink program': '[P]romoting positive body image messages to young people and the broader community through the Unilever Dove Self-Esteem Fund, in partnership with the Butterfly Foundation.'[5]

Source: [1]Unilever (2013c); [2]Unilever (2013d); [3]Unilever (2013e); [4]Learning Links (2012); [5]Unilever (2013f).

that is available, the RSPO has set sustainability criteria against which suppliers can now be certified (Unilever, 2013h).

This initiative sought to fill the void left by governments who were unable to regulate the sector or give priority towards forest preservation over economic development (Unilever, 2013h). However, while Unilever has successfully positioned itself as an enviable leader in social responsibility, remaining at this level involves constant renewal of processes and practice. This extends to its supply chain for there are reputational consequences if suppliers do not conform to ethical practices. Although Unilever works with its suppliers, persuading them to adopt sustainable practice, a report released by Greenpeace in 2008 revealed that more needed to be done.

Several of Unilever's suppliers were implicated in the Greenpeace report, 'How Unilever palm oil suppliers are burning up Borneo' (Greenpeace International, 2008a). This report criticised Unilever's lack of leadership in sustainable palm oil and lack of awareness of the practices that accompany palm oil production. The report names and shames several of Unilever's suppliers, and graphically illustrates the destructive loss of habitat, warning of the subsequent extinction risks for vulnerable animals such as orangutans (Greenpeace International, 2008a).

Alarmed by the devastating effects of deforestation on orangutan habitat in Indonesia, Greenpeace launched a geographically dispersed activism campaign on 21 April 2008. Dressed in orangutan costumes, Greenpeace activists protested at two Unilever sites in the United Kingdom, with similar protests in Netherlands and Italy (Greenpeace International, 2008b). In addition, a

Figure 6.1 Forest clearing for palm oil plantations in Riau (© Greenpeace/John Novis)

Figure 6.2 Forests action against Unilever in Liverpool (© Will Rose/Greenpeace)

creative video went viral via social media. *Dove Onslaught(er)* was a parody on Unilever's popular YouTube clip *Onslaught*.

Supported by the Dove™ self-esteem fund, the original *Onslaught* advertisement drew attention to the overwhelming number of images produced by the beauty industry that a child is exposed to as they navigate their way into adulthood. Backed by a music track, the fast-paced imagery portraying female perfectionism in the beauty industry addresses those audiences concerned about the negative impact this can have on self-esteem. The video concludes with a written caption: 'Talk to your daughter before the beauty industry does' (Piper, 2007). Greenpeace's parody replicated the fast-paced visual imagery that a child faces, yet the images are of the blatant destruction of her community and the habitat that surrounds her. The beautiful and impactful images transition into those more graphic and disturbing. The YouTube video concludes with the caption: '98% of Indonesia's lowland forest will be gone by the time Azizah is 25. Most is destroyed to make palm oil, which is used in Dove products. Talk to Dove before it's too late' (Greenpeace, 2008).

Greenpeace felt that they would achieve change more effectively by publicly exposing Unilever's involvement and responsibility towards palm oil rather than endorsing a consumer boycott campaign (Greenpeace International, 2009a).The *Dove Onslaught(er)* video has now been viewed over one and a half million times. Overall, the various tactics used by Greenpeace to draw attention to the issue were successful and the response from Unilever was swift. On 9 May 2008, Greenpeace and Unilever representatives met and agreed to the need for proactive leadership.

Averting crisis, Unilever responded within two weeks, began collaborating with Greenpeace and led the way to generate change within the sector. In a transparent act, Unilever commissioned its own independent study and published the results which had confirmed Greenpeace's original findings (Unilever, 2013i). Unilever shared the findings with its suppliers urging them to rectify their practice, suspending purchases from one supplier in particular, until they could 'provide verifiable proof that none of their plantations are contributing to the destruction of "high conservation value" forests or expanding onto peat lands' (Unilever, 2013i).

Collaboration between Greenpeace and Unilever achieved much more than a reaction to public exposure and pressure on suppliers. Accepting its status as leader within the industry, Unilever also agreed to 'support an immediate moratorium on deforestation for palm oil in South East Asia' and lobby the Indonesian government and all the major companies such as Kraft, Nestlé and Cadbury to immediately support the moratorium (Greenpeace International, 2009b).

This case presented a snapshot of two organisations that adopt proactive strategies towards issue management. The steps Unilever undertook to become a proactive leader in issue management provided a solid foundation upon which to approach impending crises. In addition, the innovativeness and responsiveness of Greenpeace is also captured through its use of clever and creative campaigning.

Conclusion

While activism prompted a reaction, the willingness of both sectors to work collaboratively demonstrates the capacity of cross-sector relationships to be able to influence and change unsustainable practices. From a tactical perspective, NPOs that are prepared to collaborate with FPOs which share the same overarching objective are well placed to encourage societal change. FPOs that are prepared to move beyond reactive strategies and invest in achieving long-term objectives may achieve reputational benefits while demonstrating leadership among their peers. Together, the two organisations in this case have demonstrated the fast pace at which sustainable change can occur.

CASE QUESTIONS

1. Collaboration has provided some well-known cross-sector relationships. Using Table 6.1, can you provide an example for each relationship type?

2. How significant is the role of Unilever in achieving sustainable solutions?
3. Why do you think Unilever responded quickly to the Greenpeace campaign?
4. Deforestation remains a significant problem; has there been any progress surrounding this issue since?

BIBLIOGRAPHY

Ählström, J. and Sjöström, E. (2005). CSOs and business partnerships: Strategies for interaction. *Business Strategy and the Environment*, 14, 230–40.

Austin, J. E. (2000a). *The collaboration challenge: How nonprofits and businesses succeed through strategic alliances*. San Francisco, CA: Jossey-Bass.

Austin, J. E. (2000b). Strategic collaboration between nonprofits and businesses. *Nonprofit and Voluntary Sector Quarterly*, 29(1), 69–97.

Bendell, J. (2000). Civil regulation: A new form of democratic governance for the global economy? In J. Bendell (ed.) *Terms for Endearment: Business, NGOs and Sustainable Development* (pp. 239–54). Sheffield, UK: Greenleaf Publishing.

Bryson, J. M., Crosby, B. C. & Middleton Stone, M. (2006). The design and implementation of cross-sector collaborations: Propositions from the literature. *Public Administration Review*, 66(6), November/December, 44–55.

Carroll, A. B. (1979). A three-dimensional conceptual model of corporate performance. *Academy of Management Review*, 4(4), 497–505.

Elkington, J. and Fennell, S. (1998). Partners for sustainability. In *Terms for Endearment: Business, NGOs and Sustainable Development*, (pp. 48–60), J. Bendell (ed.). Sheffield, UK: Greenleaf Publishing.

Googins, B. K. & Rochlin, S. A. (2000). Creating the Partnership Society: Understanding the rhetoric and reality of cross-sectoral partnerships. *Business and Society Review*, 105(1), pp. 127–44.

Gray, B. (1989). *Collaborating*. San Francisco, CA: Jossey-Bass.

Greenpeace (2008, 21 April). *Dove Onslaught(er)*. Video. Retrieved from www.youtube.com/watch?v=odI7pQFyjso.

Greenpeace International (2008a). *How Unilever palm oil suppliers are burning up Borneo*. PDF. Retrieved 10 January 2013 from www.greenpeace.org/international/Global/international/planet-2/report/2009/10/how-unilever-palm-oil-supplier.pdf.

Greenpeace International (2008b). *Unilever's 'Monkey Business': Greenpeace swings into action*. Retrieved 10 January 2013 from www.greenpeace.org/international/en/news/features/unilever-monkey-business210408.

Greenpeace International (2009a). *Unilever campaign questions and answers*. Retrieved 10 January 2013 from www.greenpeace.org/international/en/campaigns/forests/asia-pacific/dove-palmoil-action/unilever-campaign-info.

Greenpeace International (2009b). Public pressure for Indonesia's forests works, Ask Unilever Background. Retrieved 10 January 2013 from www.greenpeace.org/international/en/campaigns/forests/asia-pacific/dove-palmoil-action.

Hartman, C. L. and Stafford, E. R. (1997). Green alliances: Building new business with environmental groups. *Long Range Planning*, 30(2), 184–96.

Heap, S. (2000). *NGOs engaging with business: A world of difference and a difference to the world*. Oxford: INTRAC.

Husted, B. W. (2003). Governance choice for corporate social responsibility: To contribute, collaborate or internalize? *Long Range Planning*, 36, 481–98.

Kanter, R. M. (1994). Collaborative advantage: The art of alliances. *Harvard Business Review*, July–August: 96–108.

Learning Links (2012). *Services*. Retrieved 15 January 2013 from www.learninglinks.org.au/services-cas-reading-counting.php.

Lyons, M. (2007). Third sector opportunities and challenges: A four-sector analysis. *Third Sector Review*, 13(2), 9–26.

McDonald, S. (2010). *Cross-sector social partnerships within Australia: Strategies for success*. Unpublished PhD thesis. Graduate School of Management, La Trobe University, Melbourne.

McIntosh, M., Leipziger, D., Jones, K. and Coleman, G. (1998). *Corporate citizenship: Successful strategies for responsible companies*. London: Financial Times Pitman Publishing.

Milne, G. R., Iyer, E. S. & Gooding-Williams, S. (1996). Environmental organization alliance relationships within and across nonprofit, business, and government sectors. *Journal of Public Policy and Marketing*, 15(2), 203–15.

Murphy, D. F. & Bendell, J. (1999). Partners in time? Business, NGOs and sustainable development. *United Nations Research Institute for Social Development*, 1–86.

Piper, T. (2007, 7 October). *Beauty Pressure*. Video. Retrieved from www.youtube.com/watch?v=Ei6JvK0W60I.

Rondinelli, D. A, London, T. & O'Neill, H. (2006). Strange bedfellows: Alliances between corporations and nonprofits. In *Handbook of strategic alliances*, O. Shenkar & J. J. Reuer (eds). Thousand Oaks, CA: Sage Publications: 353–66.

Samu, S. & Wymer, W. W. (2001). Nonprofit-business alliance model formation and outcomes. *Journal of Nonprofit & Public Sector Marketing*, 9(1/2), 45–61.

Seitanidi, M. M. (2006). *Partnerships between nonprofit organisations and businesses in the UK: A critical examination of partnerships*. Doctoral thesis. International Centre for Corporate Social Responsibility (ICCSR), University of Nottingham.

Seitanidi, M. M. & Ryan, A. (2007). A critical review of forms of corporate community involvement: From philanthropy to partnerships. *International Journal of Nonprofit and Voluntary Sector Marketing*, 12: 247–66.

Unilever (2009a). About Us, *1920s*. Retrieved 5 May 2009 from www.unilever.com/aboutus/ourhistory/1920s.aspx.

Unilever (2009b). *Annual Report and Accounts 2009*. PDF. Retrieved 22 November 2010 from http://annualreport09.unilever.com/downloads/Unilever_AR09.pdf.

Unilever (2011). Annual Report and Accounts 2011. PDF. Retrieved 14 January 2013 from www.unilever.com/images/Unilever_AR11_tcm13–282960.pdf.

Unilever (2013a). View our brands. Retrieved 14 January 2013 from www.unilever.com/brands-in-action/view-brands.aspx.

Unilever (2013b). Our history. Retrieved 14 January 2013 from www.unilever.com/aboutus/ourhistory.

Unilever (2013c). Lifebuoy and USAID partnership for newborn health. Retrieved 14 January 2013 from www.unilever.com/brands-in-action/detail/Lifebuoy-and-USAID-partnership-for-newborn-health/292089/?WT.contenttype=brands%20in%20action [].

Unilever (2013d). Unilever's world dental federation partnership. Retrieved 14 January 2013 from www.unilever.com/brands-in-action/detail/Unilever-s-World-Dental-Federation-partnership/292109/?WT.contenttype=brands%20in%20action.

Unilever (2013e). Agricultural sourcing partnerships. Retrieved 14 January 2013 from www.unilever.com/sustainable-living/sustainablesourcing/agriculturalsourcingpartnerships.

Unilever (2013f). The Dove Body Think Program. Retrieved 14 January 2013 from www.unilever.com.au/brands-in-action/detail/The-Dove-BodyThink-program/311696.

Unilever (2013g). *Sustainable palm oil*. Retrieved 14 January 2013 from www.unilever.com/sustainable-living/sustainablesourcing/palmoil.

Unilever (2013h). Roundtable on sustainable palm oil (RSPO). Retrieved 14 January 2013 from www.unilever.com/sustainable-living/sustainablesourcing/palmoil/rspo.

Unilever (2013i). Working with suppliers. Retrieved 14 January 2013 from www.unilever.com/sustainable-living/sustainablesourcing/palmoil/suppliers/index.aspx.

Unilever Australasia (2009). *Our values, purpose and principles*. Retrieved 5 May 2009 from www.unilever.com.au/ourvalues/purposeandprinciples.

Waddock, S. A. (1988). Building successful social partnerships. *Sloan Management Review*, 29(4), 17–23.

Waddock, S. A. & Post, J. E. (1995). Catalytic alliances for social problem solving. *Human Relations*, 48(8), 951–73.

Wymer Jr, W. W. & Samu, S. (2003). Dimensions of business and nonprofit collaborative relationships. *Journal of Nonprofit and Public Sector Marketing*, 11(1), 3–22.

PART 4

SOCIAL MEDIA **AND CRISIS**

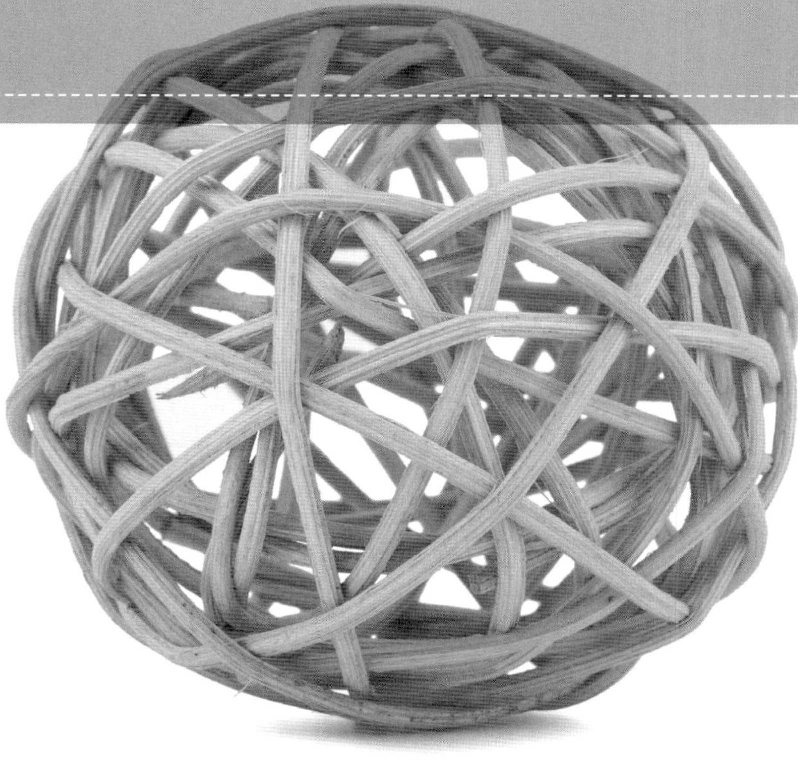

7

MEDIA TARGETS

WHEN A SPARK IN SOCIAL MEDIA DEVELOPS INTO A MAINSTREAM MEDIA FIRESTORM

Kristy Hess and Lisa Waller

Chapter objectives

This chapter aims to:

- investigate how public relations professionals can best manage social media crises of high interest to mainstream media
- explore the growing importance of social media as a source of news for mainstream media organisations and the consequences for public relations professionals when social media generates 'bad news' stories for their organisations
- examine journalists' news values and news routines and the importance of understanding how they can deepen or dissolve a social media crisis
- outline strategies to deal with a social media crisis and engage effectively with mainstream media.

Introduction

Organisations cannot forecast when an angry Facebook fan's post will spark a national debate in mainstream media, or a deluge of negative comments about a new corporate video on YouTube will catapault it onto breakfast television. However, being able to spot news value in an online forum and knowing how and why the news media might respond can help public relations professionals to deal effectively with such crises. This involves understanding and respecting the perspective of the journalist (Doorley & Garcia, 2011) and the norms and values that guide their work. Developing good relationships with journalists, understanding news cycles and having a proactive public relations plan are some of the important principles for crisis management (Regester & Larkin, 2008) and help to ensure organisations are prepared to deal with these emerging scenarios in a new media landscape. How well a social media crisis is handled will define people's perceptions of the brand, company or organisation. This chapter explores these issues through the case of Australian mass market retailer Target's 2012 media crisis over its fashions for girls aged 7–14. The controversy was sparked when a mother posted a message on the company's Facebook page asking it to sell some clothes that didn't make young girls 'look like tramps'. The case offers lessons on the importance of monitoring social media and being prepared to step in and speak up in order to steer the public conversation that now takes place across multiple platforms.

Background

The global commercial media is still coming to terms with the latest transformations of the media landscape in which corporate control is slipping and redefining itself by finding ways to meet the challenges posed by the new cultural forms, delivery systems and diversification Web 2.0 presents. The conversation now focuses on how news is defined and produced, examining what Rosen (2006) refers to as 'the people formerly known as the audience' – that is, the owners and operators of communication tools that provide the means to publish and broadcast. Such tools were once monopolised by media professionals and guaranteed their role in shaping the news. Now anyone with access to a smartphone, computer and internet connection can publish instantly, revolutionising what is considered news and how that news is produced. Jarvis (2006), for example, describes the emergence of blogging and citizen journalism as 'networked journalism' which takes into account

> the collaborative nature of journalism now: professionals and amateurs working together to get the real story, linking to each other to share facts, questions, answers, ideas, perspectives. It recognises the complex relationships that make the news. And it focuses on the process more than the product.
>
> (Jarvis, 2006)

The digital environment also means that many mainstream media outlets are becoming interactively connected, as information flows more easily across technical, social and geographical boundaries (Dueze, 2011; Jenkins, 2006). Traditional news media now work across multiple media platforms, and news and information can be produced and disseminated at a rapid pace across the globe. Changes to the business model have resulted in many radio outlets, television networks and newspapers being owned by the same media conglomerates. These news networks ensure a 'local' story can go national and global with the click of a button. It also signifies an end to the old saying 'today's newspaper is tomorrow's fish and chip wrapper', as content is archived across digital spaces, from news websites to Google and blogs.

For companies that are subjected to pillorying by social media and intense news media attention, the negative coverage is often archived and stored via one of the most powerful informational nodes of the 21st century – Google. Type 'Target Australia girls' clothing' into the Google search engine and the saga of 2012 is still likely to appear in the top search results today. This has the potential to impact on the reputation or image of a company for months or even years after a negative news story first breaks. Understanding the process by which citizen-generated social media campaigns can snowball into major media stories is essential if public relations practictioners are to effectively handle a social media crisis and retain a positive image for their organisation. Handling a crisis well involves the organisation demonstrating the skills and knowledge to assert itself as the authoritative voice by telling its own story in both social and mainstream media, and tell it fast (Regester & Larkin, 2008). This begins with being able to identify emerging issues that provide scope for wider social discussion because many people will have an opinion or experience of the topic. In order to respond quickly, public relations specialists need to be tuned in to discussions within social media and be able to spot topics that may be controversial and have high news value. They also need to be skilled in quickly developing their own robust narratives that can be used to influence public discussion.

The changing nature of information subsidies

The relationship between public relations (institutions and organisations) and journalism largely focuses on 'subsidised news' (Gandy, 1982) – news that occurs because a person, group or organisation either does something public and newsworthy, or seeks media attention. Gandy (1982) said that journalists 'favour bureaucratic sources who can provide a regular, credible and ultimately useable flow of information, insight and imagery with which to construct the news' (p. 13). Elite sources, such as those within government or powerful organisations, work to provide information subsidies with the stamp of authenticity and the appropriate news values to ensure journalists will use their material in the construction of news stories, ultimately reaching their targeted publics (Gans, 1979).

Public relations practitioners have long been understood to participate in the process of newsmaking through these subsidies, but in this chapter we argue that social media and the 'people formerly known as the audience' now have the power to serve as important sources of **news subsidy** in the digital age through media such as Twitter (Murthy, 2013) and Facebook. The reasons for this are straightforward. The mainstream news media has always survived on its ability to maintain a dialogue with contemporary cultural trends (Conboy, 2002), so it comes as little surprise that, as audiences move into social media forums, the mainstream news media are moving with them. When a YouTube clip goes viral, or a discussion thread in Facebook attracts thousands of comments in a matter of hours, the issue is guaranteed a certain level of popularity, and therefore represents a story that news organisations want high on their **news agenda**, to enable them to connect with social media users and attract even bigger audiences. It is also attractive from a **political economy perspective**. Social media sites, celebrated for their free, participatory culture, are of great interest to mainstream media because they present opportunities to **crowdsource** stories and extend the

News subsidy: Traditionally understood as information in the form of press releases or background briefings and events that provide newsmakers with material they can use in the preparation of news reports, such as press conferences, performances and public announcements. It is now more widely defined as information provided to journalists.

News agenda: The ordering of the news, which is understood to be influenced by journalists' news values.

Political economy perspective: Political economy is the study of the interrelationships between political and economic processes.

Crowdsourcing: The practice of journalists outsourcing research tasks to their audiences, who gather and help to interpret information for their use.

life of those stories outside these spaces. As we shall see with the Target example, journalists do this by contextualising the issue for audiences.

Burns (2012) indicates that while news values, which we shall discuss shortly, are useful for understanding how journalists produce news stories, they are not the only factor influencing their decisions. She cites problems such as time restraints, space and staffing – issues that stem from the commercial nature of news – that leave journalists 'taking the line of least resistance and selecting those news items that are the easiest to find and edit' (p. 30). Sissons (2006) argues that in times of cost cutting and economic rationalism, journalists have become increasingly and excessively reliant on information supplied to them as staff numbers have been reduced. Davis (2003), meanwhile, indicates that journalists feel increasingly compelled to react to what is made available free of charge rather than proactively finding and researching stories, which takes time and requires valuable editorial resources.

News values

It is important that the public relations consultant is aware of the set of collective cultural codes that assist journalists in gathering and producing the news so they can be on the look out for the types of social media conversations that can evolve into a full-blown crisis. Galtung and Ruge's (1965) study of the news outlines eight widely cited news values:

- *Impact*: The significance, importance, or consequence of an event; the greater the consequence, and the larger the number of people for whom an event is important the greater the newsworthiness.
- *Timeliness*: The more recent, the more newsworthy.
- *Prominence*: Occurrences featuring well-know individuals or institutions are newsworthy. Well-knownness may spring either from the power the person or institution possesses.
- *Proximity*: Closeness of the occurrence to the audience may be gauged either geographically or in terms of the assumed values, interest and expectations of the news audience.
- *The Bizarre*: The unusual, unorthodox or unexpected attracts attention.
- *Conflict*: Controversy and open clashes are newsworthy, inviting attention on their own, almost regardless of what the conflict is over. Conflict reveals underlying causes of disagreement between individuals and institutions in a society.
- *Currency*: Occasionally something becomes an idea whose time has come. The matter assumes a life of its own, and for a time assumes momentum in news reportage.
- *Human Interest*: Those stories that have more of an entertainment factor versus any of the above – not that some of the other news values cannot have an entertainment value.

News is often further categorised into two main types: hard news and soft news. While there is much academic debate about what the terms mean (Reinemann et al., 2012), hard news is broadly defined as the type of stories that concern serious or important topics with a sense of immediacy, such as speeches by powerful people, crimes and major weather stories such as floods and fires. Soft news, meanwhile, is understood to have a set of characteristics that include being informational, educational, emotional or entertaining. Lynch (2012) argues these are the types of stories that 'are heartwarming tales about ordinary people who overcome obstacles, do extraordinary deeds or accomplish something noteworthy' (Lynch, 2012, p. 56). They also help to provide the 'human interest angle' to hard news topics, particularly in regards to major social issues or stories about statistics, as we will see with the Target example.

Trending: Most news and social media sites now have 'trending' sections where viewers can see the most popular articles and tweets available to read.

These news values and styles, along with journalistic routines, are not stagnant and are constantly evolving in the ditial era. We suggest, for example, that what's **trending** in social media can be considered under the No. 1 traditional news value of 'Impact', a view we shall explore within the case study shortly. Commentators such as Harcup and O'Neill (2001) say as many stories are apparently manufactured, Galtung and Ruge's (1965) classic list of news values should be open to question. They argue that the dominance of celebrity and social news, the blurring of the boundary between news and reality shows and other popular culture, and the advent of citizen journalism may suggest that the nature of 'news' and news values are evolving and that traditional models of the news process are now only partially relevant. In an attempt to achieve relevance and maintain their share in a rapidly evolving market, news organisations may find themselves forced to adopt alternative news values that will attract and keep audiences. As we have already discussed, the growth of interactive media and citizen journalism is fast altering the traditional distinction between news producers and their hitherto passive audiences. Social media is already ubiquitous in the communication landscape and a wider range of media platforms are being used to identify and disseminate news. Deitz (2010) argues that Facebook, YouTube and Twitter are not replacing journalists or journalism 'but through their very existence are questioning the conventions of traditional news and current affairs, including how such conventions may constrain what and who is regarded as newsworthy' (Deitz, 2010, p. 7).

Case focus

As we have highlighted, the ability of 'everyday' audiences to use social media to immediately name and shame retailers who they think have crossed some moral boundary – and to organise highly effective and media-savvy campaigns against them – can quickly become a public relations nightmare. This case study provides a step-by-step analysis of such a crisis. It involves major Australian department store Target and a social media backlash over its range of children's clothing. It highlights some of the important practices performed by public relations experts in crisis situations and the lessons that can be learned from such a case.

In August 2012 a disgruntled Australian mother posted comments on Target's Facebook page calling on the company to stop selling clothes that promoted the sexualisation of young girls and made them look like 'tramps'. Primary school teacher Ana Amini, a mother of a six-year-old girl, wrote:

> Dear Target, Could you possibly make a range of clothing for girls 7–14 years that doesn't make them look like tramps? You have lost me as a customer when buying apparel for my daughter as I don't want her thinking shorts up her backside are the norm or fashionable.

Her open letter triggered a social media storm – attracting 44 000 responses in just over 24 hours. Within two days, the story had been picked up and was being covered by the Fairfax Media network – an Australian media conglomerate with nationwide radio, newspaper and television interests. It was only moments before the story broke in the mainstream press (about 72 hours after the initial post) that Target responded on its Facebook page with the following letter to customers:

> Hi everyone, we always appreciate your feedback on our childrenswear range. In most cases, before products are available at Target, they are reviewed and assessed by a panel of our customers and their feedback is incorporated into our design decisions. We know there is a huge diversity of opinion when it comes to children's clothing, which is why we believe in taking great care in ensuring that our range is both age appropriate and something that your kids will love. Whether it's instore or online, we always aim to provide a variety of products so that you have a choice of clothing for your children. It's very important to our childrenswear team to understand your individual concerns and suggestions about the range so that we can take them into consideration for future product decisions. If you'd like to provide us with further details about specific products, we invite you to email facebook@target.com.au. We'd like to apologise for the delay in responding to your feedback. A word in the original post was flagged by Facebook as inappropriate and therefore was hidden from our view until it was brought to our attention today. Thanks for your patience and your valuable contribution.

But by this stage the damage was done. The story was being published in local, state and national newspapers, covered by current affairs programs and gathering momentum on Twitter. Within a week, the initial post on Facebook had received more than 80 000 likes before being taken down from the Target site.

One Fairfax reader, who commented in an online poll set up by *The Age* newspaper in the wake of the story to gauge people's reaction said:

> I'm amazed that it's taken this long for this subject to hit the broadsheets because it is discussed ad infinite [sic.] by mothers and girls of this age.

This reader identifies a key point that this chapter aims to address – what makes some social media comments and campaigns more newsworthy than others? Drawing on the literature and ideas generated earlier in this chapter, there are two reasons why an issue like this received such intense media attention.

News values

The first has to do with the cultural codes and conventions that journalists use to produce the news – what we commonly refer to as news values. Harcup and O'Neill (2001) suggest that the idea of 'magnitude' is an important news value that must be considered in the generation of 'news'. Magnitude refers to stories that are perceived as 'sufficently significant either in the numbers of people involved or potential impact'. Social media serves as a barometer to the types of issues that are of interest to the public so when a story gathers thousands of 'likes' in such a short space of time it is almost guaranteed to hit the mainstream media in some shape or form. For example, we can make a reasonable assumption that 80 000 likers on Facebook will translate into a readymade commercial news media audience.

Deciding what stories to give coverage to also depends enormously on the types of news values a story satisfies. The reader above points out that the sexualisation of children and the types of clothing young girls wear is not a new issue, but the groundswell generated from a sudden social media campaign guarantees that it satisfies the news value of 'timeliness'. The story also has a dimension of conflict (angry mothers challenging the big corporation) and there are elements of prominence (Target is arguably one of Australia's most well-known mass market retailers with stores in hundreds of regional cities and metropolitan areas across the country) and proximity – it was confined largely to an Australian audience(s), although the story was picked up by international newspaper *The Irish Independent* almost a year later in discussions about suitable clothing for young girls and a similar crisis facing department stores in the United Kingdom for selling inappropriate Halloween costumes (O'Shea, 2013). The national news coverage the Target issue generated shows it was an easy story for journalists from Toowoomba to Perth to localise through interviews with mothers of young girls in their regions.

Social media

The second reason an issue such as this can draw such intense media attention is the easy accessibility of content generated via social media sites such as YouTube and Facebook. At the click of a button, journalists can accurately gauge what is popular and attracting attention. It also enables them to instantly pinpoint people they can go to for interviews and additional information. As we have highlighted, it is a new contemporary form of what Gandy (1982) refers to as 'information subsidies'. And so, when a story breaks in the social media sphere news journalists look to contextualise the issue to give the story more traction. They do this by seeking out a range of opinions from experts and they look for the hard and soft news angles to help give the story life and depth outside of social media spaces. In covering the Target story, many media outlets sought interviews with the woman who triggered the debate, while others profiled mothers who shared their experiences of raising children and today's fashion (soft news). The *Townsville Bulletin*, meanwhile, interviewed a Psychology academic to highlight the impact of sexual images and clothing in the media on children (Mosch, 2012).

PR professionals are not alone in having to learn how to work with social media in all its dimensions. Journalists are also coming to terms with the relatively new phenomenon of social media campaigns and the ways in which they evolve into major news stories (Murthy, 2013).

Verification is a major issue for journalists sourcing stories from social media. They must adhere to their professional responsibilities of ensuring that the stories they present are factual and that they have considered an issue from a range of perspectives (Burns, 2012). Correspondingly, PR professionals need to carefully monitor mainstream news coverage and be proactive in seeking corrections for any errors journalists make in their reporting of a social media crisis (Regester & Larkin, 2008).

The old imperatives of 'quality journalism' can be seen in some of the coverage of the Target case, where journalists observed that it was 'lazy' thinking to blame a single retailer for a social phenomenon such as the sexualisation of children. This led some media commentators to defend Target over the issue. One well-known Fairfax fashion journalist, in a comment piece titled 'Why blaming store for sexy kids clothes is way off target' (Safe, 2012), argued that such retailers exist to make money not act as arbiters of values.

This comment piece was orchestrated by the news media itself, not on the subtle direction of a public relations strategy. However, it served Target well in terms of deflecting the focus from the company to the wider issue of the sexualisation of children. In Australia, there have been two recent Senate inquiries (2008, 2011) that examined the issue of young children being subjected to marketing and media pressures that encourage them to be and to look 'sexy'. There has been little government action (see childrenandmedia.org.au). In the United Kingdom, the Bailey Report (2011) recommended that all images used in public places and on television needed to be more 'family-friendly'. Specifically, the report called for retailers to stop selling and marketing inappropriate clothing, products or services for children. Safe's 2012 comment piece highlighted the wider issue, showing that the news media can in fact be an ally through the practices of quality journalism, which means examining an issue beyond the immediate story or crisis. Good media commentators are keen to explore the complexities of the issue, as Safe did, and shine a light on other social factors and players in the scenario. Knowing who these leading commentators are and establishing a relationship with them is part of a good crisis management strategy. Doorley and Garcia (2011) argue that news media's attitude towards the organisation in a social media crisis can begin with a neutral attitude at worst and a sympathetic one at best. They say it is when the news media believes an organisation at the centre of the crisis is unduly slow in providing information, reticent about providing 'talking heads' for interview, or thought to be withholding information that they become hostile. From the journalists' perspective these are practical barriers to 'getting the story' in a timely way as well as reasons to lose faith or trust in the organisation and its professional communicators.

So, what can PR consultants learn from gaining the 'inside' knowledge on the news production process in times of social media-generated crisis? The Target case provides some examples of the 'to dos' and 'not to dos'.

Prevent 'crisis creep': Monitor your social media at all times and respond swiftly

Firstly, the company arguably took too long to respond to the social media storm on Facebook. Facebook is not a 9-to-5, Monday-to-Friday proposition. If your organisation wants to use social media, it also needs to monitor what is happening constantly, because social media crises must be dealt with quickly. If your company has a Facebook page or a presence on Twitter or YouTube, be aware that there are consequences to promoting the brand in these public, sometimes volatile spaces. Social media commentator Thomas Tudehope has observed that historically, organisations have looked at the social media spaces they create as 'all about their own content "what are we going to post on our page?" Now it will be the other way around – what are users going to say on our page?' (Lee, 2012). Facebook is celebrated for its ability to connect people – including those with an axe to grind. When Target finally took steps to issue an apology on Facebeook, it did the right thing by attempting to take the discussion offline, asking customers to email the store via its Facebook account, but other contact details might have been suitable to regain control of where and when individuals could respond to the issue and be seen to be taken seriously.

Make the organisation the authoritative source of information on what has happened and what is being done about it

PR professionals are the best-placed people within any organisation to take responsibility for its social media under all circumstances, and especially in a crisis, since they have the specialist knowledge and skills to manage media relations and communication with all stakeholders. Commenting on the Target case, Gabriel McDowell of Res Publica, who is an adviser to corporations on social media, said there were recent Australian examples where social media crises have been compounded by 'the wrong people' running company Facebook pages:

> Control should be taken from advertising and marketing agencies, who are used to pushing a message, and handed to PR people who are better equipped to deal with the fallout.
>
> (McDowell quoted in Lee, 2012)

The top expert – the person whom journalists, the public and other stakeholders understand as the person in charge and the principal communicator for the organisation – is the organisation's chief executive officer (Doorley & Garcia, 2011). In times of crisis, do not provide a substitute; a PR professional, however well equipped to handle the crisis, is not an authority figure in the way a CEO is, particularly in the eyes of journalists. So, when Target issued its apology to Facebook followers, it should have personalised the message with the signature of the company's CEO, to highlight how seriously it was taking the issue. The message also needs to be focused on how the organisation feels and what actions are being taken (Regester, 2005). Mainstream and social media need to be monitored closely and the organisation must act quickly to correct any errors in the reporting or public discussion.

Develop a bank of 'experts' to take control of the conversation

It is also important for organisations and companies to develop their own list of 'experts' whom they can call on for advice or develop news angles around in the wake of a crisis. Gaining the perspectives of experts is how journalists 'contextualise' stories such as this, so it would be helpful if Target had been able to steer the conversation in the mainstream media. By bringing in its own experts to write about the issue or speak to mainstream journalists, it might have deflected some attention away from the company more quickly and shifted focus to the wider issue of the sexualisation of children. It could have also sent out a press release outlining the strong sales figures for that particular clothing range and how its designs responded to popular demand.

Build and maintain good relationships with journalists and their audiences

An early and honest PR intervention can prevent a negative spark in social media from becoming a full-blown media firestorm. However, when early containment is not possible, bear in mind that mainstream news media will take an interest and it is still the most credible source of information and acts as the most important conduit to shaping people's beliefs and behavior – so PR professionals need to think about mainstream media audiences as part of any social media crisis plan. Mass media remains the most critical media form in the PR cycle and once a narrative has formed, PR professionals are thrust into damage-control mode. Maintaining a good working relationship with journalists is an important part of crisis management generally (Regester & Larkin, 2008) and can ensure organisations are prepared to deal with a social media crisis that spills over into mainstream media. Organsiations need to be constantly working on making and maintaining their relationships with journalists and media commentators. Staying in close contact with reporters during a crisis is one of the best ways for finding out what is concerning them and what news they are expecting to hear next. This can help PR professionals to shape the style and content of press conferences and what information is provided in press releases. The key idea is to make the news media and key journalists allies – a respectful and friendly relationship can provide the context for creating opportunities to discuss sensitive issues 'off the record' and to do background briefings, if needed. Honest and open communication and dialogue, as well as preparedness to be seen taking the right action in a crisis can get the media onside as an ally. This is reinforced again and again in the PR literature (Doorley & Garcia, 2011).

Consider a follow-up, proactive or damage-control campaign

Organisations can rebuild their reputation by orchestrating a campaign to improve the company's profile among social media and mainstream media audiences. Target altered its range of clothing for young girls and publicised the changes in response to the intense response from social media users and the mainstream media (Davies, 2013). It may also be sensible to consider purchasing advertising space in traditional media outlets to ensure control of the message you want to send to audiences.

Conclusion

Social media and the internet are often portrayed as heralding the democratisation of news media. However, companies and organisations are fast realising that social media has a downside and that it requires specialist PR expertise to manage. Angry customers who vent their frustrations using social media tools pose an instant threat to a company's reputation, especially when what they are saying strikes a chord with the public on Facebook and Twitter. The Target case shows that when sparks of opinion gather momentum in social media circles they can quickly turn into a firestorm once the news media – with its powerful reach across local and global information networks – steps in and amplifies the issue. A PR practitioner who is armed with the appropriate strategies and 'inside' knowledge of both the social media and the journalistic world is well placed to ease the air of discontent as quickly and as swiftly as possible.

CASE QUESTIONS

1. How would you define a 'social media crisis'?
2. Can you identify a different kind of social media crisis than the one provided here, which is an attack on the reputation of an organisation? How is a social media crisis different from just a 'media crisis'?
3. Find a recent social media crisis and research the mainstream newspaper coverage it attracted. How wide-ranging was the discussion? Was it picked up by columnists and/or opinion writers, or only mentioned in the news pages? Who was the main spokesperson for the company or organisation? Do you think the organisation managed to establish itself as the authoritative voice on the issue?
4. Which of Galtung and Ruge's (1965) news values can be seen in play in the Target example? Which of these values do you think are most relevant?
5. What key steps does a PR professional need to take to reduce the impact of negative news media attention to his or her organisation?
6. Why does a PR professional need to pay close attention to social debates, such as those surrounding the sexualisation of children in advertising and marketing? Do you think that engaging with such debates might have been helpful in Target's case?

BIBLIOGRAPHY

Bailey, R. (2011). *Letting children be children: Report of an independent review of the commercialization and sexualisation of childhood*. London: Department of Education.

Burns, L. S. (2012). *Understanding journalism*, 2nd edn. London: Sage.

Conboy, M. (2002). *The press and popular culture*. London: Sage.

Davies, L. (2013). Ready, aim – Target. Part 3. Presto: *A Blog about social media and PR. Retrieved* 9 October 2013 from www.blogs.monash.edu.

Davis, A. (2003). Public relations and news sources. In S. Cottle (ed.), *News, public relations and power* (pp. 27–42). London: Sage.

Deitz, M. (2010). *Watch this space: The future of Australian journalism*. Melbourne: Cambridge University Press.

Doorley, J. & Garcia, H. (2011). *Reputation management: The key to successful public relations and corporate communication*, 2nd edn. New York: Routledge.

Dueze, M. (2011). Journalism and convergence culture. In S. Allan (ed.), *The Routledge companion to news and journalism* (pp. 265–75), London: Routledge.

Galtung, J. & Ruge, M. (1965). The structure of foreign news: The presentation of the Congo, Cuba and Cyprus crises in four Norwegian newspapers. *Journal of Peace Research*, 2, 64–91.

Gandy, O. (1982). *Beyond agenda setting: Information subsidies and public policy*. Norwood, NJ: Ablex.

Gans, H. J. (1979). *Deciding what's news: A study of CBS evening news, NBC nightly news, Newsweek, and Time*. New York: Pantheon Books.

Harcup, T. & O'Neill, D. (2001). What is news? Galtung and Ruge revisited. *Journalism Studies*, 2(2), 277.

Hess, K. & Waller, L. (2011). Blockbusters for the YouTube generation: A new product of convergence culture. *Refractory*, 19. Retrieved 6 October 2013 from http://refractory.unimelb.edu.au/2011/08/01/blockbusters-for-the-youtube-generation-a-new-product-of-convergence-culture-%E2%80%93-kristy-hess-and-lisa-waller.

Jarvis, J. (2006). Networked journalism. Buzz Machine. Accessed 27 August 2013 from www.buzzmachine.com/2006/07/05/networked-journalism.

Jenkins, H. (2006). *Convergence culture: When news and old media collide*. New York: University Press.

Lee, J. (2012, 12 August). Target 'tramp' backlash: Why are we here? *Sydney Morning Herald*. Retrieved 8 October 2013 from www.smh.com.au/small-business/smallbiz-tech/target-tramp-backlash-why-are-we-here-20120815-247pg.html.

Lynch, L. (2012). *Exploring journalism and the media*, 2nd edn. Mason, OH: Scuth-Western Cengage Learning.

Mosch, G. (2012, 21 August). 'Trashy' clothing concerns. *Townsville Bulletin*, p. 18.

Murthy, D. (2013). *Twitter: Social communication in the Twitter age*. Cambridge: Polity.

O'Shea, J. (2013). When brands blunder. *Irish Independent*. Retrieved 10 October 2013 from www.independent.ie/lifestyle/when-brands-blunder-29630618.html.

Regester, M. & Larkin, J. (2008). *Risk Issues and Crisis Management in Public Relations: A Casebook of Best Practice*, 4th edn. London: Kogan Page.

Reinemann, C., Stanyer, J., Scherr, S. & Legnante, G. (2012). Hard and soft news: A view of concepts, operationalisations and key findings. *Journalism*, 13, 221–39.

Rosen, J. (2006). The people formerly known as the audience. Pressthink. Retrieved 9 October 2013 from http://archive.pressthink.org/2006/06/27/ppl_frmr.html.

Safe, G. (2012). Why blaming store for sexy kids' clothes is way off target. *Sydney Morning Herald*, August 14, 2012. Retrieved October 9 2013 from www.theage.com.au/federal-politics/why-blaming-store-for-sexy-kids-clothes-is-way-off-target-20120814-245sl.html.

Sissons, H. (2006). *Practical journalism: How to write news*. London: Sage.

8 HARNESSING THE POWER OF SLACKTIVISM

THE BOOM AND BUST CYCLE OF ISSUES MANAGEMENT AND CRISIS

Deirdre Quinn-Allan

Chapter objectives

This chapter aims to:

- outline the phenomenon of slacktivism on the internet and in social media
- examine forms of symbolic and token support for issues and causes and how they align with slacktivism
- explore the growing importance of supply chain activism
- explore the impact of slacktivism in issues and crisis management.

Introduction

All organisations face issues, some of which require close monitoring. Those issues ranked at the top of an organisation's list of key concerns to be researched, monitored and responded to on a regular basis are designated thus because failure to respond appropriately can see an issue morph into a full-blown crisis or lead to a slow but inexorable loss of reputation. Depending on the organisation, a crisis can have short- or long-term negative consequences, both of which represent an opportunity cost in profit forgone as the organisation diverts resources to resolve the crisis. Whether managing an issue or a crisis organisations seek to preserve reputation; Gotsi and Wilson (2001, p. 29) define reputation as:

> a stakeholder's overall evaluation of a company over time. This evaluation is based on the stakeholder's direct experiences with the company, any other form of communication and symbolism that provides information about the firm's actions and/or a comparison with the actions of other leading rivals.

Their definition provides a useful starting point for this chapter because it opens the door to examination of symbolic acts within the mix of crisis and issues management and communication within online and social media stakeholder or organisation exchanges.

Both non-profit organisations (NPOs) and for-profit organisations (FPOs) use online communication and social media to engineer stakeholder support (globally or locally) and establish their reputation and credentials. Activist NPOs use online channels to challenge organisations to change operational aspects not deemed socially or environmentally desirable. FPOs use these same channels to fight back and/or resist change for as long as possible. Alternatively, where an FPO is actively committed to corporate social responsibility beyond symbolic expressions and acts allied with corporate mission, online and social media channels facilitate collaborative and dialogic forms of communication of intent and engagement with interested and active stakeholders. See Chapter 9 for a framework for the way in which NPOs and FPOs work collaboratively to achieve socially and environmentally desirable outcomes.

Instead, this chapter examines the role of **slacktivism** in online crisis and issues management and argues against dismissing the role of slacktivists. There is need for a more complex and strategic understanding of their role and extent of influence. Collectively, symbolic acts by this group can effect change in cognitive, affective and behavioural responses of other stakeholders and directly or indirectly impact the reputation of both NPOs and FPOs. Using two different case studies, this chapter illustrates how the collective actions of slacktivists can drive an issue or cause a crisis. The first case focuses on the NPO Invisible Children and the ensuing crisis following the release of their online video Kony 12 compounded by the charity's actions. The second case examines Asia Pulp and Paper's response to slacktivism and global concerns about deforestation and impact on loss of habitat and endangered species.

Slacktivism: A pejorative term which is a compound of slacker and activism. Slacktivism is marked by symbolic or token gestures of support for an issue or cause.

Background

The internet and social media are not new media, but each year hot new trends emerge around novel ways in which they are used. The implication for public relations is that new whilst new opportunities arise to build relationships with priority publics the potential for problems increases and becomes more complex. New social media platforms emerge and others sink to obscurity. Mobile, broadband and information communication technology (ICT) advancements continue at a rapid pace with innovations driving adoption. Platforms are designed for intuitive, easy use and take advantage of users' social networks. Whilst the originators of these platforms are looking for ways to monetise their creations and capitalise on ready access to virtual communities, these communities of networked users can act as powerful change agents. Collectively, internet and social media users are able to sidestep traditional media and sustain focus on causes and issues ignored by mainstream media.

Located within an internet and social media user base of more than a billion people are the target publics, audiences and stakeholders with whom public relations professionals want to communicate. Hidden within these publics is an important group, which is often dismissed as slacktivists. The term is pejorative, a compound of slacker and activist.

Kristofferson, White & Peloza (2014) present a perspective on slacktivism, predicated on the idea that it is a form of activism which relies on tokenistic or symbolic gestures of support. On one level, this is a useful conception, in which slacktivism requires little to no sustained effort, through actions such as 'signing a petition, wearing a bracelet or pin in support of a cause, or engaging in various forms of online support such as liking or joining a page on Facebook' (pp. 1149–50). By way of contrast, activism requires substantially more effort that is sustained. Kristofferson, White and Peloza suggest volunteering by way of example. Interestingly, they also cite donating money as a form of activism. However, all things are relative, and it is reasonable to posit that Kony 12 elicited donations from people who were not going to actively commit to the cause long term. In addition, a one-off donation of $100 from someone on a low income represents a significant commitment compared with the same amount from a high-income earner.

It would be easy to adopt a binary approach; that *token support* is bad and *meaningful support* is good. Kristofferson, White & Peloza's research aimed to explore conditions that lead to token support versus meaningful support for NPOs and how token support could translate into meaningful support. This makes sense. An NPO needs to maximise meaningful support because it results in actions or behaviours that directly affect it as a going concern able to achieve its stated goals over time.

However, in the context of crisis and issues management, token support may be as important as meaningful support; it is a matter of perspective and scale. In one sense, FPOs are no different to NPOs; they too rely on forms of meaningful support derived from their base of customers who purchase their products. Consumers make purchase decision choices based on diverse functional and or psychosocial needs. Psychosocial needs present the biggest challenge to corporations and failure to meet these needs lies at the heart of many issues and crises. Consumers expect the retailers and manufacturers of the products and brands they consume to live up to their responsibilities as good and ethical corporate citizens. However, psychosocial need in the consumer manifests in many forms and which can ultimately be stronger in driving purchase behaviour than commitment to moral issues such as global warming, environmental sustainability, or preservation of human rights. For example, in developed nations few consumers would readily agree that exploitation of children in the production of a key raw ingredient is good or ethical. Consider, then, the production of cocoa beans substantially reliant on children (many as slaves) supports a multi-billion dollar global chocolate product and confectionary industry. Chocolate products are deeply embedded in social customs and consumption habits in many nations. People around the globe consume products containing cocoa on a daily basis despite the fact that the link between child slavery and cocoa bean production has been known for a long time.

So, there are many thriving companies selling products and brands which fail to live up to standards of practice underpinning sound corporate social responsibility (CSR). Bundy, Shropshire and Buchholtz (2013) point out that 'Firms and managers do not respond to stakeholder and environmental characteristics per se. Instead, they respond to specific issues and concerns advocated by stakeholders' (p. 353). Regulatory drivers aside, until consumers coalesce around an issue or cause there is little incentive for organisations to actively uphold the values they espouse until there is strategic need to do so; hence the potential importance of the slacktivist and symbolic and token acts they take in support of a cause.

Social media platforms facilitate token support because they make it easy for users to become aware of or learn about social and environmental problems. If users are persuaded, these same platforms provide quick and effortless means by which audiences may endorse a cause or criticise and punish organisations that fail to live up to expectations. For little time and effort, users can sign an online petition, put their signature to a pre-written letter condemning the actions of a company, and instantaneously send it to the CEO. They can send their friends, family and other social network contact links to rich content prepared by activists via sites such as Vimeo, Pinterest and YouTube. For a little more effort and minimal or no cost, they can tweet or post short-form criticisms via Twitter, Facebook or any social media platform which enables comment. Such effort is minimal and does not imply ongoing commitment or action. Kristofferson, White and Peloza (2014, p. 1150) also argue that 'when the initial act of token support is high in social observability (i.e. it is public), people will be less likely to engage in subsequent meaningful contributions to the cause than when the initial act of token support is low in social observability (i.e. it is private)'. The cases presented in this chapter demonstrate activists utilising both publicly visible (sharing on Facebook, tweeting) and private forms of token support such as signing an online petition. It is beyond the scope of this chapter to explore in full the research of Kristofferson, White & Peloza and conditions that can lead to slacktivism, but it is not inconsistent to argue that slacktivism and token support can be effective even if not ultimately the goal of NPOs. As the cases in this chapter demonstrate, slacktivist support can be harnessed to raise issues to top of the mind awareness in the general public on a global scale even if only for a short moment in time. Slacktivists wield power as a collective to effect change and should not be dismissed simply because they always fail to demonstrate meaningful support or commitment to a cause or issue.

Deforestation, consumers and supply chain slacktivism

NPOs have been very effective in recent years in using the internet to bring **supply chain** problems to the attention of consumers. Equally, the internet and social media have made it easier for consumers to respond and demonstrate their concern about the actions of companies, particularly in relation to supply chain problems, without actually having to make meaningful change in their behaviour. At the click of the mouse, they can take action, feel good about themselves, and share their status as concerned citizens.

Supply chain: The system employed by an organisation to secure and then transform inputs into products or services and then distribute these to customers.

But how many of those who take action online actually translate that commitment to their shopping in bricks and mortar establishments? How many are price sensitive, too busy, or creatures of habit? At the checkout, do they really consider who has suffered or what has been harmed in the production of the products they are about to purchase? Of those who do, how easy is it for them to push aside feelings of **cognitive dissonance** and continue to purchase the product of their choice at the best price? Cognitive dissonance occurs when an individual's values or beliefs come into conflict in deciding between alternative courses of action. In a purchase context (when choosing one product or brand over another), cognitive dissonance can occur pre-purchase or post-purchase. For example, when a consumer chooses a commonplace necessity such as toilet paper, he or she may experience cognitive dissonance on purchasing the product from a company he or she knows has a poor environmental record. However, if budget, convenience or some other factor has a stronger influence on the purchaser's decision-making, he or she will continue to purchase that product and rationalise the action. Decision-making in this context is essentially a private activity, not open to much scrutiny. Slacktivism presents consumers with an 'out'; they can protest online in a visible and public manner but continue business as usual in their shopping habits. In describing this type of consumer behaviour, it might then be argued that slacktivism has little merit and no impact; it is based on mere token support.

Cognitive dissonance: Occurs when an individual's values or beliefs come into conflict in deciding between alternative courses of action.

Damage done to native and old growth forests through human activity has long been a concern of environmental groups. The volunteer activists who join as members and engage in activities such as fundraising are the people who provide meaningful support. These groups have lobbied hard to build public and political support for the protection of forests (and other important ecosystems) and to promote change in the way corporations use these limited resources. No longer relegated to the green fringes of public debate, the activities of activist groups have been successful in raising the profile of many environmental concerns. The issue of deforestation, through the Kyoto Protocol, which came into effect for the period 2005–2012, has also been officially linked to climate change. Hunt (2009, p.101) identifies a raft of other agreements which variously address protection and sustainable management of ecosystems, all of which illustrate global political support through policy initiatives. However, Hunt identifies structural, political and institutional barriers which inhibit the scope of such agreements to effect rapid change, and tensions between implementation in developed and developing nations (where exploitation of ecosystems is linked to development and profit). And importantly, Hunt asserts, 'there is a severe lack of funds to establish a comprehensive global system of protected areas' (2014, p.103).

Despite growing regulatory and policy change and commitment from many nations to protect ecosystems such as forests, Greenpeace is still able to make claims such as 'Every two seconds, an area of forest the size of a football pitch is lost' (n.d). Within such contexts, enlisting token support from slacktivists has proven to be an additional but effective means of changing the behaviour of companies faster than regulatory or policy responses from governments.

Harnessing the power of slacktivism

Activist organisations have campaigned for many years on problems associated with deforestation. They have employed a diverse range of tactics which includes political lobbying as discussed above.

Supply chain slacktivism: Harnessing the power of slacktivist actions to convince organisations to change some aspect of their supply chain management to achieve improved social or environmental outcomes.

Use of the internet and social media to harness the power of slacktivism provides environmental groups with a means of engaging effectively in supply chain activism; a faster route to effect change. Examples of **supply chain slacktivism** appear to work through enlisting what Kristofferson, White & Peloza (2014) might describe as token support from consumers.

Through viral means, internet and social media can facilitate fast and global information campaigns using highly emotive tactics to inform consumers about how the products they consume are made and where raw materials are sourced. These online tactics also provide consumers with a quick and easy means of communicating their displeasure directly to other stakeholders and in some campaigns direct to the inbox of a targeted CEO. The first is a public display and the second private. Drawing on Kristofferson, White & Peloza (2014), a public manifestation of slacktivism is unlikely to translate into ongoing support; but actions such as signing online petitions or emailing direct company CEOs are inherently private acts. Although they are only token, they do indicate stronger alignment with personal values and motivation to act in the future (Kristofferson, White & Peloza, 2014). Either way, companies are finding it increasingly difficult to hide behind the rhetoric of mission and values statements and avoid responding to these tactics.

Asia Pulp and Paper

Asia Pulp and Paper (APP) is a global manufacturer of paper products. On their corporate website APP states 'Our vision is to become a leading and respected global pulp-and-paper company that provides superior values to our customers, community, employees and shareholders – responsibly and sustainably' (n.d.a). APP's customers are located in over 120 countries around the world and include both final consumers and businesses. Similarly, APP's parent company Sinar Mas (a global company which operates in six key areas: Pulp & Paper, Agri-business & Food, Financial Services, Real Estate Development, Telecommunications and Energy & Infrastructure [n.d.a]) states its vision is to provide 'a balanced approach towards the three pillars of sustainability; social, environmental and economic' (n.d.b). Similar to many global companies, Sinar Mas espouses contemporary values predicated on high ethical principles, accountability and transparency.

Like many corporations, APP has long been the subject of criticism from environmental groups. Until recently their response has been to counter criticism through traditional public relations tactics or approaches. For example, in 2006 the World Wide Fund for Nature (WWF) (2006) issued a monitoring brief to challenge a full page advertisement from APP (placed in the *New York Times* and *London Times*). The briefing paper worked through the copy of the advertisement claim by claim to refute APP's alleged efforts to **greenwash** their activities. APP has also attempted to use channels such as YouTube to communicate its green credentials. For example, in January 2010, it uploaded a video in which (among other things) it claimed that 'APP supports 500 000 hectares of forestry for conservation which acts as a massive carbon storage. . .' In 2011, it released videos designed to communicate

Greenwashing: The unethical and/or illegal misrepresentation of an organisation's environmental credentials.

how it was helping with conservation and protection of Sumatran tigers. It is worth noting that comments were disabled on these YouTube clips, thereby removing opportunity for public engagement with activists, APP customers or other stakeholders.

Around the same time, environmental activist organisations released videos highlighting the plight of Sumatran tigers that were being brought to the point of extinction by loss of habitat resulting directly from the actions of companies such as APP producing products which included household consumables such as printer paper, tissues and toilet paper. Reece Turner of Greenpeace said at the time that 'Australians deserve to know if they are wiping their bums with the habitats of critically endangered Sumatran tigers. Australian companies linked to APP should be looking to find alternative suppliers' (Greenpeace, 2011). Greenpeace released a video online in late July 2011, titled *Distressing footage: IGA linked to wiping out the endangered Sumatran Tiger*. The video was designed to elicit an emotional response showing close-up shots of the death of a tiger. Throughout the video, Greenpeace names and shames claiming that 'This destruction of habitat is being led by Asia Pulp and Paper (APP)' and 'IGA are one of APP's biggest Australian customers'. The video showed close-ups of toilet paper brands on sale in IGA supermarkets, and was followed by a call to action: 'Tell IGA to stop buying APP products.' Embedded within the video was a simple link to enable viewers to communicate directly with Metcash. The campaign was a short but highly successful example of supply chain activism leveraging slacktivist support. In just less than a month, Metcash, the owner of IGA, announced it would no longer sell toilet paper products supplied by APP.

We don't know how many consumers actively stopped buying APP manufactured brands of toilet paper, or indeed what threats they communicated to Metcash, and it doesn't really matter. This case and other similar cases demonstrate retailers are concerned enough to act and quickly. In another example, Greenpeace reported that after only three weeks of campaigning which included an online spoof advertisement and an online petition, Unilever agreed to take action to support the halt to the felling of native forest to make way for palm oil plantations. As Palazzo and Basu (2006) explain, 'Individuals participating in acts of instant solidarity, linking their life stories to the narratives written by activist groups, often times discover that consumption decisions (or, more accurately, non-consumption decisions) are an efficient means to communicate moral and political statements' (p. 339).

Returning to the IGA campaign, although the story received media attention it did not remain news for long. However, Greenpeace's videos are still online. In one video, the call to action link now takes any viewer who cares to click on the link to a new page, titled: *Success! IGA stops using rainforest destruction*. This page provides a brief synopsis of the campaign and concludes with an invitation 'Want to say thank you and congratulations to IGA/Metcash? Fill out their feedback form here'. This campaign demonstrates how token support from slacktivists can be used to influence retailers very quickly. In a country such as Australia, where a few very large corporations dominate the grocery retail landscape, NPOs can use slacktivist power to convince retailers to drop suppliers that do not meet high environmental standards. APP has now agreed to modify its practices and live up to its mission and values. As a result, in 2013 Greenpeace announced it was halting 'active campaigning against Asia Pulp & Paper (APP) following the announcement of APP's Forest Conservation Policy (FCP) . . .' A good outcome for all stakeholders and AAP.

Kony 12

The following case based on Invisible Children, an American-based NPO, presents quite a different way in which slacktivism can impact on issues and crisis management. In 2012 Invisible Children released an online video to highlight the activities of Joseph Kony, the leader of the militia group Lord's Resistance Army (LRA). In 2005, the International Criminal Court had charged Kony with war crimes and crimes against humanity. Invisible Children wanted to raise awareness of the issues surrounding the activities of Joseph Kony and the LRA and rally international support for action that would lead to Kony's arrest. They also wanted to elicit donations and raise funds to support their efforts. From an issues and crisis management perspective, practitioner and academic literature tends to focus on the way in which NPOs challenge organisations. NPOs like Invisible Children have been able to use online channels very effectively to rally support for their causes but as this case demonstrates, the internet and social media can be both friend and foe and they too need to manage issues carefully.

The Kony 12 video was released on 5 March 2012 and Raine et al. of the Pew Research Internet Project reported that eight days later 'the video had been viewed more than 76 million times on YouTube and 16 million times on Vimeo, making it one of the most viewed videos of all time on those sites' (2012). According to Invisible Children, '#STOPKONY was tweeted 1200 times per minute at its peak' (n.d.a). The research by Raine et al. (2012) also demonstrates the role of influencers in helping an online issue to gain traction; as they note, 'the amount of attention skyrocketed' after Oprah Winfrey began tweeting about the film to her 9.6 million followers on 6 March. Winfrey was not the only celebrity endorser: the video also received political support from White House Press Secretary Jay Carney, and to this day the Obama administration is still focused on the cause. In March 2014, Helene Cooper of the *New York Times* reported that 'President Obama is sending more troops and military aircraft to Uganda as part of a long-running effort to hunt down Joseph Kony' (2014).

Kony 12 provides a useful insight into the relationship between legacy media (traditional forms such as print, radio and television) and online channels. Like many other cases, Kony 12 again demonstrates that social media can quickly reach global audiences. It also shows how online audience interest drives offline media attention and can take a story to those who rely predominantly on legacy media for news. Social media users learned about the campaign via channels such as YouTube, Facebook, Vimeo, Twitter and blogs; but the media then ran with the story thereby fixing the issue as a leading item of news and commentary in many countries around the world. Unlike the Greenpeace campaign discussed above, the collective actions of slacktivists created intense media interest which ultimately led to a crisis for Invisible Children.

Invisible Children's campaign was a victim of its success, in terms both of how it raised awareness on a global scale and how it raised millions of dollars through sales of its US$30 campaign kit. Criticisms of the Kony 12 campaign emerged quickly following the video's release. Commentators and journalists around the globe began to question the accuracy of the video, some challenged the motives of Invisible Children and many argued the video over-simplified a complex issue. As Hilsum (2012) writes, 'The video provides a simple solution to a simple problem: catch the bad man who is kidnapping kids'. Invisible Children were criticised for the way in which they spent (or would spend) the millions of dollars raised from the campaign. This is an ongoing issue for NPOs. Donors looking for the feel good factor from giving to or supporting a good cause do not want to hear that funds have been wasted on administration or other expenses; they want their support to go directly to the beneficiaries.

Invisible Children should not have been surprised at the criticism. Since their inception they have been condemned in some quarters for their work. The following example from a longer post on the Wronging Rights blog is indicative: 'organizations like Invisible Children not only take up resources that could be used to fund more intelligent advocacy, they take up rhetorical space that could be used to *develop* more intelligent advocacy' (Taub & Cronin-Furman, 2009). Similarly, issues monitoring would have alerted Invisible Children to the growing concern and public interest in the ways in which charities use donations. Indeed there are NPOs dedicated to identifying and ranking other NPOs' use of donor funds. Sound issues management would have indicated to Invisible Children the need for effective information and content on their website to address concerns of key stakeholders.

Slacktivism-induced crisis

Why can slacktivism be blamed for the crisis faced by Invisible Children rather than poor issues management? Tench and Yeomans say 'crisis management is about dealing with the impact of a sudden adverse event that fractures the core of a company's operation and represents an immediate threat to its ability to stay in business' (2009, pp. 366–7).

Soon after the video's release on Vimeo and YouTube online viewers wanted to know more about Invisible Children and how to be involved. The video drove traffic to their website, which crashed as they tried to meet demand for information. But they used Facebook and Twitter to keep in touch with supporters: 'The KONY2012 site is crashing due to all of your overwhelming support! Completely awesome. Follow us on Twitter @Invisible so we can keep you up-to-date with details about when we'll be up & running' (posted on Facebook March 6, 2012). Then later that day in another Facebook post they continued to explain the problems they were having and direct website visitors in an effort to keep audiences engaged:

> You guys are making Kony famous, and you're breaking the internet. Here are the links that still work – Stop At Nothing.
> To buy action kit/bracelets: http://invisiblechildrenstore.myshopify.com/
> To make a donation: http://bit.ly/yp5Ffv
> To sign the pledge: www.causes.com/causes/227-invisible-children
> To watch the film: http://vimeo.com/37119711

Then lack of information on their website created a vacuum which the media and critics quickly moved to fill. As the campaign gathered momentum Jason Russell (co-founder of Invisible Children and film maker of Kony 12) was in high demand by the media clamouring to interview him. During this period people kept purchasing campaign kits and leaving messages of support (albeit interspersed with negative comments).

Then, just eight days after the video's release, Jason Russell had a breakdown. Video footage of Russell naked and ranting in suburban San Diego went viral. In little over a week Jason Russell's breakdown coupled with the mounting negative media attention paid to Invisible Children's tactics and use of donations replaced Joseph Kony as the main story. Invisible Children then had to spend 2012 in crisis management mode in an effort to rehabilitate their image and that of Jason Russell. Explaining his breakdown, Jason Russell has acknowledged that neither he nor Invisible Children were prepared for the scale of global interest and response. He was personally unable to cope with the intensity of media attention and media demands and they were simply catering to an audience now hungry for new angles.

The nature of the crisis faced by Invisible Children is likely to be a rare event and of a type no organisation would relish. But the coalescing of slacktivist interest and activity is a growing phenomenon and the tactics of NPOs can have significant impact regardless of whether they merely encourage short-term slacktivism or translate into meaningful activist support. At the time of writing Invisible Children have recovered from their crisis and continue with their fundraising and awareness campaigns. They continue to use similar online tactics but attract far smaller audiences than at the peak of the Kony 12 campaign.

Conclusion

The two cases presented in this chapter present different ways in which NPOs and FPOs can be affected by the collective actions of slacktivists. Although not a new concept, the ease with which people can communicate and connect with others via the internet and online has seen renewed interest in slacktivism. Issues such as global warming, sustainable practice and resource management (land, air and water) and human rights are of global concern. For any given cause, it is likely that an NPO is working to address the problems associated with that cause; many of which are low profile and small in reach and membership. However, as Kony 12 demonstrates, one cleverly crafted tactic which resonates with the social media zeitgeist can overnight turn an unknown NPO into a household name and build top of the mind awareness. If the organisation is not ready for the scale or scope of such attention, then slacktivist actions can be harmful. In the case of Kony 12, unprecedented global attention from slacktivists stretched Invisible Children's resources to breaking point, which ultimately resulted in crisis. Facing a different type of challenge through supply chain activism and slacktivism, APP and other global brands have found it difficult to resist the online tactics which sidestep traditional media and quickly and easily communicate consumer dissatisfaction with some aspect of their supply chain management.

Both cases provide insight for public relations professionals working in the field of issues and crisis management and demonstrate the power of social media to rally support around a cause or issue and build token support. Although Kristofferson, White & Peloza (2014) argue that slacktivism can be detrimental to NPOs seeking to foster ongoing and sustained meaningful support, both cases demonstrate that slacktivists can still be important audiences for both NPOs and FPOs and should not be ignored.

CASE QUESTIONS

1. Locate examples of online slacktivist activity and explain how they might represent cognitive, affective and behavioural responses.
2. Locate a recent example of an online video which demonstrates greenwashing by a global corporation and explain why the organisation might be accused of greenwashing.
3. Why do you think slacktivist actions can help to bring about FPO change quicker than environmental policy, regulation, and international agreements?
4. A colleague dismisses slacktivists and argues they don't have any lasting impact. They also argue that many activist clips on sites such as YouTube often demonstrate very low audience views. How would you respond to your colleague and what arguments could you use to counter his or her position?

BIBLIOGRAPHY

Asia Pulp and Paper (APP) (n.d.a). Mission and values. Retrieved 1 May 2014, from https://www.asiapulppaper.com/about-app/mission-values.

Asia Pulp and Paper (APP) (2010, 20 January). *Asia Pulp & Paper: Tackling climate change*. Video. Retrieved May 2014 from www.youtube.com/watch?v=kMagU7zFtP0.

Balabanis, G. (2013). Surrogate boycotts against multinational corporations: Consumers' choice of boycott targets. *British Journal Of Management*, 24(4), 515–31, Business Source Complete, EBSCO*host*. doi: 10.1111/j.1467-8551.2012.00822.x.

Bundy, J., Shropshire, C. & Buchholtz, A. K. (2013). Strategic cognition and issue salience: Toward an explanation of firm responsiveness to stakeholder concerns. *Academy of Management Review*, 38(3), 352–76. doi:10.5465/amr.2011.0179.

Cooper, H. (2014). More US troops to aid Uganda search for Kony. *New York Times*. Retrieved 1 May 2014 from www.nytimes.com/2014/03/24/world/africa/obama-is-sending-more-resources-for-joseph-kony-search.html?_r=0.

Gotsi, M. & Wilson, A. M. (2001). Corporate reputation: Seeking a definition. *Corporate Communications*, 6(1), 24–30, Emerald Insight. doi:10.1108/13563280110381189.

Greenpeace (n.d). Corporate action. Retrieved 1 May from www.greenpeace.org/international/en/campaigns/forests/solutions/Corporate.

Greenpeace (2011, 25 August). Media release: IGA supermarkets drop toilet paper made from destroyed tiger habitats. Retrieved 29 May 2014 from www.greenpeace.org/australia/en/mediacentre/media-releases/forests-media-releases/-IGA-supermarkets-drop-toilet-paper-made-from-destroyed-tiger-habitats.

Hilsum, L. (2012). Kony 2012: Inaccuracies aside, this is how to spread a message. *World News Blog Channel 4*. Retrieved 1 May 2014 from http://blogs.channel4.com/world-news-blog/kony-2012-inaccuracies-aside-this-is-how-to-spread-message/20728.

Hunt, C. (2009). *Carbon Sinks and Climate Change* [e-book]. Cheltenham, UK: Edward Elgar Publishing.

International Criminal Court (2005, 27 September). Warrant of arrest for Joseph Kony issued on 8 July 2005 as amended on 27 September 2005. Retrieved 23 May 2014 from www.icc-cpi.int/iccdocs/doc/doc97185.pdf#search=Joseph%20Kony.

Invisible Children (n.d.a). Epic progress since Kony 2012. Retrieved 1 May 2014 from http://invisiblechildren.com/kony/#epic-progress.

Kristofferson, K., White, K. & Peloza, J. (2014). The nature of slacktivism: How the social observability of an initial act of token support affects subsequent prosocial action. *Journal of Consumer Research*, 40, 1149–66, Business Source Complete, EBSCO*host*. doi:10.1086/674137.

Palazzo, G. & Basu, K. (2006). The ethical backlash of corporate branding. *Journal of Business Ethics*, 73, 4, 333–346, Business Source Complete, EBSCO*host*. doi:10.1007/s10551–006-9210–6.

Raine, L., Hitlin, P., Jurkowitz, M., Dimock, M. & Neidorf, S. (2012).The viral Kony 2012 video, *Pew Research Internet Project*. Retrieved from www.pewinternet.org/2012/03/15/the-viral-kony-2012-video/.

Sinar Mas (n.d.a). Overview. Retrieved from www.sinarmas.com/en/about-sinar-mas/#.

Sinar Mas (n.d.b). Corporate vision. Retrieved from www.sinarmas.com/en/about-sinar-mas/#.

Taub, A. & Cronin-Furman, K. (2009, 5 March). Worst idea ever? Retrieved from www.wrongingrights.com/2009/03/worst-idea-ever.html/.

Tech, R. & Yeomans, L. (2009). *Exploring Public Relations*, 2nd edn. London: FT Prentice Hall.

World Wildlife Fund Indonesia October (2006). Monitoring brief: Asia Pulp & Paper (APP) hiding destruction behind false advertisements: APP continues to ignore calls for conservation beyond 'legal compliance', and even fails on the latter. Retrieved 1 May 2014 from www.wwf.or.jp/activities/upfiles/APP_Oct06_MonitoringRpt.pdf.

Yuping, L. (2012). Seeding viral content: The role of message and network factors, *Journal Of Advertising Research*, 52, 4, 465–478, Business Source Complete, EBSCO*host*. doi:10.2501/JAR-52-4-465-478.

9

SOCIAL MEDIA ADOPTION AND RISK AVERSION

AUSTRALIAN NOT-FOR-PROFITS

Emma Bennett

Chapter objectives

This chapter aims to:

- explore the reputational risks and issues faced by Australian not-for-profit organisations in the adoption and use of social media
- determine techniques for social media risk aversion for not-for-profit organisations
- understand the importance of social media strategy implementation in navigating risk
- consider some relevant resources not-for-profit organisations may find useful in developing their approach to social media for public relations.

Introduction

Australia has some of the highest rates of **social media** usage in the world (Gupta, 2011, p. 4). As a result, organisations throughout Australia understand the need to consider social media in public relations activities. It is widely expected that social media is part of an organisation's communication strategy. Social media adoption has become less of a contentious issue than it was only five years ago. Organisations without a social media presence may be perceived as lacking transparency. Indeed, they may miss opportunities to interact with target publics and motivate action to reach their objectives. Social media has great potential for Australian **not-for-profits** (NPOs) as a tool to: help empower communities to act; inform and educate; develop effective advocacy campaigns and encourage event participation and fundraising. The aims of social media adoption for NPOs are vastly different to those of commercial organisations and so are the risks.

Social media: Online platforms used for communication purposes and connecting with individuals and organisations.

Not-for profit organisation (NPO): An organisation that does not operate for commercial purposes.

This chapter will explore some of the risks faced by Australian NPOs. Often, these are characterised by the nature of the organisation and organisational structure. NPOs face numerous (and often complex) hurdles in social media adoption and usage. As these differ between organisations, not all will be considered here. However, there are some similarities relating to resources and other priorities. Furthermore, the impact of blurred lines between personal and professional communication need to be considered. Misuse of social media for NPOs presents reputational risk. However, avoiding social media use can present an even bigger risk, where unauthorised spokespeople fill in the information gaps.

The focus is not the use of social media by NPOs during times of crisis. Rather this chapter will consider the general use of social media to meet organisational objectives. Several Australian NPO organisations are mentioned throughout this chapter (Oxfam Australia, Lifeline Australia and Brotherhood of St Laurence) to demonstrate the ways social media has been adopted, the implementation of social media strategies and whether risk can be averted. By understanding the risks associated with social media communication, NPOs can effectively develop strategies which suit their unique goals to minimise risk and deal with negative commentary.

Background

The advent of social media allowed corporations, organisations and individuals to reach wide audiences with persuasive information. Arguably, all users had the same opportunity to communicate via these channels, provided they had access to the required technology. Democratically, social media presents a range of opportunities for NPOs. Theoretically, an organisation can develop an online presence with little financial expense, regardless of its size and budget. But, with this opportunity, comes potential risk. There are often misconceptions regarding the cost of social media. Despite being able to sign up for social media sites for free, a great amount of time and expertise is required to effectively communicate via social media sites. Employees or volunteers using social media, who do not fully understand the environment in which they are communicating, face considerable reputational risk.

The purpose, objectives and structure of an organisation determine the rationale for social media adoption and use. In most cases, social media adoption makes sense for Australian NPOs, considering their reliance on their communities, as suggested by Auger (2013, p. 369), whether that be in the form of volunteers, donations, ambassadors or advocacy. It is also important to consider the sensitive nature of the work that many Australian NPOs undertake. Often, organisations are providing education and information and sometimes the messages relate to sensitive personal issues. For instance, sensitivity must be shown regarding mental health or serious illness, when analysing the adoption and use of social media.

Case focus

There are many drivers of social media adoption for NPOs. Nah and Saxton categorised these drivers into four areas: strategy, capacity, governance and environment (2012, p. 294). These same categories could be used to group together risk factors, complex issues faced by NPOs in the adoption and use of social media. Perhaps the biggest hurdle faced by NPOs relates to capacity, particularly for organisations who are dependent on a small number of employees, are without a dedicated communications resource(s) or who rely on volunteers.

Since its inception, social media has evolved rapidly. This can be intimidating. Organisations that do not believe they have the capacity to maintain social media while keeping up to date with trends, applications and technology may avoid it altogether. Additionally, in the public sphere, social media governance in the form of policies and guidelines is increasing. While this can help direct organisations to understand the ethical boundaries of social media, these too can halt progressive use of social media for smaller NPOs.

Following are some areas which present potential reputation risk to Australian NPOs in their adoption and use of social media. The approaches taken by some high-profile Australian NPOs will be explored in relation to overcoming hurdles associated with the lack of message control, expertise and resources. One of the greatest perceived risks of social media for NPOs relates to negative commentary from users external to the organisation or employees and volunteers misrepresenting the organisation online. Social media strategy development can be a key component in minimising reputational risks associated with misinformation and conflicting messages.

Social media adoption and usage

Social media has changed the communication landscape – it is dynamic, centred on user-generated content and provides a platform from which people and organisations can have their voices heard. It is increasingly difficult for organisations to justify avoiding social media altogether. This does not necessarily mean that all organisations can and should have a social media presence. There are a number of Australian NPO organisations who avoid social media for a variety of reasons.

NPOs often face unique challenges in relation to resourcing. Often, NPOs have a small number of employees whose focus and expertise are based on the core services of the organisation. Subsequently, organisations may be relying on volunteers to assist with activities. It is difficult to coordinate social media activities with conflicting priorities, limited resources and lack of communication expertise. While social media is often touted as being inexpensive and relatively quick to learn, the greatest expense is in relation to the time required to produce and curate content, engage with users, join conversations and monitor social media sites – all the while incorporating a consistent organisational approach with messaging and objectives in an ethical manner that demonstrates understanding of the specific social media sites. It is understandable that the representative(s) charged with the task of managing social media feel overwhelmed. However, this must be weighed up against the opportunities social media presents.

Importantly, many Australian NPOs have demonstrated expertise in this area, developing leading social media strategies and approaches despite the hurdles, and softening the perceived risks. Oxfam Australia uses a range of social media tools (including Facebook, Twitter, YouTube, Google +) to communicate with its target publics on relevant issues. Oxfam Australia has incorporated social media into campaigns, demonstrating social media is considered as part of a broader strategy. Oxfam's *The Grow Method* campaign encourages people to think differently about their food consumption habits (Oxfam Australia). The campaign has a dedicated website which is integrated with social media and an application on the Oxfam Australia Facebook page. This provides useful and interactive information for users, which is easy to share, demonstrating that Oxfam Australia has considered its target public and their social media habits.

In order to achieve its advocacy goals, Brotherhood of St Laurence employs a range of social media tools and incorporates them throughout organisational communications and activities. Chris Roberts (2012), Digital Manager at Brotherhood of St Laurence, highlights the importance of incorporating personal stories from the community within online advocacy campaigns. This helps to educate and engage target publics in issues prior to motivating action. This approach to social media is often adopted by organisations with a focus on advocacy (also seen in the Every Australia Counts campaign for the National Disability Insurance Scheme). This demonstrates that NPOs need to be aware of their strongest asset when using social media – the power of stories.

While other Australian NPOs may learn from these examples, the complex factors that may lead to reputational risk in social media adoption and use must be further explored.

Resources

Organisations which lack resources and are time-poor may choose to sign up to a range of social media sites to ensure they have some online presence. However, underused (social media updated and monitored sporadically) or dormant social media sites pose reputational risk. In lieu of an authoritative voice interested target publics, online activists, other organisations and even **trolls** will fill the information gap, sometimes with messages that contradict the planned messages from the organisation. This can lead to conflicts of interest, misinformation, confusion and mixed messages. Social media users will be able to judge, to varying extents, the validity of information provided on social media based on their own experiences and knowledge. The ability of users to verify authoritative information should not be overestimated, however; with no 'official' message coming from the organisation, users may have no choice but to attribute authority to unofficial messages.

Troll: Social media users who post comments and content designed specifically to aggravate and elicit an emotional response from individuals or organisations.

One or two posts on social media will most likely prove insufficient. Token posts as opposed to strategic messages and interaction demonstrates a lack of understanding of social media generally and can dissuade user engagement. Ensuring employees are educated and comfortable to use social media on behalf of the organisation can lead to positive and meaningful interactions. However, employees or volunteers posting without the knowledge or authority to do so can harm the reputation of the organisation. Messages from any representative of the organisation may be applied to the organisation as a whole, whether official or otherwise. Sometimes, the willingness to act on social media does not come from the organisation itself, which may lead to employees or volunteers taking on the task of responding to content posted about the organisation.

Understanding the social media landscape

A simple but vital area which must be understood by employees communicating on social media is that social media is a conversation. One-way messages should mostly be avoided and users should be prepared for some level of interaction. Many organisations cite community building as the main reason for social media adoption. Despite this, several studies have found 'one-way communication to be the prominent form of communication used by organisations on Facebook and Twitter' (Auger, 2013, p. 372). The risk here is that organisations are missing out on vital conversations with target publics.

Employees representing an organisation on social media need to understand the specific social media etiquette and communication trends tied to different social media sites. For example, Facebook is often used to enhance community building, where organisations should avoid bombarding users with constant messages and encourage ownership and participation from users. Alternatively, Twitter allows for more frequent updates and messages. Due to restrictions on the number of characters, abbreviations and flexible language are also acceptable. Treating all social media sites in the same way is risky (Mathos, cited in Bermudez, 2012, p. 18), for example, linking Facebook pages with Twitter accounts so they are updated simultaneously. Activity which treats social media as one 'silo' can 'lead to community fatigue and people unfollowing'.

Even to the most accomplished communications professional, keeping current with social media trends can seem overwhelming. For small NPOs this task can seem almost impossible. As a result, some organisations sign up for the most recent or popular social media sites rather than the most relevant. This highlights the importance of research in determining which social media sites should be used to reach target publics effectively. Relevancy is more important than quantity. As mentioned earlier, abandoned social media sites can pose a reputational risk. Organisations that spread themselves too thin risk 'not delivering value in each of the most important channels, which of course is determined by your demographics, your strategy, and your objectives' (Mathos, cited in Bermudez, 2012, p. 18).

The lack of control over messages presented by social media is often a major perceived risk for NPOs. It is important that organisations understand and accept this aspect of social media as changing the way they need to communicate and interact with target publics. There will be some conflict between the planned messages from the organisation and the unplanned messages from users. Active user participation is vital and, essentially, is the purpose of social media. According to Quain (2010, p. 37), organisations need to lead by example: 'blogging and posting pictures and videos to encourage others to participate ... there's one thing technology hasn't changed about public service: it takes time and effort.'

Social media has necessitated organisational transparency. Organisations without a social media presence or who restrict online activity could be viewed as being less transparent. This trend towards transparency has resulted in an increased amount of information about NPO activities being available online. Consequently, there is a risk that messages from an organisation will be drowned out. Rosenberg (cited in Michaels, 2008, p. 2) highlights the importance of understanding audiences in order to cut through the **noise**:

Noise: An extraneous variable in the communication process which can impact the way a message is received.

> you have to understand your audience, what message you're trying to communicate and how best to do that – and as more and more people look to the web to connect, there's an explosive growth in competition for people's minds and energy.

Effectively, potential risks must be acknowledged, considered, prepared for and dealt with, if employees are to gain the required experience to handle social media issues which may present themselves again. As organisations become more immersed in social media, the messaging will become more consistent, the voice stronger and communication via these channels appears less risky – enhancing the opportunity to build communities.

The impact of the nature of organisations

While there are many ways to categorise types of organisations, whether based on their aims (e.g. fundraising, advocacy, information) or nature (health and wellness, community, animal welfare and so on), it is important to take these factors into consideration when assessing potential risk.

Organisations focusing on advocacy (e.g. Brotherhood of St Laurence, GetUp, People with Disability, Animals Australia) may publish messages which appear biased due to the passions of those involved with the cause (Pattie & Johnston, cited in Auger, 2013, p. 370). As the aim of many of these organisations is to persuade and influence, the tone adopted for online communication must help to demonstrate the immediacy of action and encourage change. However, as is the case with all forms of communication, organisations must communicate ethically via social media and avoid using a propaganda approach, which conflicts with the ideals of social media.

The risks for organisations related to health and wellbeing are complex. Organisations such as beyondblue, the Heart Foundation and the Cancer Council provide important information both to people affected by illness and to the families of those affected. If people who are experiencing hardship turn to social media for advice, the risks of misinformation goes far beyond the reputation of the organisation. For some organisations, these risks and the lack of specific regulation has led to trepidation. However, as Popovic, Smith and Hellebusch (2013, p. 26) point out, avoiding social media altogether 'is not an effective long-term strategy that benefits the general public'. To combat the constant bombardment of messages relating to lifestyle and health from commercial organisations, government, individuals and other NPOs, it is important that NPOs in this area take a sophisticated and authoritative approach.

Some use social media to assist in fundraising activities. For example, Movember Australia focuses on recruiting Mo Bros to become fundraisers. There are risks associated with focusing messages on fundraising, as opposed to information or education. However, these depend on the type of organisation and the expectations of users. Movember is a fundraising campaign, raising money for beyondblue and Prostate Cancer Foundation of Australia. Therefore, the approach to social media messaging is different to the approach of these organisations. Constant calls for donations via social media can lead to confusion over messages and objectives as well as fatigue of users who will choose to unfollow or unsubscribe.

The specific target publics of an organisation will impact on the way social media is adopted. If we consider the restrictions and limitations of particular sites for people living with disabilities, there is often a risk that some people will miss out on the level of engagement and interaction the organisation hopes for through the use of social media. In 2011, Media Access Australia and the Australian Communications Consumer Action Network developed the resource 'Sociability: Social media for people with a disability'. This resource provides information regarding specific social media sites (such as Facebook and Twitter) with the objective of helping people with disabilities to use 'popular social media tools' (MAA/ACAN, 2011, p. 3). This guide is also a useful reference for organisations who advocate on behalf of people with disabilities to ensure that communications via social media take important factors into consideration regarding accessibility. Without taking accessibility into account, some NPOs risk deficient communication with their most important target publics.

The structure of an organisation and its decision-making hierarchy will evidently impact the adoption and use of social media. The opinions, ideals and fears of decision-makers will have a flow-on effect and impact upon social media strategy and use. According to research by Nah and Saxton, organisations with a top-down structure are less likely to use social media (2012, p. 299). This may be due to restrictions placed on employees or lack of understanding regarding potential for social media communication in line with organisational objectives. Alternatively, it may be due to the sensitive nature of the work undertaken by the organisation which narrows the scope for social media use.

The blurred lines between personal and professional

Social media has blurred the distinction between personal and professional communications. The complex nature of many NPOs means that often guidelines do not necessarily apply to unique situations. For example, if an employee from a service-oriented NPO befriends a client and the client is then offended by content posted by the employee, it raises questions of when, how and if the organisation should intervene.

Employees must be aware of who within the organisation has the authority to represent the organisation officially online. Browning (cited in Quainton, 2012, p. 28) believes that a common mistake made by NPOs is choosing one individual to take responsibility for all social media activity. This is risky for NPOs given the amount of time required to effectively monitor social media and the size of the teams responsible for communications activity. When social media platforms were still relatively new in 2008, Fest (cited in Michaels, 2008, p. 2) understood the real cost of Web 2.0 tools: 'this is not a trivial thing to do ... it takes a lot of staff time'. Fine (2011) takes this a step further, suggesting that it should not be the responsibility of the communications department alone. Rather, all departments within an organisation should implement a strategic approach to social media and social media activity should be incorporated into many aspects and areas of the organisation. This can enhance the ability of the organisation to present its most valuable assets: the stories from within.

As the lines between personal and professional communication blur, there is a great risk for NPOs, in relation to what their employees say about them online. Holland (2011) suggests that the only way to counteract these issues is to provide education and training which is backed up by strong policies. However, this becomes a hurdle without dedicated and trained employees who are able to provide this guidance, or a lack of funding to bring in external parties to assist in this process.

Social media as a stand-alone tactic

It goes without saying that social media should be part of an integrated approach to public relations and communication. This is to ensure consistency of messages and approach throughout the organisation, rather than social media being a stand-alone tactic. As mentioned earlier, both Oxfam Australia and Brotherhood of St Laurence incorporate elements of social media into campaign activities.

The consistency of organisational messages is key. This consistency should also be reflected in the offline relationships forged between organisations, whether these are other NPOs, government agencies or corporations. The importance placed on corporate social responsibility means that many NPOs are supported financially via corporate donations. One of the most prominent examples in Australia is the relationship between Mount Franklin Water and the McGrath Foundation. Here, it is important that the McGrath Foundation recognises this relationship on social media (this can be achieved by 'liking' and interacting with the Mount Franklin page, mentioning them, and other responses) to ensure consistency. Failure to do so could lead to a breakdown of an important relationship.

The role of strategy development in risk aversion

While some organisations have developed strong social media policies, guidelines or strategies, others avoid this approach due to the unpredictable nature of the medium. Mathos and Norman (cited in Bermudez, 2012) cite the importance of developing a clear social media strategy to avoid 'a lot of activity with no real purpose'.

When developing social media strategy, it is vital that the organisation determines the specific reasons for using social media sites as a communications tool. This may be to publicise fundraising events, call supporters to action, influence change, raise awareness and so on. Oxfam Australia (cited in Wirth Consulting, 2012) states three reasons why it uses social media: to increase awareness, promote active citizenship and increase online donations.

While a strategy will help to direct the communication coming from the organisation and the way the organisation handles enquiries from users, it is important to note that the organisation does not have control over social media. As a result, the way the community interacts on Facebook pages (for example) may contradict the original aims of the organisation's approach to the site. As the organisation does not own the sites they are using, it is important that organisations treat these as social spaces and abide by each site's terms of use and the unwritten **rules of engagement**. Ensuring content is interactive, engaging and relevant to the users, means avoiding one-way communication. Organisations should always expect that someone will interact with the content – this is desirable and essential in building an online community. As Jennings (2011, p. 42) emphasises, organisations need to acknowledge that they are communicating with people, with individuals, rather than markets or whole target publics. And often, these people are impassioned about the same issues the organisation is communicating about.

Rules of engagement: Informal norms and customs which determine acceptable hehaviour for a given social media platform and which evolve over time.

The way an organisation will approach social media strategy will depend on their purpose and nature. Some organisations, such as Lifeline Australia, choose to make their social media guidelines publicly available. Other organisations may see social media policies and guidelines as a roadblock which actually discourages the participation sought when they signed up for social media sites. Due to the sensitive nature of some of the content posted by Lifeline online and the impact it may have on users, it is imperative that employees communicating online are equipped with information and advice as to responses. Making this information publicly available also ensures that social media users understand their responsibilities online.

One area where social media guidelines or policies and procedures can create a greater sense of control is in relation to dealing with negative feedback. Sometimes, when faced with negative comments on social media sites, the initial reaction of an administrator may be to delete the comment. However, this itself poses many risks. For example, what if the comment was genuine and constructive? What if the person posting was genuinely upset and the deleted comment encouraged them to become more upset? Each 'negative' post should be considered uniquely and assessed. Sometimes negative comments actually provide an opportunity for the organisation to educate and inform. Many employees of NPOs are impassioned about the work they do. This is what makes internal resources of NPOs so vital to the cause. However, this can also lead to employees taking negative posts personally. When responding to negative posts, administrators should keep in mind that they are not personal attacks. It can often help to develop a response using specific guidelines and ask for feedback from another employee before posting to ensure the response demonstrates a reasoned, rather than defensive, approach. Administrators must make the decision to deal with negative posts, as if not responded to they can escalate into an issue.

In addition to developing response guidelines, organisations should also incorporate information regarding to appropriate tone. To demonstrate understanding of social media, social media etiquette and the target publics, an organisation should develop a voice that is used when communicating using social media. Generally, this should be informative and friendly.

Social media resources for NPOs

In 2012, the Advertising Standards Board ruled that Facebook pages are now classified as advertising. As a result, companies and organisations are responsible for inappropriate content posted on the Facebook page, either from the administrators or user-generated comments (Lee, 2012). Evidently, it is vital that those responsible for administrating social media for NPOs monitor sites regularly. However, the risks are increased for NPOs without a dedicated team of communicators responsible for this task. This move raised many questions regarding the onus on organisations regarding third-party content and their responsibility to guide users in what they post online, contrasting the perceived 'open' nature of social media, where people often feel safe to provide commentary that may be deemed offensive. As a result of these changes, the Communications Council developed a Social Media Code of Conduct. While many of the guidelines are directed at commercial organisations, it includes useful information for employees in their personal use of social media, maintaining privacy and professionalism.

Other changes to social media have impacted on the opportunities for NPOs. The social networking sites Facebook, Twitter and Instagram are using paid posts and advertising. While this may be necessary in ensuring their prominence online through revenue, it may lead to a less democratic space. What drew organisations to social media originally was the seemingly cost-effective way to reach large numbers of people with messages. Now, NPOs are competing with paid content, which many of them cannot afford. Size and budget did not so greatly influence social media adoption and usage before the enterprise became more commercial, but now, large organisations with large budgets have the most opportunity to have their voices heard. Therefore, in order to cut through the noise, NPOs need to ensure they are engaging the right people with interesting, effective content.

Often guidelines such as these can feel restrictive to NPO employees communicating online. Especially in an era where trial and error of messages is important in developing strategy and determining the best way to engage audiences.

Conclusion

A range of complex issues are associated with social media use for NPOs. Education and research is vital so organisations ensure they are communicating with the most appropriate tools. Understanding organisational capacity and planning for social media becomes imperative. Organisations also need to demonstrate understanding of the mediums in which they are communicating, using spaces for interaction and listening to conversations as well as posting and publishing content.

Neglecting social media presents risks associated with misinformation and also ignores opportunities to connect with target publics and influence change. This is particularly important for organisations dealing with health and wellness issues. Developing social media strategies and guidelines around negative commentary can go some way to minimising risks. Education, understanding and preparation will ensure that employees using social media understand the nature of the medium and develop a consistent approach.

Auger (2013) has written that 'No longer can organisations allow information to remain static but the information they provide must compete with many more voices in the vast online communities of cyberspace, and the information must be timely, responsive, persuasive and transparent to compete within this large marketplace of ideas' (p. 370). Perhaps the biggest risk NPOs can take is to make little or no use of social media in communicating with their target publics. It could be considered that the perceived risks of social media can outweigh the opportunities, and this can be a tremendous hurdle for NPOs in the adoption and use of social media. Missing opportunities to connect with target publics is the greatest risk. Social media provides organisations and ambassadors a platform from which they can engage communities and motivate change. Ensuring that planned messages coming from the organisation are included in the conversation is vital.

CASE QUESTIONS

1. What are the biggest risks facing NPOs in relation to communicating via social media?
2. Find an example of an Australian NPO using Facebook or Twitter. Find a negative comment posted by a user and how it was handled by the organisation. Would you take the same approach?
3. Why is the development and implementation of a social media strategy important in minimising risk?
4. Why are the types of social media sites used by an NPO more important than the number of sites being used?

BIBLIOGRAPHY

Auger, G. A. (2013). Fostering democracy through social media: Evaluating diametrically opposed non-profit advocacy organisations' use of Facebook, Twitter, and YouTube. *Public Relations Review*, 39, 369–76.

Bermudez, C. (2012). Nonprofits need to get smarter about using social media, say authors. *Chronicle of Philanthropy*, 24(10), 18.

Brotherhood of St Laurence, website, www.bsl.org.au. Retrieved 3 November 2013.

Communications Council (2012). Communications Council Best Practice Guide: Social Media Code of Conduct.

Fine, A. (2011). Social media are no longer optional. *Chronicle of Philanthropy* 23(17).

Gupta, S. (2011). Exploring social responsibility through social media. *Global Media Journal: Indian Edition*, June.

Holland, P. (2011, 12 August). Social networks weave uneasy web for workers, *Sydney Morning Herald*. Retrieved 22 August 2012 from www.smh.com.au/business/social-networks-weave-uneasy-web-for-workers-20110811–1iorn.html.

Jennings, A. (2011). How to ruin social media strategy for your company: What happens if they don't 'like you?' *Home Business*, November/December, 42.

Lee, J. (2012, 6 August). Watchdog clamps down on Facebook, *The Age*, retrieved 22 August 2012 from www.theage.com/id=3530134.

Lifeline Australia (2012). *Social Media Policy: Version 1.0*, November, retrieved 6 November 2013 from www.lifeline.org.au/ . . . /18/Social%20Media%20Policy.pdf.aspx.

Media Access Australia & The Australian Consumer Action Network (MAA/ACAN) 2011, Sociability: Social Media for People with a Disability.

Michaels, M. (2008, 5 January). Finding their voice, *Chronicle of Philanthropy*, 20(14), 2.

Nah, S. & Saxton, G. D. (2012). Modeling the adoption and use of social media by non-profit organisations. *New Media and Society*, 15 (2), 294–313.

Oxfam Australia, website, https://www.oxfam.org.au/, viewed 1 November 2013.

Popovic, K., Smith, C. & Hellebusch, S. J. (2013). Attitudes on the use of social media in healthcare communications. *Journal of Communication in Healthcare*, 6(1), 22–8.

Quain, J. R. (2012). Social network cause and effect, *US World and News Report*, November, 36–7.

Quainton, G. (2012, 20 March). Charities great and small can use social media. *Third Sector Magazine*, 28.

Roberts, C. (2012, 11 December). Integrating social media into advocacy campaigns: What's the right mix? Connecting Up. Retrieved 3 November 2013 from www.connectingup.org/learn/articles/integrating-social-media-advocacy-campaigns-whats-right-mix.

Wirth Consulting (2012). The state of social media use in Australian non profit organisations, July. Retrieved 30 October 2013 from www.wirthconsulting.com.au/component/phocadownload/category/5-research-papers?download=8:the-state-of-social-media-use-in-australian-non-profits-h1-2012.

PART 5

NATURAL **DISASTERS**

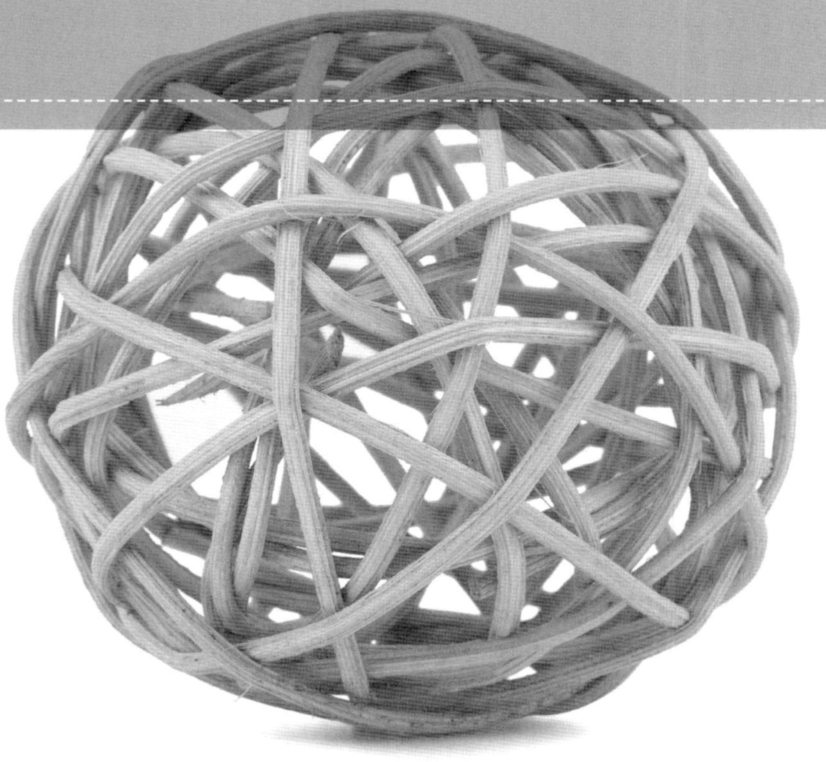

10

COMMUNICATING DURING DISASTERS

INSIGHTS FROM THE 2013 BUNDABERG FLOOD

Amisha Mehta and Dominique A. Greer

Chapter objectives

This chapter aims to:

- define and establish the significance and outcomes of risk communication
- discuss the role of risk communication across crisis and disaster phases
- identify message components of risk communication
- identify advantages and disadvantages of communicating risk across a range of media channels.

Introduction

In January 2013, ex-Tropical Cyclone (TC) Oswald triggered a series of extreme weather events across the east cost of Queensland. The Wide Bay–Burnett region, located between 120 and 400 kilometres north of Brisbane, felt the particular effects of ex-TC Oswald, which included mini tornadoes, thunderstorms and strong wind gusts that killed several people and caused significant damage to infrastructure. Two years earlier, Queensland had experienced similar extreme weather events, during which social media acted as an information hub when websites for organisations including emergency services struggled to cope with the increased user demand. However, in the main town in the Wide Bay–Burnett region, Bundaberg, the extreme weather of January 2013 created a unique communication challenge for emergency services and the community: while Queenslanders had become accustomed to using social media to communicate during natural hazards, Bundaberg is home to the second-largest number of older Australians and thus social media usage in this region is low. This issue made communicating risk, warnings and instructions to individuals, communities and businesses more complex.

This chapter introduces the key concepts of risk communication during natural disasters and examines their usefulness in the case of the 2013 Bundaberg flood. In this chapter, a working knowledge of the content and phases of risk communication during natural disasters is developed. To support this working knowledge, it introduces key theories that explain how individuals interpret and process messages. This knowledge is important because the increasing complexities of natural disasters present challenges for communicating and connecting communities, governments and businesses.

Background

This chapter focuses on the risk communication strategies employed during extreme weather events that affected the regional Australian city of Bundaberg in 2013. Bundaberg is located almost 400 kilometres north of Brisbane, the capital city of Queensland. Often described as the 'lifestyle capital of Queensland', the region attracts retirees and older residents. The Wide Bay–Burnett region, which includes Bundaberg and its surrounds, is the second most popular residential area for older Australians, with 46 per cent of its population expected to be aged 55 years or older in 2021 (Alouat, 2013). Bundaberg is the gateway to the southern Great Barrier Reef and is situated around the Burnett River on a fertile flood plain. In the 19th century, Bundaberg was a prosperous sugar town, which led to the emergence of two iconic companies: Bundaberg Sugar and Bundaberg Rum (both now owned by overseas companies).

The Bundaberg Regional Local Government Area encompasses a population of approximately 93 000 people (Queensland Treasury and Trade, n.d.). While the weather in Bundaberg usually attracts extra visitors to the region, the town experienced severe weather-related events in 1942, 1974 and 2011. In 2013, the town flooded after rain fell continuously for 24 hours in the catchment area around Bundaberg (Fraser, 2013). While only 10 per cent of the city was flooded, the event destroyed many homes and businesses, which presented a challenge for recovery and reconstruction (Fraser, 2013). According to Fraser (2013), however, while 1500 people were left without homes, only 200 were accommodated in evacuation centres. Friends and family accommodated the majority of evacuees.

Several government bodies were responsible for communicating with residents during the severe weather events. The Bundaberg Regional Council has a Local Disaster Management Group (LDMG), which acts as the local arm of the Queensland Government's disaster management operations. LDMGs work with local councils, state government and related emergency services agencies to review and update disaster management plans; build community awareness to prevent, prepare for, respond to and recover from disasters; and manage disaster operations on behalf of the district and the state. At state level, the disaster management arrangements connect local communities with government departments, agencies such as State Emergency Services, government-owned corporations such as power companies and the corporate sector. This whole-of-government approach operated during the 2013 events to encourage coordination and consistency in disaster planning, response, recovery and reconstruction. But just how well did these organisations really communicate? What communication challenges did they face during this event?

What is risk communication during disasters?

In order to explore this case, the chapter begins with an examination of how risk communication works. Risk communication has been described as a 'point of intersection of social communication, practical management and policy-making' (Boholm, 2008, p. 1). This intersection is particularly meaningful during emergent natural disasters, where practical management and policy are being continually reworked and implemented as the disaster gains certainty. Risk communication is 'any purposeful exchange of information about health or environmental risks between interested parties' (Kellens et al., 2013, p. 25). Such communication aims to educate individuals, groups and organisations and so to stimulate their interest, increase their knowledge, inform their decision-making and/or alter their attitudes and behaviour (Boholm, 2008).

Traditionally, risk communication was perceived to be a one-way process (Kellens et al., 2013). Experts would assess the risks of a disaster using complex statistical analysis and then communicate these calculated risks to the public (Kellens et al., 2013). From this perspective, communication during disasters was fairly straightforward: expert meteorologists, hydrologists, engineers and disaster management officials would simply form an expert judgement of the risks of the disaster, then inform the public so that they could make well-informed behavioural choices.

The problem with this approach, however, is that it fails to account for how the public interpret expert risk assessments when forming their own risk perceptions. Slovic (1986) found that public risk perceptions suffer from three key problems. First, people distort their judgement of risk when a similar prior event is still particularly memorable or vividly imaginable (Slovic, 1986). This would most certainly have been an issue for the residents of Bundaberg because many of them had only recently recovered from the 2011 flood they had experienced. Second, people are likely to ignore frightening risk messages when they are faced with uncertainty (Slovic, 1986). As natural disasters are extremely uncertain events, this would also have shaped the way Bundaberg residents would have interpreted risk communications during the floods. Third, if risk messages contradict people's strongly held opinions, they are often ignored; conversely, if people lack strong opinions about the event, they are highly suggestible to different message framing (Slovic, 1986). Together, these factors distort how the public interpret expert risk assessments and result in varied interpretations of emergency messages.

Due to the limited success of this approach, risk communication has now evolved to be a more interactive, collaborative learning process (Kellens et al., 2013). Risk communication strategies now focus on 'structuring dialogue' to 'develop shared understandings about risk and its acceptability' (Salter, 2002, p. 4). This dialogue forms the foundation for designing and implementing disaster interventions (Salter, 2002). Internationally, risk communication is now perceived to be

> an interactive process of exchange of information and opinion among individuals, groups and institutions; often involving multiple messages about the nature of risk or expressing concerns, opinions or reactions to risk messages or to legal and institutional arrangements for risk management.
>
> (Salter, 2002)

Risk communication across the four phases of disasters

Most Australian disaster management agencies and operations partition natural disasters into four phases (Rogers, 2011). The first phase, **prevention**, refers to the time period when community members and businesses can take action to limit the impact of potential disasters. In Bundaberg, this phase involved building or relocating homes away from flood-prone areas. The second phase, **preparation**, refers to the time period when community members and businesses can undertake activities to prepare for an imminent event; in Bundaberg, residents were encouraged to prepare a flood survival kit prior to the summer storm season. The third phase, **response**, refers to the time period when governments and emergency organisations work with affected stakeholders to respond to the emerging event. In Bundaberg, this phase involved evacuating residents to safety and providing time-critical weather forecasting. The final phase, **recovery**, refers to the time period when governments, emergency organisations and communities work together to rebuild and recover from the immediate event. In Bundaberg, this phase involved rebuilding damaged infrastructure and providing permanent accommodation to displaced residents.

Prevention: As the first stage in the disaster cycle, prevention refers to the steps that community members and businesses can take to limit damage from events, including building homes away from flood areas.

Preparation: As the second stage in the disaster cycle, preparation refers to the activities that communities can undertake to prepare for an event, such as having a flood survival kit.

Response: As the third stage in the disaster cycle, response refers to the way government or organisations work with affected stakeholders to respond to the event.

Recovery: As the fourth stage in the disaster cycle, recovery refers to the way governments, organisations and communities work together to rebuild and recover from the event.

Risk communication plays an essential role across all four phases of the disaster spectrum. The content of communication comprises three types of information, used in different ways during prevention, preparation, response and recovery phases (Sturges, 1994):

1. instructing information
2. adjusting information
3. internalising information.

According to Sturges (1994), instructing information contains content to advise people about how to physically react to the event. This kind of information is often delivered as a warning or instruction that directs people to respond with specific and immediate behaviours during a disaster or crisis (Sturges, 1994). For example, residents could be warned to prepare for disaster season by undertaking specific preparatory activities. The second type of communication content is adjusting information. This includes content that helps people psychologically cope with the event (Sturges, 1994). For example, government leaders could reassure people that their homes and businesses would be rebuilt. The third type of communication content is internalising information, which helps people formulate an image about the organisation (Sturges, 1994). For example, government leaders could recognise the work of emergency services teams in responding to the event. Internalising information is more commonly recognised in the public relations literature as a means to help restore or improve the image or reputation of organisations involved in disasters or crises.

One factor that influences the choice of communication content is the phase of the disaster or crisis. During natural disasters, instructing information is essential across all phases of disaster, although it is most critical during preparation, response and recovery. Instructions are often issued by multiple organisations during the crisis. These organisations are typically seeking compliance from individuals, households and businesses.

Multiple information sources and channels are used to communicate during disasters. Recent research demonstrates that it is important to integrate both expert information sources and formal social interactions, such as communicating updates from fire authorities using mass media, with non-expert information sources and informal interactions, such as hearing about a neighbour's actions via social media (Brenkert-Smith et al., 2012). Research suggests that local sources and one-to-one interaction are valued more highly than media sources because they provide personalised, localised information (Brenkert-Smith et al., 2012). Communication channel options include face-to-face, radio, social media, television, online and print newspapers and organisational websites. The message and channel choice are determined by factors including the recognition of audiences, availability of power, time and resources.

Research has also investigated how to make instructional messages more effective and persuasive. This research recommends that instructional messages should be tailored to audience learning styles, as well as demographic factors such as gender, age and ethnicity (Sellnow et al., 2012). Persuasion is best achieved when people receive messages that align to their preferred learning style.

Drawing on the cycle of learning model developed by Kolb (1984, cited in Sellnow et al., 2012) and their research, Sellnow et al. provide constructive advice for designing instructional messages and make explicit potential differences in the preferences of thinkers, watchers, feelers and doers. For example, thinkers process instructional messages cognitively and will respond to messages which are based on 'certainty, expert opinion, accuracy, caution and a single correct answer' (2012, p.641). Watchers appear to be motivated by both cognitive and affective drivers and will respond to succinct messages which assign blame and/or responsibility for risk or crisis. This suggests a balance is needed between long-form and short-form instructional messages to meet the needs of these two distinct groups.

The third group, feelers, demonstrate affective responses to instructional messages; that is, they are seeking engagement on an emotional, visceral level (Sellnow et al., 2012, p.641). Interestingly, Sellnow et al. suggest that fear appeals can be effective for this group. The final group, the doers, want to know what is being asked of them, what actions they must perform to avoid risk and/or deal with the crisis to keep safe.

Risk communication in Bundaberg: Across the four phases

Warnings about the acute flooding in Bundaberg began on the eve of Australia Day 2013, a time that normally signals preparation for parties to bring together friends and families (see Table 10.1). For some members of this community, learning this news in the face of only recently rebuilding from the 2011 flood brought immense stress. Others responded with **resilience**, vowing to rebuild after the event. The Bundaberg Regional Council, the Bureau of Meteorology, State Government and emergency services agencies began communicating with communities in earnest, providing information about weather updates, warnings and instructions for residents across the east coast of Queensland.

Resilience: The extent to which individuals, communities and organisations can manage stress and uncertainty associated with a disaster and work to rebuild their future.

Table 10.1 Timeline of Bundaberg flood events

Disaster Phase	Date	Events
Preparation Phase	January 24	Warnings issued to residents in Bundaberg and surrounding areas.
	January 25	Warnings issued to residents in Bundaberg and surrounding areas. Australia Day events cancelled.
Response Phase	January 27	More than 1000 homes and 200 businesses expect to be swamped as the Burnett River is predicted to peak at 9m.
	January 28	Residents of North Bundaberg are rescued by boat and helicopter as the Burnett River continues to rise. Hundreds are evacuated to the AgroTrend grounds.
	January 29	Burnett River peaks at 9.525m – the highest in recorded history. 7500 people displaced as 3000 houses damaged by floodwaters.
	January 30	More than 200 Army soldiers arrive in Bundaberg to help. Citrus damage bill expected to top $100 million.
	January 31	North Bundaberg declared an exclusion zone. Call goes out for people to volunteer for the Mud Army.
Recovery Phase	February 1	North Bundaberg opens to residents so they can assess the damage to their homes.
	February 4	The Mud Army begins to clean up in North Bundaberg – one of the worst affected areas.
	February 8	Army is farewelled by residents and presented with certificates of appreciation from Mayor Mal Forman.
	February 14	The Tallon Bridge reopens.

Source: *Fighting back: Our road to recovery*, 2013

For Bundaberg, there were a number of communication challenges during the preparation, response and recovery phases. While communication case studies and research articles about the 2011 Queensland floods have focused on the power of social media to inform and connect communities, social media was a complementary focus for Bundaberg residents, businesses and tourists. In addition, because the flood event had implications for a number of regions and cities across Queensland, communication strategies drew on messages from state and local governments as well as emergency services agencies. Despite integrating expert sources, residents remained uncertain about which areas the floods would impact. Another communication challenge related to the demographics of Bundaberg's population, which comprises a high proportion of older Australians. These demographics had implications for the type of messages and communication channels used by emergency service organisations and volunteers during preparation and response. However, not all of the preparation and response phase communication challenges are unique to Bundaberg. During most natural disasters in most regions, emergency service organisations must communicate instructions and information to guide appropriate behaviour during the disaster, while attempting to prevent inappropriate behaviour.

The preparation phase

Floods can be either expected or unexpected events. While the severe flash flooding in Toowoomba, sometimes referred to as an 'inland tsunami', highlights the unexpectedness of floods, the 2013 Bundaberg flood was an anticipated event, which allowed residents to take preventative action. The immediate preparation phase comprised two days. On 24 January 2013, the Bureau of Meteorology issued severe weather warnings for the Queensland coast and flood warnings for a number of rivers and streams in these areas. This message was reinforced by Emergency Management Queensland, which recommended that residents who required assistance to evacuate should contact State Emergency Services. Locally, the Bundaberg Regional Council asked residents to be mindful of the weather and to prepare emergency kits. The council gave specific instructions to builders and those people living in caravans, requesting that properties be secured by removing or properly storing loose items.

On 25 January 2013, as weather continued to affect the region, the first disaster management alert was issued. The LDMG was moved to an Alert level as localised flash flooding was anticipated. At the same time, some of the council's planned Australia Day celebration activities were cancelled. On 26 January 2013, the disaster moved into the response phase following mini tornadoes at nearby Bargara, Burnett Heads, Coonarr and Avenell Heights. The LDMG warned residents of power outages and to take care near fallen power lines. They also advised of potential sewage overflows due to electricity outages and set up an evacuation centre at the Civic Centre in Bundaberg.

Dealing with problems of compliance

Despite the best efforts of emergency service organisations, not everyone complied with the instructional messages issued during the preparation and response phases. This is a common issue during the preparedness phase – many households or businesses fail to plan for disasters – but is particularly concerning during the response phase. In past natural disasters, people often didn't believe (or simply ignored) the warnings and refused to evacuate their properties, only to face life-threatening situations without the possibility for rescue. For example, during Cyclone Yasi in 2011, North Queensland residents that chose to refuse to evacuate were warned that emergency services would not be able to attend to them until the cyclone had passed.

At the same time as coordinating community evacuations and managing the imminent event, emergency services in Bundaberg also issued warnings to potential spectators of the flood. Drivers were specifically instructed to not drive through floodwaters or onto flooded roads. People were warned to avoid playing near, swimming or boating in waterways such as dams, creeks and rivers. In Queensland, non-compliance with these instructions is so problematic that a campaign was designed to encourage people to do the right thing. The campaign, which used the slogan 'If it's flooded, forget it', warned drivers and their passengers to never enter floodwaters regardless of their assumed knowledge of the road or reliability of their vehicle. Swift water changes everything a driver might have known about a road: it can split roads, carry heavy or sharp objects, transport chemicals, or be contaminated with sewage. Water can also severely damage cars, affecting the engine and their ability to manoeuvre. People who drive through floodwaters often die or need swift-water rescue. Both of these consequences put emergency service crews in dangerous situations, too.

During the 2013 Queensland floods, the Queensland Fire and Rescue Service responded to 20 calls for swift-water rescue in one night. Most official messages relating to the event include some sort of warning about these activities. Below is an example of floodwater warnings presented in a media release issued by the Queensland Government:

> Before you hit the road, check the current conditions and map out an alternative route if there is a chance you may come across floodwaters. Flash flooding can occur quickly and catch motorists and pedestrians unaware. In most cases, swift-water rescues are preventable and there is absolutely no excuse for motorists who deliberately drive or walk past a road closed sign and into floodwaters.
>
> (Queensland Government, 2013)

The response phase

As the weather continued to cause infrastructure damage, the LDMG issued a number of advisories and media alerts on 27 January about both the expected levels of the Burnett River and the streets likely to be flood-affected. The advisories contained conflicting information, which reflects the uncertain and emergent nature of disasters. This conflicting information confused residents. The first advisory suggested the river would peak at 7 metres and that residents at risk, particularly those in North Bundaberg, were to seek higher ground or relocate to friends' and family members' homes located outside of the inundation area. Using this information, the local council used its website and other channels to advise residents of the streets and roads that were likely to be flooded.

Later that day, a revised media alert said the Burnett River was expected to reach 8.5 metres, significantly higher than the previously reported level and the 7.92 metre level experienced in the 2010/11 floods. A similar message came from the Bureau of Meteorology, which provided comparisons between the 2013 and 2010/11 events. In addition to the alert that identified the streets most likely to be at risk, a one-sentence media update was posted:

> Based on previous reports/updates – streets indicated as having the potential for flooding is NOT an exclusive list and we advise all residents to be vigilant and prepare themselves.
>
> (http://bundaberg.qld.gov.au/news/2013/01/27/update-street-flooding)

On 28 January, as the Burnett River continued to rise to levels higher than predicted, the response focus shifted to evacuating residents in North Bundaberg. The Burnett River had reached 9.1 metres and was anticipated to rise to 9.5 metres, an additional metre above the levels reported the previous day. A high priority alert was issued to notify North Bundaberg residents to evacuate immediately to Oakwood State School. The Bundaberg Region Disaster Management's Facebook page reported that there were residents on roofs waiting to be rescued. Approximately 11 000 people were evacuated over several hours. This exercise represents the largest air evacuation in Australia's history, including periods of war. Over the course of the day, reports about the rising river levels and updates about evacuation points for North Bundaberg continued to flow through a range of media outlets and on the ground.

At the same time as communicating instructions to North Bundaberg residents, the LDMG was also dealing with unfounded rumours about water supply. While flooding had affected water treatment plants, water was still available and safe. These myths were addressed using social media, the council website and the news media:

> Unfounded rumours are rife that Bundaberg's water supply is being 'cut-off'.
>
> The rumours are false. There is no issue with the quality or quantity of Bundaberg's water supply. Contact Bundaberg Regional Council on 1300 883 699 if further advice is required.
>
> Authorised by Peter Byrne, Local Disaster Co-ordinator, Bundaberg Disaster Management Group, 3.30pm.
>
> (http://bundaberg.qld.gov.au/news/2013/01/28/bundabergs-water-supply)

While the weather had isolated communities and triggered power outages, some residents were relatively unaffected by the event and wanted to volunteer to support their local communities. Managing community donations is essential to recovery but can place a significant strain on the resources required to manage the immediate response phase of the natural disaster.

The recovery phase begins

The recovery efforts began on 30 January 2014, only a handful of days after the event began. During this time, communication focused on the effects of the flood in terms of human life and injury and damage to property. Messages helped to set expectations for community members. In the interests of community safety, North Bundaberg was declared an exclusion zone. Residents and the general public were forbidden to enter the area while search and rescue teams conducted a survey. Flood information updates reported that approximately 20 homes were severely damaged. Entire sections of sewage lines in North Bundaberg had been destroyed. Some parts of North Bundaberg were yet to be accessed by search and rescue teams as they were still inundated with water. Meetings were held with North Bundaberg residents to explain the situation: there was no water, no power and no sewage in the exclusion zone.

When residents were allowed to return to clean their homes, a call to mobilise the 'mud army' was issued by the Bundaberg Regional Council. The 'mud army' was the name given to the community members who volunteered their time to help friends, family and strangers following the flood events in 2011. The Council also continued to provide updates to the community about how to dispose of rubbish and travel and transportation access.

Final assessments of more than 3500 homes in Bundaberg showed that 38 homes were uninhabitable, more than 350 were severely damaged and almost 1000 experienced damage caused by floodwaters rising above powerpoints. A number of people were without homes and while most were accommodated by friends and family, an affectionately named 'tent city' was established at the local showgrounds to provide air-conditioned living spaces and a communal kitchen to displaced residents. This phase also represented a time of communication transition, when messages from emergency services were issued less often and other organisations became more engaged with Bundaberg communities. For example, Ergon Energy, the major supplier of electricity to the area, provided safety advice to residents when cleaning up debris after floodwaters. They issued a community power update to provide guidance around the safe use of generators and reported on repair efforts. As the focus of the community shifted towards recovery and reconstruction, insurance agencies came into the town to assess properties and support customers. Red Cross also provided support to the area and information to guide the clean-up process.

Local, national and international media covered the events of January 2013, with Australian networks broadcasting live or posting live blogs, but as recovery and reconstruction efforts began, the communication strategy shifted. For emergency services organisations, communication shifted from disaster-based approaches towards providing ongoing support and making connections with the community. Even now, the Bundaberg Regional Council provides regular advice about recovery through newsletters and community reference groups. Other emergency services agencies set up meetings to help learn from this event and inform strategies for future natural disasters.

Communication via social media

Although social media played a complementary role to traditional media during the events in Bundaberg, analyses demonstrate that social media provided an outlet for two-way risk

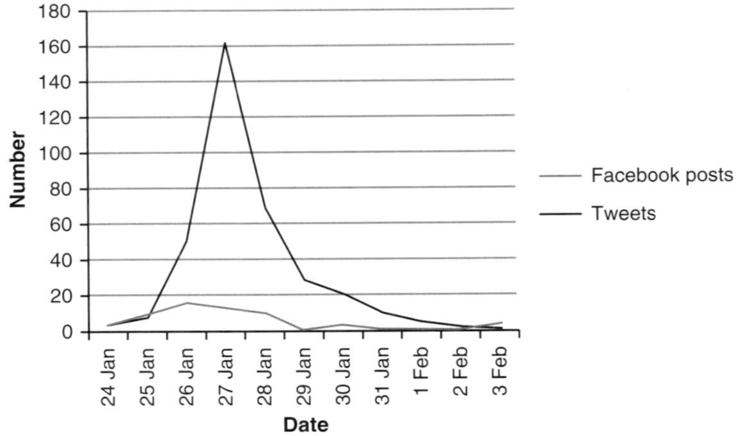

Figure 10.1 Social media communication before, during and after the flood event

communication to be socially constructed in real-time. Figure 10.1 illustrates the number of tweets posted to #bigwet, #qldfloods and #bundaberg, as well as the number of posts on the Bundaberg Region Disaster Management Facebook page over the event period. Across both types of media, there was a steep increase in the number of alerts issued from 26 January onward. While #qldfloods was the primary Twitter hashtag in the 2010/11 floods, it only accounted for 67 tweets in 2013. In 2013, #bigwet accounted for 325 tweets.

The timing of these messages aligns with the disaster phases; thus, social media messages were dominated by **instructional communication** from government agencies and media. Adjusting information or messages of reassurance and support were most often expressed by people living outside of the at-risk area. There were very few messages that drew on image-based content. During the event, very few tweets were made by Bundaberg residents. However, more residents used the Bundaberg Region Disaster Management Facebook page to post photographs of damaged property. Both channels show a marked drop off in the number of tweets or posts following the peak of the event.

Instructional communication: The content or messages used by authorities or trusted sources to guide an individual, community or organisational response to a disaster.

Risk, crisis and communication lessons learned

From a theoretical perspective, communication across disaster phases ideally should include a blend of instructing, adjusting and internalising (image-building) content (Sturges, 1994). By examining this case study, particularly its social media messages across these three content types, there are some clear issues to be resolved. In Bundaberg, much of the disaster communication focused on providing instructions (e.g. warnings or updates delivered via social media, telephone and face-to-face channels) to influence the behaviours of the community. In addition, adjusting information was provided largely by individuals outside of Bundaberg. However, there was limited inclusion of internalising or image-building content across this flood disaster. One explanation for the lack of image-based content is the nature of disasters. Given the devastating effect of disasters and the long-term recovery implications for the local community, messages that remind people of the good work of emergency services might seem self-important and self-promotional rather than respectful of the affected individuals and businesses.

However, there is still a need for image-based communication, when the time is right, from emergency services. One of the challenges that can face emergency services is the media agenda. During the event response and immediate recovery phase, emergency services are portrayed as the heroes of the day: saving lives, protecting property and managing disaster response. However, media framing can shift from 'fame to blame' post-disaster and highlight the faults or inadequacies of the emergency service response. This portrayal has implications for the public's perception of trust and credibility in emergency services, which may negatively affect their behaviour in subsequent disasters.

Although instructional messaging dominates disaster communication, it is important to understand how messages are delivered in the context of an unfolding and unpredictable event. For example, on 27 January, when the Burnett River at Bundaberg was rising, the predicted flood levels changed a number of times in one day, making it difficult for the local council to provide an accurate list of streets expected to be inundated. Rather than providing definitive messages during disasters, organisations should view media updates and social media posts organically and incorporate messages about potential changes to instructions or impact areas to reflect the uncertainty of the event.

At the same time, localising the message and channel to the audience is critical. This case study highlights some interesting problems in relying too heavily on one channel. First, Bundaberg is home to a large number of older Australians, which reduced the uptake of social media as a primary source for communication. Second, the loss of power limited the community's ability to stay connected on social media. This case demonstrates that multi-channel, localised messages are critical during disaster management, even if certain channels have been successful in managing similar disasters elsewhere.

Figures 10.1 and 10.2 highlight the significant number of updates or bulletins either issued or monitored by the Bundaberg Regional Council. While this represents a large amount of social media information, it does not take into account other sources of information, such as meetings, briefings, or other public relations and communications activities. It is critical to consider the resourcing of the public relations/media relations teams during disaster in order to manage fatigue and ensure that messages remain consistent following shift changes.

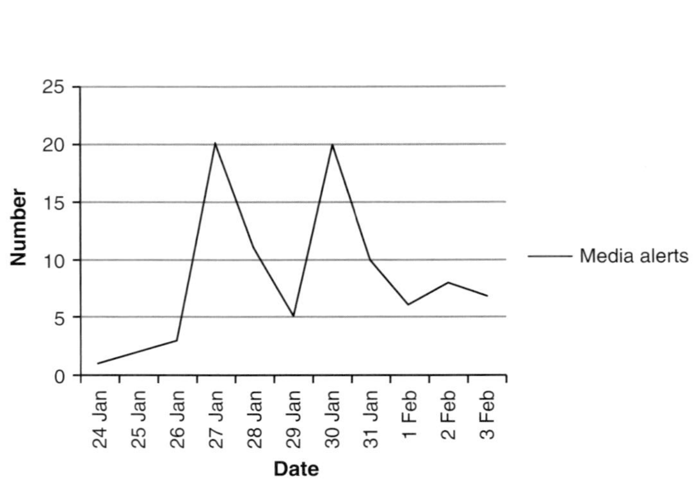

Figure 10.2 Communication alerts issued by Bundaberg Regional Council

Conclusion

Effective communication about natural disasters begins well before an event occurs. Advanced preparation for disaster events can save lives and protect property, which helps people rebuild and become more resilient to disaster events. In addition, communicating about appropriate behaviour during disaster response can help improve compliance to warnings. One strategy that aims to help people prepare for events is the Queensland Government's *Get Ready Queensland* initiative. Following the 2010/11 disasters, the Queensland Government initiated a public education campaign that now runs in October of each year to encourage preparation and build resilience among Queenslanders. The *Get Ready Queensland* campaign includes a booklet mailed to all households and aims to help prepare residents for cyclones, floods, severe storms and tsunamis. It encourages people to sign up to a program of weekly updates that remind you to prepare for disasters. More information can be found via http://getready.qld.gov.au/.

Online and social media have become go-to channels before, during and after natural disasters. However, it is important to monitor the changing media landscape to understand what this means for risk communication during disasters. While online and social media are useful for preparation and (in some cases) disaster response, they may not suit all populations or disasters. Disaster and risk communication must always align channel, medium and message to help individuals and communities prepare for, respond to and recover from natural disasters.

CASE QUESTIONS

1. What are some ways that internalising or image-based messages could be introduced into disaster communication?

2. Disaster-based communication necessarily involves government departments and agencies. What are two businesses that are involved before, during and after disasters, and how can they be part of community engagement around natural disasters?
3. Consider the definition of risk communication (see discussion of Salter, 2002, in the text). What are some of the ways social media can contribute to this process and in this context, what are the advantages and disadvantages of this channel?
4. The case study identifies the challenge of dealing with compliance during disasters. For example, people still engage in dangerous driving through floodwaters, which puts them and emergency services crews at risk. The Queensland Government developed one campaign to manage this issue ('If it's flooded, forget it'), but what other strategies could be used to increase compliance?

BIBLIOGRAPHY

Alouat, J. (2013, 29 July). Elderly numbers rise but care is limited. *Bundaberg News Mail*, www.news-mail.com.au/news/elderly-numbers-rise-but-care-is-limited/1961887.

Boholm A. (2008). New perspectives on risk communication: Uncertainty in a complex society. *Journal of Risk Research*, 11(1–2), 1–3.

Brenkert-Smith, H., Dickinson, K. L., Champ, P. A. & Flores, N.(2012). Social Amplification of Wildfire Risk: The Role of Social Interactions and Information Sources. *Risk Analysis*, 1–17.

Fighting back: Our road to recovery (2013, 16 February). *News Mail Bundaberg* 31.

Fraser, A.(2013, February 11). Despair after the flood, *The Australian*, 11.

Kellens, W., Terpstra, T. & De Maeyer, P. (2012). Perception and communication of flood risks: A systematic review of empirical research. *Risk Analysis*, 33(1), 24–49.

Queensland Government (2013). Media alert. Be prepared for a wet Australia Day long weekend. www.disaster.qld.gov.au/News/view.asp?id=9000&s=scdo.

Queensland Treasury and Trade (n.d.). http://statistics.oesr.qld.gov.au/report-viewer/run?__report=qld-reg-snapshot.rptdesign&sessionId=4IKZSXBV00IODIU0JHA011IDI80Y1VY8DHPQPWLMII Z4H9CF83OB0FUNRKYUTA3DH7F2FGN1095JAVTQCPA2BTV41NKI7O0ZQE7XP0H8DUU BBOE498W54ZHJV0LN5N1R&__format=pdf.

Rogers, P.(2011). Development of resilient Australia: Enhancing the PPRR approach with anticipation, assessment and registration of risks. *Australian Journal of Emergency Management*, 26(1), 54–5.

Sellnow, T. L., Sellnow, D. D., Lane, D. R. & Littlefield, R. S.(2012). The value of instructional communication in crisis situations: Restoring order to chaos. *Risk Analysis*, 32, 633–43.

Slovic, P. (1986). Informing and educating the public about risk. *Risk Analysis*, 6(4), 403–15.

Sturges, D. L. (1994). Communicating through crisis: A strategy for organisational survival. *Management Communication Quarterly*, 7, 297–316.

11

GOVERNMENT ROLES IN EMERGENCY COMMUNICATION RESPONSE

Jordi Xifra and Mark Sheehan

Chapter objectives

This chapter aims to:

- examine government communication responses in emergency crises particularly in bushfires
- explore the role of planning and chain of command in crisis communication
- examine the implications of social media for government crisis communicators.

Introduction

This chapter looks primarily at the bushfires (sometimes called 'wildfires' or 'forest fires') in the Catalonian province of Spain and the resulting lessons learnt in managing the communication during these crises. In doing so, it also reflects, where applicable, on the lessons of the catastrophic fires in the state of Victoria in Australia in 2009. These two populous regions represent some of the most fire prone areas of the world.

Examining a crisis

On 22 July 2012, two wildfires broke out in the Alt Empordá county of Catalonia which is situated in the northeast of Spain adjacent to the French border. The first fire started inland at La Jonquera and the second near the seaside town of Portbou which, as the crow flies, is located approximately 30 kilometres west of La Jonquera.

It was quickly apparent that the severity and threat posed by the two fires was significant. The region was in drought and hot dry Tramuntana winds were gusting at high speed. The conditions were set for disaster and Catalonian Directorate General of Civil Protection invoked phase 2 of the Infocat Plan (the highest level) (324a, 23 July 2012). The Infocat Plan establishes operational procedures for emergency services and state response to declared wild fire emergencies (Generalitat de Catalunya, 2012, p. 4). Infocat also sets out the state's responsibilities for liaising with the media and informing the general public about declared fire emergencies.

Both fires caused significant damage to farmland, forests and homes, and worse resulted in four deaths and many serious and life-threatening injuries including burns. (324b, 27 July 2012). At Portbou, residents and tourists fleeing the fire took refuge on the beach. Tragically, a French father and daughter, unable to make their way safely to the beach, died in attempt to escape the flames by leaping off a cliff (*The Guardian*, 23 July 2012). The La Jonquera fire claimed a further two lives.

The La Jonquera fire was the worst of the two fires, burning for three days. In just over 24 hours from the time the La Jonquera fire was declared it was reported to have burned more than 9000 hectares (BBC, 23 July 2012). The Portbou fire was brought under control within a few hours, but combined both fires destroyed just over 13 000 hectares of land. In addition to the loss of life the fires caused major disruption to local residents and tourists. A tweet from the Civil Protection Directorate General of the Government of Catalonia reported that 3200 homes were without power and 1700 experienced loss of phone services (*Ara*, 22 July 2012). During the crisis over 1000 residents were forced out of their homes to seek refuge in designated shelters. Major roads were closed and rail travel in the region was disrupted including closure of the rail tunnel connecting Portbou with France. Smoke from the fires reached as far south as Barcelona, 150 kilometres away.

These two fires represented the worst fire season experienced by the region in over a decade. Catalonia has a Mediterranean climate, experiencing moist to wet winters and dry summers. Similar to Victoria, Catalonia can experience weather extremes marked by high summer temperatures, prolonged periods of drought and hot, dry winds which gust in excess of 100 kilometres an hour. However, these conditions are not the sole cause of fire emergencies. Catalonia, faces similar problems to Victoria in terms of forest and land management and associated biomass accumulation generated in years of normal or high rainfall and 'social pressure within the forest-urban interface area, due to high demand for nature spaces for recreational uses and accommodation' (Pastor et al., 2006, p. 24). As in Victoria, debate has raged over the mitigating effects of *burning off* during cooler/wetter months to reduce the fuel loads. Burning off is the land management practice of intentionally setting fire to vegetation to reduce fuel load or create potential fire breaks. Pastor et al. reported in 2006 that this practice had not been part of Catalonia's fire prevention strategy for some decades with the government preferring to resource fire fighting (extinction) rather than prevention. However, at the time of the 2012 fires both fire prevention and fire extinction strategies were in place. Again, parallels can be drawn with the Victorian context in that the causes and prevention of devastating and catastrophic fires are complex despite what is known. The only certainty is that under the right conditions in these regions wild fires will occur. And communities affected will look to the authorities for help and information in dealing with the crisis.

Media coverage

National media provided live coverage of the developing fire during the night, including *TV3*, *Canal 3/24*, *Radio Girona*, *Catalunya Radio*, *Catalunya Informació*, *RAC1*, and the weekly journal *Alt Empordà* and many newspapers also discussed the fire. The following day, the fire was front-page news in every Catalan newspaper, with in-depth coverage in the following pages. Similar lead coverage occurred in TV and radio news programs, with live broadcasts from the affected municipalities. The story also made international headlines, including reports in *Le Monde* (2012), in *The Guardian* (2012), and at the BBC News (2012) and Al Jazeera (2012) websites.

Background of the crisis

Emergency situations create conflicts between media professionals and institutional managers. This conflict has sometimes taken a public dimension in Catalonia in recent years.

In emergency situations, the contentious negotiation of information distribution arises between policy-makers, or public managers, and journalists (and, indirectly, the public opinion and those stakeholders involved in a crisis). As Pont (2012) points out, explicitly, the stakeholders in these situations clash because of:

1. the limited access of journalists to certain areas: government authorities ban journalists' access to all points of the crisis
2. too much media attention: the strong competition implies that media companies and professionals don't pay attention to the rigour in information dissemination
3. the differentiation between media: the authorities do not always provide assistance to ensure a diligent and equal treatment of different mass media
4. repeated violations of ethical standards by the journalists: the mass media violate some ethical standards set by regulatory bodies, professional associations and press associations.

The Catalan government heeded this advice and ensured none of these factors occurred during the crisis management of the fires of Alt Empordà. Furthermore, Pont's study examines how to manage emergency communications, and the uses of **social media** in such a situation (2013). Additionally, in consideration of Pont's third and fourth points, there is evidence that journalists will often follow crisis management routines (Moeller, 1999; Muller & Gawenda, 2009). Burns and Eltham (2010) have suggested that 'Crisis management routines, institutional practices and professional ethics helped journalists to frame their Black Saturday coverage, influenced how they conducted interviews and dealt with trauma and survivors, and affected what they decided to omit' (p. 96).

Social media: Includes mobile telephonic technology, websites and networks, whereby citizens acts as sources for disaster communication updates and government promulgates and categorises disaster information.

When reflecting on the Spanish authorities' responses to the Alt Empordà fires, it is also worth considering the broader communication lessons from the catastrophic 2009 bushfire in the

Australian state of Victoria. The analysis of the Victorian Government's haphazard response by Galloway and Kwanash-Aidoo (2012) suggests five points that emergency authorities should contemplate as they face crisis:

1. Communication is central to pre-crisis, crisis event and post crisis management.
2. For communication to be effective, it has to be timely and must reach its intended audience.
3. Authorities must understand what constitutes effective communication *from the point of view of the message recipients*.
4. If the crisis is sufficiently severe (affecting a high number of people with major property damage) it is not possible to deflect attention to the future until the immediate past has been analysed.
5. Publics expect authorities to keep them safe but differ as to how that should be done.

(Galloway & Kwanash-Aidoo, 2012)

Implicit in successfully implementing these suggestions is the role of mass media and social media. The advice proffered by Galloway and Kwanash-Aidoo (2012) relies on the authorities conscripting media into the crisis for the greater common good. It is also critical that the authorities gain the trust of the community by ensuring vital information is received promptly (Spooner, 2014).

Responsibility of government agencies

The organisation of civil protection in Catalonia depends on the Directorate of Civil Protection and the Directorate of Prevention and Fire Extinction and Rescue. Both directorates are branches of the Ministry of Home Affairs. According to the Basic Regulations of Civil Protection (*Normativa Básica de Protección Civil*, NBPC) of Spain, each region has to create and regulate their own plans, which in the case of Catalonia is done by the Civil Protection Plan (PROCICAT). However, there is also a requirement for the development of special risk plans; the special plan to deal with forest fire emergencies is Infocat.

In Spain, the authority for dealing with risks and emergencies generated in nuclear power plants, as well as risks and calamities arising from military conflict, are the exclusive responsibility of the central state. Despite these situations, the Catalan Government can participate in the development of plans and emergency committees created to deal with emergencies in the geographical area of Catalonia.

Specific emergency plans

PROCICAT has three levels of emergency declaration: 'Alert', 'Emergency' and 'Activation of the Plan'. The latter refers to the implementation of special plans for the most common situations that occur in Catalonia. The government has drawn up plans, whose nature requires some appropriate technical and scientific methods for evaluation and treatment. There are special protocols for situations, such as wildfires, snowstorms, floods and earthquakes, and other risks due to chemical and nuclear industry.

One of the most important organisations in the public management of crisis situations is the Emergency Centre of Catalonia (*Centre d'Emergències de Catalunya*, CECAT), which aims to centralise all information during an emergency and maintain the **chain of command**. Its responsibilities include the following:

1. To maximise the collaboration between the different governmental branches and public organisations.
2. To decide the declarations: alert, emergency and activation of the plan.
3. To practise management functions (public relations function included).
4. To transfer the leadership to the central state, in case of national interest.
5. To guarantee the informative tasks of the Press Office.

Chain of command: In essence, who is responsible for which functions in an emergency or disaster. It has been recognised as the weakest link in disaster planning. Uncertainty of roles leads to confused objectives – often this can result in a tragic loss of life.

CECAT operates 24 hours a day, every day of the year; in Australia, the equivalent organisation is Emergency Management Australia (EMA).

As Pont (2013) points out, one of the pillars of the organisational chart of emergencies in Catalonia are the centres of advanced control (*Centres de Control Avançat*, CAC) formed by all of the senior management executives in charge of especially adverse situations *in situ*. These are coordinated by the Service of Firefighting and Rescue of the Catalan Government. One of the primary functions of the CCA is supplying detailed information on current and/or evolving risks or calamities through the CECAT, and the distribution of instructions to manage the crisis.

Also included in the organisational structure of emergency services in Catalonia are the action groups of 'citizens and any administration staff operating directly at the place of risk or disaster'. These are arranged in various sectors, including firefighting bodies; the local police, *Mossos d'Esquadra* (literally 'Squad Lads'); the police force of Catalonia; the public and private healthcare services of Catalonia; the state security bodies and forces (National Police and Civil Guard); rural service actors; voluntary associations; Red Cross staff; and road maintenance teams from all involved administrations. The organisation of these troops is collected from four basic groups:

1. Intervention groups: Service of Firefighting and Rescue.
2. Health groups: Catalan Health Service.
3. Logistics groups: Management of Civil Protection.
4. Groups of order: The authority corresponding to the real deployment of police forces in each territory.

Their responsibilities given by the Civil Protection Act of Catalonia are:

- to evaluate firstly and in real time the situation of the risk or calamity
- to control, reduce or reverse the effects

- to come to the rescue of people and properties
- to recognise and evaluate the associated risks.

They also have to determine the area of intervention and communicate it to the other groups, set up the advanced command centre (*Centre de Comandament Avançat*, CCA) from where the coordination of action groups takes place, and from where the director of the plan is kept informed. Input from these stakeholders should be considered in light of the recommendations made by Galloway and Kwanash-Aidoo (2012).

Managing communication

The growth of social media has increased the number of people working in emergency information management in organisations. Today, the importance of operational tasks of adverse situations is as critical as the communication tasks; poor communication management can nullify successful emergency management by government and the other professional bodies involved in a crisis.

The **Information Office** of the Emergency Committee of Catalonia has two modes of operation: in the first mode, it responds to daily requests from the media about small incidents and provides historical information about incidents; in the second, proactive mode, it activates an emergency plan, for example when there is a danger of heavy snowfall, and its media office disseminates information through the mass media to the population about how to proceed to minimise risk. The most important functions of the Office of Information are to:

- gather information on the risk or crisis and its evolution
- elaborate announcements, orders and recommendations for the population
- disseminate status updates on behalf of the director (i.e. Alert, Emergency Activation Plan), and oversee the completion of each of these
- direct research information of the media and correct erroneous information
- provide information to the families of citizens personally affected.

Information Office: Administrative units specifically set up to respond to a crisis. These offices function as a clearing house for information coming in from a number of sources and being redistributed to media and stakeholders.

The Information Office is, according to the Civil Protection Act of Catalonia, the only source and coordinator for all information production and distribution. The Information Office has the power to unify the content of the information to be provided to the media in order to avoid confusion or contradictions and establish media releases models to both the mass media and the population. The Civil Protection Act of Catalonia compels the media to disseminate such media releases:

> In emergency situations regulated by this Act, public and private mass media are obliged to cooperate with the Civil Protection authorities and officials, and must disseminate or, if appropriate, publish, as a priority, immediately – if the emergency requires it – and free of charges, information, warnings and instructions that these authorities provide them. In all cases, the civil protection authority that generates the information must be identified.
>
> (*Civil Protection Act of Catalonia*, article 11)

In Victoria, a similar structure exists:

> The Information Unit deals not only with collection of information from the fireground and from media and state and regional levels of emergency management but also with dissemination of information to fireground personnel, other agencies and the community (via agency websites and the media).
>
> (2009 Bushfire Royal Commission, 2010)

The dissemination of information to Catalonian citizens through new information technologies is structured through the website of the Ministry of Home Affairs (Generalitat de Catalunya, n.d.). This website details the different plans, the organisational structure of the Ministry, and the task forces and persons in charge the management.

In some sections, there is information specific to municipalities and local authorities, aimed at allowing them to establish emergency plans. In others, public service information is provided, together with a range of data on what to do in an emergency; however, as Pont notes (2013), this information can be difficult to locate (Pont, 2013). The websites of the Government of Catalonia, and many of the Spanish authorities managing emergency services, give only limited advice to citizens. In contrast, the Victorian Government's VicEmergency website (http://emergency.vic.gov.au/map#prepare-fire), although still being refined, provides a wealth of information and contact points through Apps, Facebook, Twitter and specific radio broadcasters on the website.

Social media: A critical tool

The new information technologies and new media allow that interaction can take place despite time and physical space. This technological ubiquity opens great opportunities for information in emergency situations, but also poses great challenges to the government and journalists (Pont, Codina & Pedraza, 2009). The accelerating digitisation has entailed a new communicative space. As Murdock (2010) argues, the interactive and converged network system transforms all, confusing the boundaries of immediacy, intimacy, public and private, local and global, personal and collective, mediated and interpersonal.

The new media have enabled a significant increase in the number of users that broadcast information, breaking the exclusivity of traditional channels of disseminating news: press, radio and television. But the multiplication of information may not always produce multiple benefits. The hoaxes, rumours and false information that have been disseminated can undermine the potential of social media in emergency communication. Perrow (1999) suggests that technological solutions are vulnerable during crises. Burns and Eltham (2010) have noted that, in the context of Black Saturday, 'Australian news media organisations are still far more conservative in using social media platforms, even compared with international conglomerates' (p. 96).

In the context of risk and crisis communication, we must take into account the idea that the network society no longer distinguishes between message sender and emissary. In the network society emerges a new user model, called by some authors 'prosumer or proactive user' (Pont, 2013,

p. 83). Users, interacting with websites, participate in the public debate and convert websites into content platforms, including blogs and microblogs (Twitter, Facebook and so on) and video (YouTube). In crisis situations, these new media have been powerfully useful (Aced, 2013).

To the advantages expressed above, we have to add that the internet and social media can be more technically effective in the face of crises. Mobile telephony has been especially useful since it came into use in the last decades of the 20th century, though in an emergency it can suffer from the same practical problem as landline telephony, as mobile services become quickly jammed by panicked friends and relatives trying to reach loved ones (Burns & Eltham, 2010, p. 92). It has been shown to be vulnerable in fire emergency, leaving portions or the entire area without coverage where mobile phone towers are destroyed. Likewise, where disaster-affected communities are left without power or phone they lose the ability to connect to the internet.

Murdock, Horlick-Jones and Petts (2001) have argued strongly for a paradigm shift in risk and emergency communication, asserting that technologies should be understood as an opportunity rather than a problem, mainly because citizens can now access public space not only through radio, press and television, but also through the internet and new media. When Web 2.0 emerged, users moved from passively observing content to interacting with it in a collaborative way, contributing content of all kinds. This development provides a great opportunity but also a serious challenge in emergency situations, especially in the control of information. Once again we should consider Galloway and Kwanash-Aidoo's (2012) advice in managing this information.

The majority of civil protection protocols include the use of information systems, which, when well used, have helped citizens to better confront critical situations. However, many of the guidelines or protocols have become outdated by the rapid and constant emergence of new media, which are consolidated in parallel to traditional media. Therefore, the emergence of the internet and, in particular, Web 2.0, as an element of information and interaction for crises is increasingly used by citizens. Pont (2012) refers to studies and surveys commissioned by various Western governments in support of this. This practice should also give increased attention to the 'mobile internet', which combines the advantages of the network with the mobile phone technology, allowing high connectivity and interaction between people, governments and informers.

With the emergence of social media, in particular, the communication of messages in a crisis is no longer exclusive to the authorities and the mass media – citizens participate actively disseminating contents of their own emergency or crisis. Participation focuses on social networking, a proactive process, especially so when there are emergencies and crises situations of all kinds (Pont, Codina & Pedraza, 2009).

In Spain, there have been many examples of what we might call *mobile and 2.0 mobilisation*. Short messages from cellular telephones helped create the large demonstrations after the terrorist attack on Madrid's Atocha train station in 2004. The use of social media not only by citizens, but also by politicians and journalists, was a milestone in the cooperative and participatory conception of information in crisis situations.

Since the emergence of Web 2.0, when an emergency occurs in the mass media, the public are called upon to participate and contribute their pictures, comments and videos. If this participation is based on the principle of matching the veracity of the messages, following the ethical standards of journalism, then it can be a good journalistic contribution that supplements the work of professional media. Burns and Eltham (2010) alert us to this with reference to the Australian Broadcasting Corporation's investigative TV program *Four Corners*, which 'highlighted the power of "convergent media" via mobile phone footage of fires approaching Kinglake's Kangaroo Ground Oval'. They posed the question 'Can citizen journalists act as more than just "first responders?"' (p. 96), indicating a dual role in media and emergency information.

In March 2010, the Government of Catalonia created the Twitter account @emergenciescat, which became continuously operational in October of that year. The account has more than 40 000 followers (Pont, 2013). According to Pont (2013), the followers can be sorted in four clearly recognisable groups:

1. people linked to the world of emergencies
2. mayors, authorities and institutional profiles
3. journalists and mass media
4. citizens.

According to Marc Homedes, Press Director and Community Manager of the Directorate of Civil Protection of the Catalan Government: 'The fact that we are a profile reference causes that people not only are aware of what happens, but people report emergencies' (cited by Pont, 2013, p. 90). The government also uses the emergency phone Twitter account @112.

Emergency public relations managers claim that new media allows instant reporting of risk situations to a large number of individuals who in turn can relay (thanks to retweets) vital information. As Marc Homedes has stated:

> Emergencies are changing and Twitter allows us to be much more agile in the information process. It helps to inform many parallel parts of the emergency; a useful information for citizens. For example, if there are power outages or gas as a result of a fire or a flood and how long can the affectation [sic.] last.
>
> (Cited by Pont, 2013, p. 90)

The government's responsibility for communication stresses that Facebook allows, in addition to detailing all the alerts, it to publicise activities and provide educative safety tips: 'It's less viral but it reinforces the task' (Homedes, cited by Pont, 2013, p. 90).

A number of disasters in recent years have shown that the new media has the potential to locate people. People want to be cared for when there is an emergency. That is, they want to be provided with the ability of making decisions on what transport to take or what supplies are needed to deal with a particular crisis. Today, this task is facilitated by social media (Pont, 2013).

Media officers usually manage the internet accounts of Spanish civil protection administrations, expanding the role of journalists in managing social networks. Marc Homedes recalls that 'it is said that social media are free and this is false. They cost what it costs to have people investing time in managing them effectively, not only when it suits us. This channel has the same relevance as press releases' (cited by Pont, 2013, p. 88).

Most administrations have incorporated institutional management of social media as another routine task. The fires in the Alt Empordà are a paradigm of this.

> We focus almost all our work in reporting from @emergenciescat, without forgetting press releases and telephone hotlines, but pivoting on Twitter. We informed about that to the reporters. They agreed and thanked us for the information we put on the social net. We had some tweets with over 1600 retweets.
>
> (Homedes, cited by Pont, 2013, p. 98)

So, when the Alt Empordà fires struck, there were 12 official Twitter accounts providing live information about what was happening.

Conclusion

Social media is now a crucial source of information and assistance during the fires, in addition to governmental tools, and supplementing mass media coverage by both traditional journalists and citizen journalists. On Twitter, Alt Empordà was a worldwide trending topic: five of the 10 trending topics in the morning of 23 July referred to the fires: #focempordà, Alt Empordà, Junquera, Portbou and Ap-7 (the name of the affected highway). A campaign created through Twitter, 'Un català, un arbre' ('One Catalan, one tree') collected more than 9000 signatures. In Victoria, the leader of communications for the Justice Department's Government 2.0 activities of the online response following the Black Saturday bushfires has identified more than 30 free and paid social media platforms that can be utilised in emergencies (http://twitter.com/darrenwhitelaw).

The communication management of the emergency of Alt Empordà fires was perceived as so effective that members of the governments of Holland and Belgium, as well as the London police force, have enquired about the communication management processes (Pont, 2013). According to Pont (2013), 'The communication crisis management of the Alt Empordà fire showed the importance of taking into account the contributions of public relations in the management of such emergencies' (p. 99). In the Black Saturday fires in Victoria, the acute role of PR was also in evidence whether in government agencies or hospital emergency and trauma centres (Cameron et al., 2009).

Social media allows emergency communication to expedite decision-making. In this sense, the managers of this crisis assessed and responded – the two basic steps of what Aced (2013) has called 'public relations 2.0'. The Catalan Government assessed its activities, and defined its strategy, through analysis of the following variables: nature of the message, type of emitter, scope and amplification. In addition, the government acted quickly to prevent the crisis spreading. Furthermore, it cultivated a community that had previously been created around the social media of the government. In managing the crisis of the fires of Alt Empordà, social media was the crucial tool, providing a more effective way for people in Catalonia to manage issues, risks, emergencies and crises. Although, as we have seen in this chapter, government can react appropriately in times of emergency through well-defined chains of command and communication, all agencies should be prepared for a major catastrophe, such as Victoria's Black Saturday. In the short space of three years, from Black Saturday in 2009 to Alt Empordà in 2012, the rise of social media has changed the way emergency communication takes place, increasing the degree of preparedness a public expects of its government and their agencies in time of acute emergency.

CASE QUESTIONS

1. What differences do you see between planning for a large-scale disaster and planning for a smaller crisis?
2. What are the dangers inherent in using social media in a crisis?
3. How does a government's role in crisis communication differ to that of a corporation?
4. Does the number of government agencies involved in emergencies create communication problems?

The authors wish to acknowledge the website <www.324.cat>, which they consulted at various times in preparing this chapter for publication.

BIBLIOGRAPHY

Aced, C. (2013). Relaciones públicas 2.0. Cómo gestionar la comunicación corporativa en el entorno digital. Barcelona: UOC.

Al Jazeera (2012, 23 July). Thousands flee deadly wildfires in Spain. www.aljazeera.com//news/europe/2012/07/20127232314174423.html.

Ara (2012, 22 July), Incendi a la jonquera 3.200 abonats es queden sense llum i 1.700 sense telèfon. Retrieved from www.ara.cat/societat/abonats-queden-linies-telefon-afectades-incendi-jonquera_0_741526039.html.

BBC News (2012, 23 July). Spain wildfires: Four killed in Catalonia. www.bbc.co.uk/news/world-europe-18949400.

Burns, A. & Eltham, B. (2010). 'Catastrophic failure' theories: Evaluating media explanations of the Black Saturday bushfires. *Media International Australia*, 137, 90–9.

Cameron P., Mitra B., Fitzgerald M., Scheinkestel C., Stripp A., Batey C., Niggemeyer L., Truesdale M., Holman P., Mehra R., Wasiak J. and Cleland H. (2009). Black Saturday: The immediate impact of the February 2009 bushfires in Victoria, Australia. *Medical Journal of Australia*, 191(1), 11–16.

Castells, M. (1996). *The rise of the network society: The information age – Economy, society and culture*. Oxford: Blackwell.

Galloway C. & Kwansah-Aidoo K. (2012). Victoria burning: Confronting the 2009 catastrophic bushfires in Australia. In A. George & C. Pratt (eds), *Case studies in crisis communication: International perspectives on hits and misses* (pp. 279–82). New York, Routledge.

Generalitat de Catalunya (2012). PLA especial d'emergències per incendis forestals de Catalunya (INFOCAT). Retrieved 17 September 2014 from www20.gencat.cat/portal/site/interior/menuitem.c8dca3082ff3fddf65d789a2b0c0e1a0/?vgnextoid=75a5bded8ced4210VgnVCM10

00008d0c1e0aRCRD&vgnextchannel=75a5bded8ced4210VgnVCM1000008d0c1e0aRCRD&vgnextfmt=default.

The Guardian (2012, 23 July). Spanish wildfires kill father and daughter. www.theguardian.com/world/2012/jul/23/spanish-wildfires-kill-three.

Le Monde (2012, 23 July). Un immense incendie tue quatre Français dans le nord-est de l'Espagne. www.lemonde.fr/europe/article/2012/07/23/un-immense-incendie-hors-de-controle-fait-3-morts-dans-le-nord-est-de-l-espagne_1736888_3214.html.

McLuhan, M. (1964). *Understanding media: The extensions of man*. New York: McGraw-Hill.

Moeller, S, (1999). *Compassion Fatigue: How the Media Sell Disease, Famine, War and Death*. Routledge, New York.

Muller, D. & Gawenda, M. (2009). *The Black Saturday Bushfires: How The Media Covered Australia's Worst Peace-Time Disaster*. Centre for Advanced Journalism, University of Melbourne, Australia.

Murdock, G. (2010). Shifting anxieties, altered media: Risk communication in networked times. *Catalan Journal of Communication & Cultural Studies*, 2(2), 159–76.

Murdock, G., Horlick-Jones, T. & Petts, J. (2001). *Social amplification of risk: The media and the public*. Contract Research Report. Health & Safety Executive (HSE). Retrieved 26 November 2013 from www.hse.gov.uk/research/crr_pdf/2001/crr01329.pdf.

Pastor, E., Pérez, Y., Miralles, M. & Planas, E. (2009). Prescribed burning in Catalonia: Fire management and research. *Proceedings of The Royal Society Of Queensland*, 115, 23–7.

Perrow, C. (1999). *Normal Accidents: Living with High-Risk Technologies*. Princeton University Press, NJ.

Pont, C. (2012). Las nuevas tecnologías y la percepción de los ciudadanos ante la comunicación de emergencias. *Hipertext.net*, 10. Retrieved 4 November 2013 from www.upf.edu/hipertextnet/numero-10/nuevas-tecnologias-percepcion-ciudadanos-comunicacion-emergencias.html.

Pont, C. (2013). *Comunicar las emergencias*. Barcelona: UOC.

Pont, C. & Cortiñas, S. (2011). Journalistic practice in risk and crisis situations: Significant examples from Spain. *Journalism: Theory, Practice and Criticism*, 12(8), 1052–66.

Pont, C., Codina, L. & Pedraza, R. (2009). Comunicación de riesgo y sistemas de información en la web: Cinco modelos informativos. *El Profesional de la Información*, 18(4), 389–97.

Solidaritat Catalana (2012). IMPACTANT: Crida desperada dels bombers, a petició de SI i altres grups, el passat febrer 2012. YouTube, https://www.youtube.com/watch?v=y35J2C8lEK4.

Spooner, R. (2014, 6 June). Hazelwood inquiry told of communication woes. *The Age*.

12

POST-CRISIS

REBUILDING A COMPANY, A REPUTATION, A COMMUNITY

Mark Sheehan and Biagio Oppi

Chapter objectives

This chapter aims to:

- demonstrate the importance of planning and response during disaster emergency situations
- introduce key considerations in determining a disaster response strategy
- understand the comparable elements of crisis and disaster communication
- understand some of the principles of recovery from the adverse public relations effects of the disaster
- understand what sort of organisational change can take place as the result of the crisis
- explore the role of communication in disaster recovery.

Introduction

It is well recognised that when an organisation experiences a crisis caused by a natural disaster, publics are less likely to apportion responsibility to that organisation. This contrasts with crises involving events such as product tampering, accidents or management transgressions where the level of organisational control is perceived or judged to be greater (Coombs, 2000, p. 86). In 2012, biomedical company Gambro's manufacturing plant, based in Medolla, a small town of 6000 in the Modena region of Italy, was hit by a devastating series of earthquakes. Damage to the plant had significant and immediate impact for employees, customers and other key stakeholders, as operations ceased in the wake of the earthquakes.

This chapter will reflect on Gambro's crisis management response and their crisis communication strategies in response to the earthquakes and the ensuing rumours. An analysis of Gambro's crisis response shows they acted to counteract stakeholder concerns and leverage well-established stakeholder relationships. As Coombs (2000, 2006, 2007a, 2007b) makes clear, relationships are central to effective crisis management, and, although stakeholders often view a natural disaster as being removed from the organisation's responsibility, this concession may not exist in a prolonged recovery period or where the stakeholders face a life or death outcome. These were the very conditions Gambro faced. So, a relational approach can add depth to the attributional analysis of such a crisis (Coombs 2000, p. 86). To extend the analysis of crises caused by natural disaster and Gambro's crisis response, the chapter will also examine crisis communication strategies of similar disaster case studies.

The international medical-technical company Gambro, headquartered in Sweden, has 13 production facilities in more than 90 countries, and employs more than 8000 people worldwide. Gambro has operated in the Medolla region of Emilia-Romagna since the early 1960s.

Physical or sudden crisis

Unlike many other crisis case studies in this text, this case study focuses on an emergency or disaster caused by natural disaster (events beyond human control) – sometimes referred to as a 'physical crisis' or 'sudden crisis'. As Xavier (2014) has observed, a physical crisis differs from a management or operational crisis, which tends to arise from a 'smouldering issue' that grows over 'many years before becoming public, and then involve[s] a response played out over many months'. Physical crises 'can happen in a matter of minutes, leaving little planning time for the organisations involved' (p. 202). This classification of crises into 'emergencies' and 'smouldering crises' has been quantified by US research between 1999 and 2008, which found that:

> two thirds of all crises (64%) had been smouldering rather than striking suddenly without any warning . . . records of thousands of US crises reported by print media in the decade 1999 to 2008 showed that about 51% of all crises were mainly caused by management, while employees caused about 31% and external forces around 18%.
>
> (Harrison, 2011, p. 824)

A complication Gambro faced in the aftermath of the immediate emergency was that the 'aftershocks' once again encouraged rumours of plant closure and panic for those publics whose life depended on **kidney dialysis**, using the bloodline components Gambro produced.

Kidney dialysis: The removal of unwanted matter from the blood performed by a machine.

There are many definitions of crisis; for example, 'it is a major occurrence with a potentially negative outcome affecting the organisation, company or industry as well as its publics, products, goods, services or good name' (Fearn-Banks, 2002, p. 2). In terms of the emergency crisis some exceptions need to be made – a disaster leaves little doubt of 'potential' damage – it is highly visible. More appropriate, in part, for the emergency crisis is

> an event, revelation, allegation or set of circumstances which threatens the integrity, reputation or survival of an individual or organisation. It challenges the publics' sense of safety, values or appropriateness the actual or potential damage to the organisation is considerable and the organisation cannot on its own, put an end to it.
>
> (International Association of Business Communicators, cited in Sapriel, 2003, p. 348)

Table 12.1 Public relations/emergency management terms

Public relations/crisis management terms (after Fink, 1986)	Emergency management terms
Boundary spanner	Prevention: risk, mitigation or reduction
Crisis build-up	Disaster preparedness, readiness
Crisis breakout	Emergency; disaster
Abatement	Response; consequence management
Termination	Consequence management; recovery
Issues management	Recovery

Source: Nicholls & Glenny (2005)

It is also worthwhile to place crisis terms with which you are you are familiar in the context of emergency management terms, as shown in Table 12.1.

In comparing the crisis terms and emergency terms Nicholls and Glenny (2005) made the distinction that is as equally applicable to the Medolla earthquake as it was to the Canberra bushfires of 2003. They state that, in a community disaster,

> which of its nature, is a profound, extensive social, psychosocial, economic, infrastructural and environmental disruption of whole populations (Norman, 2004), it makes sense to distinguish between crisis and disaster and to look at the aftermath of disaster – recovery – as a discrete category rather than a continuation of issues management or indeed as abatement and termination.
>
> (Nicholls & Glenny, 2005, p. 42)

The last time a major earthquake had hit this region was in the 16th century, so it was a completely unpredictable event. Twenty-nine people were killed in the Medolla earthquakes, including four at a nearby medical plant.

A positive aspect, in a sense, for emergency crises is that the attribution for responsibility for the crisis is lifted from the organisation in the first instance. It is critical to recovery, as noted in Coombs (2000). Verhoeven et al. (2012, p. 501) also found that, while 'the effectiveness of crisis response strategies and variations in crisis communication affects reputation and trust differently on different levels', trust is eroded to a lesser extent when the organisation announces an accidental crisis (compared with a preventable crisis). The conclusion is that differing types of crises can leave organisations partially exonerated for the consequences of the crisis or disaster when stakeholders judge the event causing the crisis as accidental. Gambro stakeholders could assess the shortage of product as directly caused by the earthquake. However, other crises after-effects can play a significant role and impact on recovery unless dealt with swiftly. The role of rumour among Gambro employee publics is such an example.

In the context of natural disaster, the crisis may be more severe and wide-reaching. Not only are an organisation's operations affected; the whole community may also be in danger. In Medolla, there was significant structural damage to buildings and loss of life. Similarly, in the horrific bushfires in Victoria in 2009 and Canberra in 2003, 'homes were destroyed, serious infrastructure damage had occurred and many people's livelihoods had been critically impaired' (Nicholls & Glenny, 2005 p. 41). Despite the wonders of modern technology, it is worthwhile noting that in such situations the very infrastructure needed to keep first-response disaster communication operational can be destroyed. This was the disaster that faced the community of Medolla in May 2012, and one of the town's major employers, Gambro.

A crisis on three fronts

In the 2012 earthquakes in Modena, the immediate and local stakeholders (employees, suppliers and local government) all understood the difficulty faced by every organisation in the region and this relational framework allowed for great empathy. However, the first front on which Gambro faced a crisis related to the nature of the company's manufacturing facility. It posed no environmental challenges, although some had supposed that it might, but the interruption to the production and distribution of dialysis monitors and bloodlines could have posed a life-threatening crisis to its user stakeholders. Bloodlines are specially and precisely manufactured tubes that run a patient's blood to the dialysis machine (monitor) and back to the patient. The dialysis machine (also manufactured and pioneered by Gambro) performs the function of the kidneys in instances where they have been injured or diseased – the machine is an artificial kidney. While monitors themselves could be sourced from other manufacturers or run for longer periods (although dialysis is a prolonged process taking many hours up to three times weekly) without supplies of bloodlines kidney dialysis machines are inoperable. The earthquakes interrupted production, which meant that dialysis patients reliant on Gambro products faced potentially life-threatening delays.

Manufacturing of biomedical products has been undertaken successfully in the Emilia-Romagna region of Italy since the early 1960s. The engineering heritage of the region is well credentialed with the headquarters of Ferrari, Maserati and Ducati located in the region. Italy is recognised for its cluster approach to manufacturing as identified by Porter in his seminal work *The Competitive Advantage of Nations* (1990). He wrote that related and supported industries in a region create advantages based on close working relationships, because suppliers and end users located near each other can take advantage of short lines of communication, quick and constant flow of information and an ongoing exchange of ideas leading to innovation. This led the Medolla region in Emilia-Romagna to become a world leader in the manufacturing and development of biomedical products and in biomedical engineering. These specialities grew out of the work done at the Universities of Bologna and Modena respectively, with the Sant'Orsola-Malpighi Hospital in Bologna reputedly having one of the best nephrology (study of kidney disease) units in the world. Gambro pioneered the medical technology innovation in the region, and more than 200 companies are now involved in medical-technical research and production based in Emilia-Romagna.

The second crisis front related to the fact that, for many years, Italy has suffered from political and economic instability. As a direct result, the Italian hospital system faced strict financial constraints. While hospitals formerly carried sufficient supplies of the bloodlines to cover some months, in 2012 they only maintained enough stock to last a few weeks or even a few days. Hospitals relied on Gambro to warehouse the bulk of stock and distribute that stock efficiently and quickly. Now, Gambro was facing crisis on a new front; not only had the production facility been damaged but the earthquake had also shut down the warehouse operations containing the bloodlines. To gain an understanding of the severity of the impact, consider these statistics: more than 65 per cent of Italy's dialysis patients are treated by products manufactured in the Medolla region, and 50 per cent of Italy's 24 000 kidney disease patients are treated by Gambro products made in Medolla (according to Gambro internal documents).

Gambro now had to decide (and quickly) whether to move manufacturing operations from the earthquake-ruined complex in Medolla to a more secure site. If they chose this option they would remove a key economic driver from the local economy still recovering from the global financial crisis (GFC); the long-term consequences to the community of Medolla would be severe. Gambro also had to deal with the immediate need to reassure kidney dialysis patients, their families, and attendant medical staff around Italy that dialysis treatments could continue and not be stalled by lack of access to Gambro's bloodline products.

The third crisis front related to the company itself. Timing is everything, and the earthquakes could not have happened at a more delicate time. In the 18 months before the earthquake, Gambro had embarked on a restructuring exercise, which included changes to processes affecting bloodline production. Gambro initially announced a complete shutdown of bloodline manufacturing in Medolla, but then decided to implement only a partial reduction in manufacturing. Their first approach was to 'let go' most of the contract labour force. This decision was then altered to downsizing a segment of the workforce.

The restructuring was an industrial process that involved the introduction of new production labour-saving techniques and the removal of some production lines and plant and machinery to alternative sites within the region and overseas to Mexico. The announced restructuring in 2011 affected 400 people, employees and contractors. At this point, no full time employees were made redundant; however, 160 contract workers did not have their contract renewed. This process created an anxious workforce who, when the earthquakes occurred, began to speculate on the future of the plant in Medolla. If production had already been removed to other sites could this occur again? Would Gambro consider it easier to close the damaged Medolla plant and relocate to other factories? Would it be too expensive to repair the damaged plant and cheaper to relocate overseas to Mexico? Was the region now considered earthquake prone and not suitable for production of such life-saving materials?

The company's restructure and strategic changes created an environment conducive to rumours. As the largest employer in Medolla, Gambro's actions were closely watched by the community. In the wake of the earthquakes, old fears resurfaced and the rumour mill started up again. Foremost among the gossip was the story that Gambro would cease production in the region completely. So, on this third crisis front, misinformation and rumour threatened to damage Gambro's relationship with the very community that would play an important role in **disaster** recovery. The media, having exhausted the human interest angle of the earthquake (for example, the sad loss of life and historic buildings), began to pursue the corporate angle. It picked up the story from the 2011 restructure that Gambro might leave the region – a story that was likely to panic the already-fragile population after the earthquake.

Disaster: A physical event leading to crisis – normally not initiated by human interaction – such as earthquake, tsunami and bushfires.

However, strong communication channels and the long-term stakeholder relationships were used to contradict the rumour and assuage fears of such a development at a pivotal time in the region's history. In addition the quick recovery at the plant and stakeholder belief in the company's assurances were based on the relational framework and trust Gambro had developed since establishing itself in the region in the 1960s.

The earthquakes: From one disaster to another

On 21 May 2012, a major earthquake of 5.9 magnitude hit the Medolla region. Gambro's monitor and bloodline production buildings and distribution centre were damaged in the earthquake and the injection moulding (**bloodline**) production areas of the facility could not be accessed. It was fortunate that as it was a Sunday there were limited staff on the premises. The plant was able to recover partially. Less than five days after the earthquake limited production of dialysis monitors commenced and Gambro was able to begin distribution from its warehouse in Medolla.

Bloodlines: Specially manufactured, highly specified tubes that run a patient's blood to the dialysis machine (monitor) and back to the patient.

Just as Gambro Medolla and its Crisis Task Force Team (CTFT) were coming to terms with the devastation and handling the situation as laid down in the company's crisis management plan and procedures, a second earthquake hit. This quake happened on 29 May 2012, at a magnitude of 5.8, and Medolla was at its epicentre, much closer to the factory; the result was devastating. To make matters worse, in the weeks that followed the second quake, the region was subject to several hundred aftershocks, which affected those buildings that had not already been damaged or destroyed. Gambro's plant and distribution were similarly affected. Distribution ceased and the factory went in shutdown mode, operating with a skeleton staff, including the CTFT.

Although before 20 May, Gambro was ready for crisis situations, including restructure, takeover and earthquake, no amount of planning can fully prepare an organisation for a total dislocation caused by such a disaster. Although no Gambro employees were injured, life was difficult. Many local residents in Medolla had been sleeping in cars and tents since the first earthquake, and the second forced many more from their homes. Other factors of a more intangible nature were also evident; an Italian Red Cross spokesperson stated that 'The psychological impact of having two earthquakes in a row is a tough one. Now it's going to be very difficult for us to convince people to go back to their houses' (Momigliano 2012).

Target publics

From the outset, Gambro's Medolla CTFT had clearly defined primary and secondary publics to target in the event of a crisis. Primary targets included dialysis users (and by default their supporters – both family and clinical); medical practitioners throughout Italy and Europe; local Gambro employees; and the Medolla community.

Secondary publics included trade unions; local authorities and local, regional and national government; neighbouring communities; and other Gambro employees in the rest of the world. The Italian public was also important, since natural disasters tend to sustain ongoing and extensive media coverage. The company and CTFT quickly realised that the primary publics required the utmost reassurance from the company.

'One Voice': Coordinated crisis communication

Message distribution is critical in a time of crisis – but in a disaster it can be hampered by the need to consider how messages may impact on the broader community. How then did the company communicate with its staff, quell the rumours of total closure, and show real concern for the plight of its workers, as well as for the situation of kidney disease patients?

The disaster strategy was implemented by two coordinated teams operating at global and local (on the ground) levels. The global team consisted of senior managers impacted by the event and chaired/managed by Vice President of Operations (also on this team was the Medolla plant manager, the global supply manager and director, the distribution manager and director, the quality bloodline and quality monitor directors, the insurance and finance director, the communication director, legal counsel, marketing EMEA, and others). The combination of expertise and role focus ensured that company objectives, stakeholder needs and community concerns were equally addressed.

The focus of the local team was to deal with employee stakeholders and the community to allay concerns. At the local level the team consisted of the same functions and the local key plant functions (purchasing, human resources, sales and marketing) and chaired/managed by the Site Manager.

A number of task forces were also established to ensure a quick and prioritised recovery. The key role of the task forces was to ensure impact to customers was minimised and that patients were not affected. The sales force followed a day-by-day plan of focused distribution and stock monitoring, guided by a 'round table' involving all main stakeholders: Gambro; its competitors; local and national governments; the national healthcare system; the Italian Society of Nephrology; and patients' associations.

The communication strategy was encapsulated under the theme 'One Voice'. The goal was to prevent media-induced panic and to dispel people's belief that the situation was escalating out of control. Attention of this nature in the wake of the earthquakes would represent an unhelpful distraction and could impact on restoring product supply and distribution. Gambro wanted to focus its energies on disaster recovery, not unwanted and unhelpful media diversions.

The strategy focused on ensuring total alignment of internal and external communication. Implementing the 'One Voice' strategy, a single external communicator was appointed to speak on behalf of Gambro. There was a clear strategy to ensure there was no communication vacuum, and that corporate and industry leaders were involved. The crisis management plan had emphasised and made explicit the need to control communication through distributing clear and consistent messages to the media. Gambro avoided certain parts of the media; for example, talk shows, live-to-air transmission and media outlets, and any journalist who might seek a sensational angle on the story. Gambro recognised that stakeholders needed reassurance and action. Key messages needed to communicate to stakeholders the details of Gambro's recovery activities and (importantly) their progress.

The media was crucial for targeting both internal and external publics. All meetings with stakeholders (trade unions, workers committees etc.), with both internal and external stakeholders, and the outcomes of these meetings were always confirmed with media. Gambro chose not to use media releases (and in the immediate aftermath of the 20 and 29 May earthquakes this was not an option) but in the immediate recovery period chose mobile phone calls and, when there was a resumption of infrastructure, through email and social media.

For employees, Gambro's CTFT faced a challenge with traditional media forms compromised due to the earthquakes and the fact that many stakeholders were no longer able to access media due to the destruction of their homes and the loss of infrastructure services. Harrison (2011) has described exactly this situation as likely in a disaster: essential services are threatened or cut and that 'the internet is not going to be available and it is therefore essential to have a fall-back position' (p. 843).

Surprisingly in the digital age the first medium utilised was posters outside the plant in the early hours of the earthquake. Within 24 hours, mobile phone contact with key stakeholders occurred, which led to daily SMS updates. Face-to-face communication with key community leaders and a large group of employees (in the car park outside the Gambro plant) was also utilised as a medium of showing concern. The two-way nature of these meetings alerted Gambro's CTFT to the needs of its employee stakeholders.

Internal communication was intensified in the first days, in an attempt to coordinate and restart the production of life-saving products as soon as possible. This message was targeted at employees but also at the external audiences that need to be reassured with a communication consistent with the commitment taken by the management.

An employee donor campaign was initiated by the senior Management Team with a contribution of €100 000. The campaign gained strength as awareness and concern for Medolla employees grew. Internal company communication and international media coverage brought images of the devastation to the broader company community. Gambro doubled all employee contributions, resulting in a grand total of funds of €300 000. Children of affected workers were given summer holidays. The generosity of their colleagues was not lost on the Medolla Gambro employees and many letters received by the Donation Program committee testify to the gratitude and empathy expressed by the worldwide Gambro community to their colleagues in Medolla.

The network of Gambro sales forces throughout the nation ensured message delivery was widespread and stakeholder clients were kept updated not just on the reinstatement of the production facility but the township's recovery.

Paradoxically, the earthquake presented the company with the opportunity to finally quell the persistent but totally unfounded rumour of its departure from Medolla (or even Italy) by reinforcing its intention to remain and announcing it would rebuild the damaged plant and distribution centre and reinvest in its current production facility.

By 5 June, Gambro was posting media releases in the online social media newsroom and public relations (PR) platform mynewsdesk delivering its key messages.

Conclusion: Outcomes and recovery

Gambro set up task forces, which were intended to:

- manage day by day the demands from medical stakeholders
- salvage products and machinery from damaged production facilities
- find two new premises in the region to commence temporary manufacturing (for bloodlines and monitors) and one R&D facility
- ensure critical supply demands were met.

Fire brigades and salvage contractors took control of the restricted areas of the plant to salvage stock and machinery from the damaged manufacturing plants. After three and half months 28 000 pallets were removed from the distribution centre and machinery was moved to the temporary plants.

Interim production was set up and long-term solutions were developed that proved successful in the aftermath of the earthquakes. Just one month after the first quake, spare parts were delivered to hospitals; a brand new bloodline was designed by the R&D team in a few days, and prototyped, tested, approved and manufactured at the company's Tijuana plant in Mexico, within three weeks. These actions guaranteed high volumes of production to begin very quickly, while a bloodline plant was set up near Medolla, starting its activities at the beginning of August.

The estimated impact of the disaster and aftermath on Gambro's reputation were measured by its communication team from early June to the laying of the foundation stone for the new facility in December 2013. The team monitored a wide variety of external sources, including local and national print media and the leading news media such as Italy's leading finance media outlet. Over this period, a positive impression of Gambro of 60 per cent was registered, with a neutral impression at 30 per cent. Internally, the work of the company in reinstating its plant and facility was seen as a positive, but even greater was the impact in rebuilding the community and in assisting employees to recommence their lives. The work of piecing together a community after a disaster could take decades but initiatives by key agents gives hope. Gambro's successful results on the reputation index demonstrate to the world not only its continuing viability and effective management, but also its ability to rebuild and substantially commit to the future in a town where hope is a key asset in rebuilding a community.

CASE QUESTIONS

1. In what ways do crisis management and communication differ from disaster communication?
2. Do publics regard organisational responses differently in a disaster than a company-induced crisis?
3. In Table 12.1, the authors equate the Crisis Management term 'issues management' with the Emergency Management term 'recovery' – is this an accurate comparison?

BIBLIOGRAPHY

Bentele, G. (2003). *Public trust: Theory and empirical results in Germany*, 10th International Public Relations Research Symposium, BledCom, 4–6 July 2003, Bled, Slovenia.

Coombs, W. T. (2000). Crisis management: Advantages of a relational perspective. In J. Ledingham & S. Bruning (eds), *Public relations as relationship management: A relational approach to the study and practice of public relations* (pp. 73–93). Mahwah, NJ: Lawrence Erlbaum Associates.

Coombs, W. T. (2006). Crisis management: A communicative approach in Botan & Hazleton (eds) *Public relations Theory II* (pp. 171–198), Mahwah, NJ: Lawrence Erlbaum Associates.

Coombs, W. T. (2007a).*Ongoing crisis communication: Planning, managing, and responding*, 2nd edn. Thousand Oaks, CA: Sage.

Coombs, W. T. (2007b). Crisis management and communications. Gainsville FL, Institute of Public Relations, www.instituteforpr.org/topics/crisis-management-and-communications.

Fearn-Banks, K. (2002). *Crisis communication: A casebook approach*, 3rd edn. Mahwah, NJ: Lawrence Erlbaum Associates.

Galloway, C. & Kwanash-Aidoo, K. (2005). *Public relations Issues and crisis management*, Melbourne: Thomson Social Science Press.

Galloway C. & Kwansah-Aidoo K. (2012). Victoria burning: Confronting the 2009 catastrophic bushfires in Australia. In A. George & C. Pratt (eds), *Case studies in crisis communication: International perspectives on hits and misses* (pp. 279–82). New York, Routledge.

Gambro (n.d.). Website. Retrieved 1 March 2014 from www.gambro.com/en/global/About-Gambro/Gambro-in-brief.

Harrison, K. (2011). *Strategic public relations: A practical guide to success*. South Yarra, Vic.: Palgrave.

Huang, Y. -H. (2008). Trust and relational commitment in corporate crisis: The effects of crisis communicative strategy and forms of crisis response. *Journal of Public Relations Research*, 20, 297–327.

Momigliano, A. (2012, 30 May). Two earthquakes in two weeks test Italians' morale. *Christian Science Monitor*. Retrieved 1 March 2014 from www.csmonitor.com/World/Europe/2012/0530/Two-earthquakes-in-two-weeks-test-Italians-morale.

Nicholls, S. & Glenny, L. (2005). Communication for recovery: A case study in communication between the Australian Capital Territory Government and the ACT community after the ACT bushfires, January 2003. In C. Galloway & K. Kwanash-Aidoo (eds), *Public relations: Issues and crisis management* (pp. 41–58). Melbourne: Thomson Social Science Press.

Norman, S. (2004). *NZ Recovery Symposium 04 Proceedings*, Wellington, NZ: Ministry of Civil Defence and Emergency Management.

Porter, M. (1990). The competitive advantage of nations. *Harvard Business Review,* March–April, 73–93.

Sapriel, C. (2003). Effective crisis management: Tools and best practice for the millennium, *Journal of Communication Management*, 7(4) 348–55.

Sommerfeldt, E. (2012). The civility of social capital: Public relations in the public sphere, civil society and democracy. *Public Relations Review* 39(4), 280–9.

Verhoven, J., Van Hoof, J., Keurs, H. T. & Van Vuuren, H. A. (2012). Effects of apologies and crisis responsibility on corporate and spokesperson reputation. *Public Relations Review*, 38, 501–4.

Xavier, R. (2014). Emergency crisis communication: Returning power to Collinsville. In M. Sheehan M and R. Xavier (eds), *Public relations campaigns* (pp. 206–15), 2nd edn. Melbourne: Oxford University Press.

APPENDIX: ANSWERS TO CASE QUESTIONS

Introduction

1. *Identify the risks of nationalisation for Australia's banks in the period following the Second World War.*

   Nationalisation would mean all private banks would be sold to the Commonwealth Bank (at that time government owned) – so the private banking community would be completely lost to a monopoly. In harsh terms it would mean that the private banks would cease to exist in Australia.
2. *How are McConnan's activities reflected in the quote from author and practitioner Ray Ewing?*

   The issue of control of the banks had been simmering for some time. While it was considered necessary during the war it was assumed this would cease in 1945 at the conclusion of the Second World War. Ewing determines pre-1970s IM as 'an ad hoc process, not a planned and continuous process' yet in 1944 McConnan was preparing for this battle and although it took him some time to persuade his colleagues ultimately it resulted in a concerted effort from all of Australia's private banks 1946 to 1949. So in this regard we could regard the bank nationalisation campaign as one of the earliest if not the first IM campaign in Australia.
3. *Thinking about the bank nationalisation case, why did the banks continue their campaign when they had already been successful in the High Court?*

   It is recognised that a victory in a court of law does not necessarily translate to a victory in the court of public opinion. In this case the private banks required the defeat of the Labor Government and so maintained a campaign leading up to the 1949 election where the issue was a key determinant in the electoral success of the Liberal Government of Robert Menzies.

Chapter 1

1. *Conduct an online search of the following crises and categorise these crises according to Lerbinger's three crisis typologies:*
   - *Burger King: An employee posted a photograph online of someone standing on two containers of lettuce with the caption: 'This is the lettuce you eat at Burger King.'*
   - *Commonwealth Bank of Australia (CBA): Rogue financial planners at the CBA have been accused of lying and providing poor financial planning advice to the bank's customers putting profit and commission ahead of best interests of these clients.*
   - *Telstra Warrnambool Exchange Fire: In November 2012, a fire in Telstra's Warrnambool exchange left the Southwest region of Victoria without access to telecommunication services. More than 60 000 customers were affected, unable to make phone calls or use the internet. The worst-affected customers were without services for up to 20 days.*

Burger King: This can be categorised as a human climate or management failure crisis. Justification for the former would include the argument that the employee was directly targeting Burger King and the employees' actions (the photographer, the photographed, and the poster) was intended to harm the organisation. It could also be argued that management failure such as social media training and policy led to failure to clearly communicate to employees their rights and responsibilities when communicating about their employer (Burger King). It could also be argued that poor management or supervision of employees in the actual workplace contributed to the crisis.

Commonwealth Bank of Australia: This is a clear case of management failure. Organisational culture which emphasised profit and sales encouraged employee misconduct.

Telstra Warrnambool exchange fire: The cause stemmed from the physical world and the extent of the damage to the exchange caused by the fire meant Telstra was unable to quickly resume services until the exchange was rebuilt.

2. *Why are a crisis audit and pre-crisis planning important?*

The chapter outlines many reasons. Importantly, crises often unfold very quickly and without crisis auditing and planning an organisation may miss the warning signs of an imminent crisis (which they might have been able to avert). Also if a crisis does occur pre-planning and preparedness helps to mitigate damage to reputation, maintain trust with key target publics and where possible keep up normal operations. The organisation will know:

- that the crisis communication plan has CEO and senior management approval and can be implemented
- who has authority and responsibility to act
- with whom the organisation needs to communicate, and when and how to do so (e.g. media, publics, regulatory bodies, emergency services, support services and so on)
- what resources are required.

3. *Why should employees refrain from communicating with the media in times of organisational crisis?*

Common reasons include lack of training in dealing with media who are seeking newsworthy angles, which may be at odds with legal or regulatory limitations on communication. Poorly phrased or miscommunicated information may inflame the crisis or cause emotional harm to friends and families of those affected by the crisis. Too many employee comments can divert media attention away from the authorised media contact, making if difficult for the organisation to communicate clear, timely and accurate information.

4. *Why might organisations avoid issuing an apology in time of crisis?*

This is an extension question, and requires a review of the term *apologia*, which is discussed in the chapter. In responding, reference should be made to ethics, relational trust and reputation management, and possible legal and financial reasons that make issuing a full apology problematic.

Chapter 2

1. *Can you give an example of a risk that has become a crisis, other than the Coode Island example? What risk communication was used and with which publics? How did those involved prevent a risk becoming a crisis?*

   In 2011, tropical cyclone Yasi battered Northern Queensland and caused an estimated $3.6 billion worth of damage (Reuters, 3 February 2011). It impacted on tourism, and destroyed infrastructure, homes and was a major Australian disaster. Tropical cyclones remain an ever-present risk in northern Australia and other parts of the country. Following Yasi and other devastating events that occurred during this time, the Queensland Reconstruction Authority launched a major communication campaign targeting local and regionally based schools, businesses, community groups, service clubs, emergency services, volunteers, councils, 'vulnerable communities' and remote indigenous communities. A key aim was to provide risk communication to improve resilience and community preparedness for future disasters, so that future crises caused by natural disasters could be lessened and minimised.

2. *Thinking of how risk perception can be magnified, can you think of a risk that is overly magnified in the public mind? What risk communication strategies would you put in place to reduce public alarm?*

   With a number of recent airline disasters in the public mind, there is increasing concern about airline safety and heightened anxieties about flying. Yet according to international figures, the odds of being killed on an airline flight are one in 3.4 million (Planecrashinfo, n.d.), compared to 1 in 492 for death in a car crash (National Safety Council, 2010). Airlines may therefore put in place measures to reduce the 'dread' of air travel; these might include testimonials from passengers, celebrities and safety experts about the performance, professionalism and efficiency of airlines. Recognising that internal communication is also important developing loyalty and trust with staff at the front line of customer service may be important in ensuring that 'word of mouth' communication remains positive.

3. *Can you think of some public authorities or corporations that have used Sandman's strategies for outrage reduction? What techniques were used? How successful were these techniques with the relevant publics?*

   Arguably the Victorian Government has used a number of Peter Sandman's techniques to sell its controversial East–West link project which encompasses a new 18 kilometre freeway that will link Melbourne's east and west. The Linking Melbourne Authority has tried to improve the knowability of the project by holding public information sessions and conducting an open social impact assessment with public involvement, it has tried to explain the shared benefits to the public of improved road transport and traffic flow and it perhaps has allowed limited ways for the public to 'share the knife' and public participation by providing online forums for 'engagement'. These techniques, however, have not been totally successful with polls showing that it is is one of the least supported government projects currently being implemented (Tomazin, 2014). Critics have continued to raise concerns about large growth of traffic on suburban roads, pollution, lack of focus on public transport as an alternative solution, and the failure of the supposed benefits of the project to deliver. These techniques may not have worked because they have insufficiently in Sandman's approach provided community participation in the management of the project and so outrage has not been reduced. However, another explanation might also be that this is a case where 'experts disagree' and the project is simply not acceptable because there is not enough consensus for the project to move forward without controversy and therefore without reduced risk perception.

4. *What are some other examples of risk communication as consensus communication? How was risk communication used to inform and encourage groups to work together to reach a decision about how the risk would be managed, prevented or mitigated?*
   The Australian HIV-AIDS campaign is often cited as a very successful example of consensus risk communication because it involved affected communities and focused on grass-roots as well as government organisations and was fundamentally different from the top-down approaches used in other countries such as the United States. In 1987, following a long and sometimes acrimonious debate, a newly elected Labor Government initiated an HIV-AIDS campaign directly funded community groups and established a consultative structure for consulting the community on AIDS and affected vulnerable groups. This was particularly important in spreading the word and preventing risk because it meant that the representatives of vulnerable groups were participating in the management of the campaign and distributing messages and materials to those who most needed this information.
5. *How would you develop a longitudinal risk communication program over a 20-year period? What would be important? Can you think of any examples of such programs?*
   A longitudinal risk communication program should be developed like any other public relations program and contain a stage of formative research followed by program planning. Program planning involves identification of publics and stakeholders, goals and objectives; development of strategies, tactics and messages and consideration of other issues such as budget, materials and a schedule for implementation. At the end of the program, the success of the program should be evaluated. The difference between a short-term risk communication program and a longitudinal one is that a longitudinal program will be made up of a number of staged programs rather than just one. At the end of each program, the program will be evaluated and new objectives, strategies and publics developed for the next program or next development part of the longitudinal communication program. For example, government anti-tobacco campaigning has been developed continuously since the early 1980s. The original Australian National Tobacco campaign targeted smokers aged 18–40 years. Further research and evaluation following this campaign, however, established that younger people needed to be more specifically targeted with health messages. In addition it was decided that more graphic measures were needed such as plain packaged cigarettes with graphic health warnings to change the behaviours of hardened smokers. Following program stages were therefore tweaked to target these groups in different relevant campaign stages.

Chapter 3

1. *What is meant by the definition of reputation as 'anticipated corporate conduct' based on meeting stakeholder expectations (Helm & Gray, 2009)?*

   Helm and Gray point out that there is not yet consensus on defining corporate reputation as a 'construct' (2009, p. 67). Instead it can be useful to recognise the impact of divergent stakeholder expectations and that these need to be integrated into organisational planning and decisions related to operational and risk management. Where organisations are able to achieve this there may be positive benefits which flow to reputation. This is because the organisation adapts its behaviours in a way which is consistent and expected. As Helm and Gray point out, 'Reputation is thus "measured" by stakeholders who assess the degree to which anticipated outcomes, based on historical perceptions of an organisation's ethics, motives, communications and actions, are in line with actual experiences' (2009, p. 67). Therefore, the perception of Fonterra as a 'serial offender' following two other scares could be perceived by some stakeholders as evidence of automatic guilt.

2. *Why is reputation difficult to measure?*

   As the case demonstrates, reputation is an aggregate measure of stakeholder perceptions and expectations. The case identifies many stakeholders such as business customers, consumers, regulators, shareholders and both New Zealand and international media. These stakeholders hold divergent views and levels of informed (or not) and privileged information. Even within different stakeholder groups there will be different perceptions, attitudes and knowledge of the facts of the case.

3. *Risk management is generally discussed in the context of a single organisation. Why was the crisis and damage to Fonterra's reputation a matter of national interest and allied to New Zealand's reputation?*

   To respond to this question, an understanding is needed of New Zealand's competitive advantage and positioning within global markets as a producer of high quality food which is safe from contaminants. As a small economy, New Zealand is heavily reliant on tourism, high-tech manufacturing, service provision and food production. Because Fonterra is such a high profile organisation globally, quite apart from its economic contribution, its sound reputation is vital to protect the New Zealand brand of '100% Pure'. See also examples given in the chapter, which make clear the economic and brand links between New Zealand and Fonterra.

4. *Although Fonterra's initial testing identified the presence of potentially dangerous bacteria which produce the botulism toxin, subsequent testing in overseas laboratories found there was no contamination and therefore no risk. Review the case and list the reasons attributed to Fonterra for their failure to manage the crisis. What could they have done differently?*

   This is an extended exercise on a complex case, and the focus should be on the communication elements rather than any legal obligations or duties. For example, as the case discusses, Fonterra was accused of focusing on the science behind food safety and testing rather than communicating with customers to allay their fears.

Chapter 4

1. *Why is it important that elite athletes value the relationship with their social media fan base?*
   Using social media platforms, such as Twitter, sports fans build a relationship with elite athletes. This relationship, like any other, is based on communication and trust. A loyal fan base can support an athlete during a crisis, or it can just as easily turn against an athlete who has neglected to nurture the relationship.
2. *What are the ramifications for an athlete who confesses to wrongdoing but fails to apologise without reservation?*
   The 'confession' can be seen as self-serving because the athlete has failed to take full responsibility for the transgression. As discussed in the chapter, scholars agree that one of the worst positions in a reputational crisis is to have caused a crisis that could have been prevented. In this situation often the best approach is to 'fess up and fix it'. Taking responsibility and apologising without reservation helps rebuild credibility and trust.
3. *Describe one benefit and one risk of the social media micro-blogging platform Twitter in a crisis?*
   The real-time speed of Twitter enables information, although restricted to 140 characters, to spread quickly to key stakeholders. Tweets can also contain links to other social media platforms, such as blogs, that contain more information. Although the velocity of Twitter can be helpful, a risk is the information may be wrong which can cause more reputational harm.
4. *Armstrong adopted the strategy of 'stealing thunder' to confess on the Oprah Winfrey Show. Why is 'stealing thunder' considered a useful strategy to reduce reputational damage?*
   'Stealing thunder' can reduce the attribution of blame by stakeholders. Studies have shown that damaging information has less impact when it is self-disclosed by the transgressor, rather than exposed by other parties, such as the media.

Chapter 5

1. *What key issues did KFC need to consider in this situation?*
   Answers may include the following:
   - The nature of complaints against KFC the organisation versus the product.
   - The vulnerability of the organisation to viral attacks online.
   - The active complainants/supporters of KFC online.
   - The degree of involvement of the different KFC stakeholders in the incident.
   - The level of dissatisfaction of stakeholders and the type of responses they seek from KFC.
   - The type of communication channels, including social media channels that are open to KFC to communicate its efforts to resolve the problem and the implementation of these channels.
2. *What makes a company in a multi-ethnic society vulnerable from a communications standpoint?*

Answers may include the following:

- KFC needs to consider the expectations of the local communities in which it operates. KFC should have a better understanding of the socio-political environment in which it operates.
- Currently in Malaysia, a multi-racial/religious society, any small incident or perceived grievance or conflict between parties of different religions/races can be blown out of proportion, especially within an active social media environment.
- Considering that most political parties in Malaysia also tend to be set up along racial lines, the likelihood of an issue becoming politicised is also very high.
- When under the public microscope, the organisation's communication must ensure it does not aggravate the socio-political conflict and instead remains neutral by focusing on the business angle and daily operations. For example KFC could pay more attention to improving its customer service.

3. *In what ways could KFC have managed the situation in a risk management context?*

KFC needed to emphasise professionalism in its customer service, for example:

- grooming better trained customer service staff that practise courtesy at all times, especially the frontline staff, which often consists of young, part-time staff
- ensuring that on-site management and supervisory staff have a hands-on approach; in monitoring crowds and being early with communications about availability of products
- ensuring a quick response to customer grievances: a speedy response by senior management directly to aggrieved parties is a must, no matter how small the incident may be, especially when it is obvious the incident is going viral; there is no point in hoping the problem will just blow over without organisation involvement, and social media is unpredictable
- remaining vigilant about online conversations about the related industry and the particular organisation, and to respond speedily
- seeking swift closure, whether by issuing an apology or offering compensation.

4. *Would you have resolved the case differently from KFC Malaysia's approach? What recommendations would you suggest?*

KFC avoided being dragged into the racial or political aspects of the incident online, which is as it should be. It focused on appeasing its current and potential clientele, while at the same time coming to terms with the aggrieved parties.

Unfortunately, KFC was a little slow in its response to the incident, which went viral very quickly, especially since the opposing parties in the incident were of different racial backgrounds, and there was political interference by fundamentalist race-based parties.

Recommendations:

1. Have a strong social media communications team that actively engages with stakeholders, especially customers.
2. The social media team should be trained and empowered to respond immediately to online discussions involving the organisation.

Chapter 6

1. *Collaboration has provided some well-known cross-sector relationships. Using Table 6.1, can you provide an example for each relationship type?*

   There are many examples of localised philanthropy and sponsorship. An exemplar of a cross-sector social partnership is FPO Timberland and the NPO City Year.

2. *How significant is the role of Unilever in achieving sustainable solutions?*

   The problem begins further along the supply chain but Unilever are in a powerful position. Unilever is a large user/purchaser of palm oil and if an organisation this large does not purchase from the palm oil producers, it has obvious financial consequences. By placing pressure on Unilever (and other large purchasers) to change their policy, Greenpeace have been able to influence a change in policy further along the supply chain. An organisation driven by a profit imperative will have to consider its bottom line; if income ceases, changes have to be made. Deforestation remains a significant problem – this was a positive step towards a moratorium on deforestation in Indonesia.

3. *Why do you think Unilever responded quickly to the Greenpeace campaign?*

   Similar to the rationale in question 1, yet the focus is on Unilever's stakeholders. It received pressure from various stakeholder groups and responded promptly to the communication generated via social media. It would be appropriate to map the stakeholders and identify who would have had the most pressure/impact on Unilever. If could be considered a good strategy to minimise the period of time the issue remains at a crisis level until a suitable response has been provided.

4. *Deforestation remains a significant problem; has there been any progress surrounding this issue since?*

   Answers should examine the stakeholders, and explore what actions have occurred lately to help resolve the problems surrounding habitat destruction and palm oil production.

Chapter 7

1. *How would you define a 'social media crisis'?*

   A social media crisis is an issue that arises in or is amplified by social media, and results in negative mainstream media coverage, and/or a change in business process, or financial loss.

2. *Can you identify a different kind of social media crisis than the one provided here, which is an attack on the reputation of an organisation? How is a social media crisis different from just a 'media crisis'?*

   Another kind of social media crisis from the Target example is where someone from within an organisation publishes material that damages the brand, rather than an 'attack' from outside.

   A social media crisis is different from a media crisis because publics are more directly involved – also the crisis is 'viral', meaning it spreads very quickly and is difficult to address or contain.

3. *Find a recent social media crisis and research the mainstream newspaper coverage it attracted. How wide-ranging was the discussion? Was it picked up by columnists and/or opinion writers, or only mentioned in the news pages? Who was the main spokesperson for the company or organisation? Do you think the organisation managed to establish itself as the authoritative voice on the issue?*

   Students should access <http://oursocialtimes.com/6-examples-of-social-media-crises-what-can-we-learn> and search online for mainstream media coverage of one of the recent cases listed to examine possible solutions.
4. *Which of Galtung and Ruge's (1965) news values can be seen in play in the Target example? Which of these values do you think are most relevant?*

   Those at play include timeliness, prominence, frequency, proximity and conflict. Proximity is probably the most relevant.
5. *What key steps does a PR professional need to take to reduce the impact of negative news media attention to his or her organisation?*
   a. Prevent 'crisis creep': Monitor your social media at all times and respond swiftly.
   b. Establish the organisation at the centre of the crisis as the single authoritative source of information about what has happened and what is being done about it.
   c. Develop a bank of 'experts' to take control of the conversation.
   d. Build and maintain good relationships with journalists and their audiences.
   e. Consider a follow-up, proactive or damage control campaign.
6. *Why does a PR professional need to pay close attention to social debates, such as those surrounding the sexualisation of children in advertising and marketing? Do you think that engaging with such debates might have been helpful in Target's case?*

   They need to be able to spot topics that may be controversial and have high news value and respond quickly. Engaging with the debate could have helped in Target's case as a way of deflecting attention away from the company and on to the wider issue.

Chapter 8

1. *Locate examples of online slacktivist activity and explain how they might represent cognitive, affective and behavioural responses.*

   In answering, define the terms *cognitive*, *affective* and *behavioural*.

   Cognitive responses cannot be seen because they are the thoughts a receiver has while listening to a message. Cognitive responses may be inferred where they manifest in beliefs or opinions expressed via means such as a comment left in response to an online video or the sharing of a link via social media networks.

   Affective response refers to the feelings or emotions generated in response to stimuli. A simple example of a symbolic affective response is to 'like' a cause on Facebook.

Behavioural response refers to the actions taken by an individual in response to stimuli. An example of a behavioural response includes such actions as leaving a comment in response to an online tactic, forwarding and sharing content within social media networks.

2. *Locate a recent example of an online video which demonstrates greenwashing by a global corporation and explain why the organisation might be accused of greenwashing.*
   Responses to this question will require you to develop a mini-case study and conduct research. Review the corporate mission and values of the organisation, and look for media articles, online discussion, and other relevant resources that help to illustrate the issues over time. You should consider whether the allegations are accurate or whether there is evidence that the organisation is taking genuine action to effect change.
3. *Why do you think slacktivist actions can help to bring about FPO change quicker than environmental policy, regulation, and international agreements?*
   NPOs can use social media tactics such as online petitions to link slacktivist directly to key organisational decision-makers such as CEOs.
4. *A colleague dismisses slacktivists and argues they don't have any lasting impact. They also argue that many activist clips on sites such as YouTube often demonstrate very low audience views. How would you respond to your colleague and what arguments could you use to counter his or her position?*
   On the one hand, many organisations are resistant to change – but a review of NPO campaigns demonstrates global organisations can respond very quickly to pressure from online tactics. Review Greenpeace's website for examples. In response to low viewing numbers, you can point out that your colleague has ignored networking effects of social media tactics. Viewing statistics or other metrics such as likes only provide a measure of a particular instance of a tactic and do not capture all the transactions and activities which take place online.

Chapter 9

1. *What are the biggest risks facing NPOs in relation to communicating via social media?*
   a. Misinformation or lack of authoritative voice.
   b. Lack of strategic approach.
   c. Avoiding or under-using social media sites, or focusing on the wrong sites/spreading themselves too thin.
2. *Find an example of an Australian NPO using Facebook or Twitter. Find a negative comment posted by a user and how it was handled by the organisation. Would you take the same approach?*
   Negative posts should be handled professionally, authoritatively and, wherever possible, with a friendly tone. Organisations should avoid removing negative posts and the responses should not demonstrate that the administrator has taken the post personally.

3. *Why is the development and implementation of a social media strategy important in minimising risk?*

   It can help to formulate the type of tone used by the organisation and develop response guidelines for dealing with negative comments. It also ensures there is organisational understanding of why social media has been adopted and appropriate use, and who has the authority to post on behalf of the organisation.

4. *Why are the types of social media sites more important than the number of sites being used?*

   It is important that organisations use social media strategically to connect and engage with the right people. Organisations should not spread themselves too thin; instead they should focus on the most appropriate social media sites to reach their unique objectives.

Chapter 10

1. *What are some ways that internalising or image-based messages could be introduced into disaster communication?*

   As elaborated in the conclusion to this chapter, while it may not be appropriate for emergency services to communicate internalising or image-based messages following a disaster, other sources can commend the work of these agencies. For example, political leaders or businesses like insurance agencies could operate as third-party endorsers for the work of emergency services.

2. *Disaster-based communication necessarily involves government departments and agencies. What are two businesses that are involved before, during and after disasters, and how can they be part of community engagement around natural disasters?*

   Answers could include supermarkets (e.g. Woolworths, Coles) and insurance agencies (e.g. Suncorp, CGU, Westpac). Both types of companies are involved in all phases of disaster management and can be involved in communicating disaster preparedness messages before events and support messages following events. Supermarkets are essential to community recovery and managing logistics and power are essential to restocking shelves. Insurance agencies are interested in ensuring homes and businesses are adequately insured for disasters in order to address reconstruction efforts (see the Australian Business Roundtable for further information: <australianbusinessroundtable.com.au>). Insurance agencies ensure call centres and staff are on the ground in the response phase to support customers. They can later come under scrutiny for increased insurance premiums.

3. *Consider the definition of risk communication (see discussion of Salter, 2002, in the text). What are some of the ways social media can contribute to this process and, in this context, what are the advantages and disadvantages of this channel?*

   In considering risk communication, social media is a good channel for interaction and exchange of ideas. This has advantages for discussion during the preparedness phase of disasters as it helps build support for and engagement in risk mitigation. Social media can be more of a challenge during the response phase if powerlines are down. In addition, the response phase is very time sensitive, and there's often little time for the negotiation or dialogue around risk. In this phase, it is important to provide clear, concise, and accurate instructions.

4. *The case study identifies the challenge of dealing with compliance during disasters. For example, people still engage in dangerous driving through floodwaters, which puts them and emergency services crews at risk. The Queensland Government developed one campaign to manage this issue ('If it's flooded, forget it'), but what other strategies could be used to increase compliance?*
   Campaigns could consider different types of messages or angles. The existing campaign targets dangerous driving but others could look at how to teach parents or children about the dangers of playing in floodwaters. Campaigns could also show images of swift-water rescues, showing the risks to people, or perhaps include statistics about injuries or deaths that occur as a result of driving through floodwaters.

Chapter 11

1. *What differences do you see between planning for a large-scale disaster and planning for a smaller crisis?*
   There is no difference. The public relations manager should always apply the principles of crisis communication no matter what degree of crisis occurs. A small crisis can spin off in to a larger one in a brief period of time. As this case shows, the fire at La Jonquera was greater in scale compared with the fire in Portbou. However, the potential existed for both to form a united fire front and with catastrophic results.
2. *What are the dangers inherent in using social media in a crisis?*
   The examples of social media abound in crisis situations. Despite its advantages of timeliness and accessibility it can result in conflicting information if publics are responding to individual communication rather than a more reliable source such as government authorities.
3. *How does a government's role in crisis communication differ to that of a corporation?*
   A corporate entity will be responsible for communicating to its immediate primary stakeholder base. Employees, and customers if required, are the primary stakeholders. It will then deliver communication to the broader community, who are secondary stakeholders. In most cases, these messages will be constructed to meet the communication requirements of the specific target publics. Government communication must be delivered by consistent and contemporaneous channels to all publics. Messages will be uniform for these public ensuring each public receives the same message.
4. *Does the number of government agencies involved in emergencies create communication problems?*
   Yes, when a number of agencies are involved, this can lead to message confusion and contradictory statements, as each authority issues information that may unintentionally vary as they focus on their particular area of responsibility.

Chapter 12

1. *In what ways do crisis management and communication differ from disaster communication?*
   In a disaster situation, all efforts are primarily focused on a community, not on an organisation. The disaster coordination will be the responsibility of a government appointed authority and will include the State Emergency Services. It may also involve several NGOs – such as the Red Cross, Salvation Army, or St Johns Ambulance. Communication will be controlled through a central spokesperson, who is a government appointee.
2. *Do publics regard organisational responses differently in a disaster than a company-induced crisis?*
   If an organisation experiences a crisis caused by a natural disaster, its stakeholder publics are unlikely to apportion responsibility for the crisis to that organisation. However this judgement is affected by organisational response and recovery where it concerns the stakeholders.
3. *In Table 12.1, the authors equate the Crisis Management term 'issues management' with the Emergency Management term 'recovery' – is this an accurate comparison?*
   Under the strict definition of IM in the book's introduction, it would not appear so. However, the recovery phase may give rise to ongoing issues, for example the distribution of donated funds to disaster survivors may need to be administered through an independent body to avoid accusations of bias or favouritism.

INDEX

activism, 109, 110
Advertising Standards Board, 128
AgResearch, 49
Amini, Ana, 98
ANZ Bank, 48
apologia theory, 23–6
  denial strategies, 24
  developments in, 24–5
Aristotle, 24
Armstrong, Lance, 61–2
  'attacking the accuser' defence, 65
  confession on Oprah Winfrey's television program, 61, 65–6, 67
  diverting of attention, 68
  failure to apologise, 61
  inspirational and iconic status, 62, 67
  Livestrong Foundation, 62, 67, 69
  sponsors of, 62
  strategic use of Twitter, 63, 69
  unfair treatment, 68, 69
  use of social media, 63
Asia Pulp and Paper, 108, 112–13, 116
  criticism by environmental groups, 112
  Forest Conservation Policy, 113
  and the Sumatran tiger, 113
attribution theory, 26
Auger, G. A., 129
Austin, J. E., 83
Australia
  adoption of social media, 119
  banking system, 5–6
  not-for-profit organisations, 122
Australian Communications Consumer Action Network, 125
Australian Responsible Care Program, 34

Bagrie, Cameron, 48
Bailey Report (UK), 101
Banking Act, 5, 6–8
  High Court challenge to, 7
banks, Australian, 5–6
beyondblue, 124, 125
Billings, A., 65
biomedical products, manufacture of, 161–2
blogging, 95; *see also* social media
bloodline products, 159, 162
botulism, 41, 45
Brotherhood of St Laurence, 122, 126
Brown, N., 60, 63, 65
Bundaberg, 133
  assessments of damage, 141
  communication challenges, 138
  communication strategy, 141–2, 151–2
  demographics of, 138, 143
  floods and disaster communication, 132–45
  floodwater warnings, 139
  instructional information, 138, 142
  power outages, 140
  preparation phase, 138
  problems of compliance, 138–9
  recovery phase, 140–1
  Regional Local Government Area, 133
  response phase, 139–40
  responsibility for disaster communication, 133
  risk communication in, 137–42
  spectators of the flood, 139
  swift-water rescues, 139
  timeline of flood events, 137
  water supply, 140
Bundaberg Regional Council, 137, 138
  and the 'mud army', 141
Bundaberg Regional Council Local Disaster Management Group, 133, 138
  advisories and media alerts, 139, 144
  conflicting information, 139
  Facebook page, 140, 142
Bureau of Meteorology, 137, 138, 140
Burns, A., 148, 152, 154
bushfires in Catalonia, 146–57
  development of, 146–7

Canberra bushfires, 160
Cancer Council, 124
Carney, Jay, 114
Catalan Government, 148
Catalonia
  Basic Regulations of Civil Protection, 149
  Civil Protection Act, 150, 151
  Civil Protection Directorate General tweets, 147
  Civil Protection Plan, 149
  climate of, 147
  Directorate of Civil Protection, 149
  Directorate of Prevention and Fire Extinction and Rescue, 149
  Emergency Centre of Catalonia, 150
  forest and land management, 147
  government assessment of its activities, 155
  government Twitter account, 154
  Infocat plan, 146
  Information Office of the Emergency Committee, 151
  Ministry of Home Affairs, 152

Catalonia, bushfires in, 146–57
action groups of citizens and others, 150–1
background of the crisis, 148–9
chain of command, 150, 155
communication management, 155
communication strategy, 152
damage caused by, 147
fire prevention and extinction strategies, 150
management of internet accounts, 154
media coverage of, 148
responsibility of government agencies, 149
specific emergency plans, 149–51
use of social media, 148, 152–5
Chase, Howard, 4, 5
Chifley, Ben, 5, 6, 7
China and the Fonterra botulism scare, 43, 46, 48, 49
citizen experts, 33
citizen journalism, 95, 98
Clinton, President Bill, 66
cognitive dissonance, 111
Coleridge, Chris, 50
Commonwealth Bank, 6
communication management, role of public relations in, 2
Communications Council Social Media Code of Conduct, 128
consensus communication, 30–40
definition, 33
outcomes of, 37, 38
consumer behaviour, 109
Coode Island chemical fire, 31–3
crisis communication, 32, 33
issues analysis, 31–2
risk communication, 32
Coode Island Community Consultative Committee, 31, 33–5
functions of, 37
issues covered by, 36
membership, 34, 36
objectives, 33
outrage management, 37
Coombs, T., 26, 27, 158, 160
apologia theory, 24
crisis typology, 15
impression management, 25
responses to a crisis, 19, 66
corporate social responsibility, 80, 81, 108, 126
corporations
response to complaints, 73
and social media, 73
Creech, Wyatt, 45
crises
attribution of responsibility for, 160
definition, 159
emergency crisis, 159
natural disasters, 132–45, 159–61
types of, 159
crisis communication, 1
'dark sites' emergency websites, 18
definition, 32
government roles in, 146–57
lessons from the Bundaberg flood, 142–3
public participation in, 153
responsibility for, 102, 153, 154
social media, 18, 153
speed of, 73
and stakeholder negativity, 5
training for, 17–18
websites and online newsrooms, 18
crisis communication planning, 12, 17
crisis creep, prevention of, 101–4
crisis, impact of, 1
crisis management, 4–5, 67
authoritative source of information, 102
boom and bust cycles, 107–18
the crisis team, 17
definition of the type of crisis, 15–16
facilities needed, 18–19
image restoration theory, 25
impression management, 25
and issue management, 4
maintenance of relationships with journalists, 103
models and procedures, 15–23
post-crisis period, 15, 22–3
pre-crisis phase, 15–19
pro-active damage control, 103–4
protection of interests, 23
ranking of threats, 17
response phase, 15, 19–22
ripple effect of a crisis, 42
role of public relations in, 12–28
role of slacktivism, 108
sequencing, 15
situational crisis communication theory, 26
skills and knowledge needed, 96
and slacktivism, 115
and social media, 116
stakeholders in, 148
token support and, 109
training for crisis communication, 17–18
use of experts to control social media conversations, 103
crisis response, 15
communication with internal audiences, 20–1
cooperation with authorities, 20
employee morale and trust, 21

crisis response (cont.)
  goals of, 19
  monitoring the crisis, 20
  news conferences, 21–2
  protection of victims, 19–20
  recording of queries, 22
  review of, 23
  speed of news release, 21
crisis situations
  avoidance of, 5–6
  role of public relations in, 2
  types of, 15–16, 21
cross-sector collaboration, 80–91
  types of, 82, 83–4
crowdsourcing, 96
cycle of learning model, 136
Cyclone Yasi, 139

Danone (company), 42, 46
dark sites (websites), 18
deforestation and orangutans, 86, 87
Doorley, J., 101, 102, 103

elite athletes
  confessions by, 65
  diverting of attention, 68
  reputation and, 60
  'stealing the thunder' strategy, 66
  tolerance of transgressions by, 64–5
Elkington, J., 82
Eltham, B., 148, 152, 154
emergency communication, 146–57
Emergency Management Australia, 150
English, Bill, 44, 45
environmental activism, meaningful support for, 111
environmental agreements, 111
Ergon Energy, 141
Every Australian Counts campaign, 122
Ewing, Ray, 4, 5
experts, 33, 36–8
  citizen experts, 33
  disagreement among, 37
  expert publics, 33
  risk assessments, 134

Facebook, 101, 102, 123
Fan, Zhang, 48
Fearn-Banks, K., 3, 4
Fennell, S., 82
Ferrari, Dr Michele, 62
Fonterra (company), 41
  communication management, 50
  compensation demands, 42
  crisis communication, 46, 50, 52, 53
  crisis management, 52
  failure of its apology, 47–8
  false positive tests, 42, 44, 46, 49
  financial cost of the crisis, 50
  food contamination crises, 43
  interpretation of the crisis, 49–50
  media reaction to the crisis, 46–7
  perspective on the food contamination crisis, 45–6
  product recalls, 42
  reliance on science, 50–1
  reputational damage, 41, 42–5, 50, 51, 53
  risk management, 52
  stakeholders' perceptions of, 51–2
  trade implications of the crisis, 47
food safety, 41, 43, 48
for-profit organisations, 80
  cross-sector collaboration, 88
  online communication and social media, 108
forest and land management
  burning off, 147
  fire prevention and extinction strategies, 147
Fotheringham, William, 67

Galloway, C., 3, 149, 151, 153
Galtung, J., 97, 98
Gambro (company), 158
  communication with employees, 165
  crises affecting, 161–3
  crisis communication, 158, 164–6
  crisis management, 158, 165
  earthquakes and, 163–4
  employee donor campaign, 165
  and the global financial crisis, 162
  interim production arrangements, 166
  nature of the manufacturing facility, 161, 162
  'One Voice' communication strategy, 164–6
  outcomes and recovery, 166–7
  relationship with the community, 163
  reputational impact, 166
  restructuring process, 162
  round table of stakeholders, 164
  rumours about, 162, 166
  sales network, 166
  target publics of, 164
  task forces, 164, 166
  use of media, 165
Gandy, O., 96, 100
Geelong Chemical Action Network, 31
Gibson, Neil, 51
Glenny, L. 160
Good Agricultural Practice Guidelines for Palm Oil, 85
Gray, B., 49, 53
Greenberg and Elliott, 45, 51

Greenpeace, 80–91, 111
- activism on deforestation, 86
- campaign against Asia Pulp and Paper, 113
- campaign against Unilever, 87, 88
- collaboration with Unilever, 88
- issue management, 88
- online videos, 113

greenwashing, 112
Groser, Tim, 47
Grunig, James, 13, 14, 23, 26

Hambrick, M., 63
Hamilton, Tyler, 67
Harrison, K., 3, 159, 165
Hartland, Colleen, 31
Hearit, Keith, 24
Heart Foundation, 124
Heath, R., 4, 7, 8, 13
Helm, S., 51
Homedes, Marc, 154
Hunt, T., 14

image restoration theory, 25
impression management, 25
information subsidies, 100
Invisible Children, 108, 114–16
- negative media attention, 116
- results of its campaign, 114
- and slacktivism, 115–16
- use of Facebook and Twitter, 115
- website management, 115

issue management, 1, 3–4, 5–6
- boom and bust cycles, 107–18
- and crisis management, 4
- criteria for monitoring issues, 7
- and cross-sector collaboration, 81–4
- through cross-sector collaboration, 80–91
- functions in, 4
- proactive, 80
- as a public policy role, 5
- responsibility for, 81
- role of slacktivism, 108
- role in strategic planning, 4
- and social media, 116
- token support and, 109
- tools for, 1

issues communication, 1
Italy
- manufacture of biomedical products, 161–2
- political and economic instability in, 162

Iyer, E. S., 84

journalism
- quality journalism, 101
- verification and social media stories, 100

journalists
- and crisis management routines, 148
- factors affecting decisions, 97
- news values, 97–8

Kemp, Charles, 6
Key, John, 44, 47
KFC
- apology to Danny Ng, 76
- co-creation strategy, 78
- containment strategy, 77–8
- crisis communication, 77
- crisis management, 77–8
- 'KFC finds love again' campaign, 78
- recruitment of radio DJs, 78
- strategy of containment, co-creation and convincing, 77
- strategy to convince, 78

kidney dialysis, 159
Klout score, 12
Kony 12 campaign, 114–16
- criticisms of, 114

Kony, Joseph, 114
Kristofferson, K., 109, 110, 112
Kwanash-Aidoo, K., 3, 149, 151, 153
Kyoto Protocol, 111

Landy, John, 31
lay publics, 33, 36
Lerbinger, Otto, 15–16, 21, 25
Lifeline Australia, 127
Livestrong Foundation, 62, 67, 69
Lord's Resistance Army, 114

Malaysia
- background on the i-City KFC fight, 75–6
- breadth of use of social media, 74
- cultural, racial and religious diversity of, 74
- issues in the KFC fight, 76–7
- KFC i-City fight, 73–9
- public reaction to the video clip of the fight, 75
- racial stability in, 74, 76
- youth reliance on social media for news, 74

Malaysian Airways flight MH370, 20
McConnan, Sir Leslie, 5, 6, 7, 8
McDowell, Gabriel, 102
McGrath Foundation, 126
McMullin, Ross, 6
Media Access Australia, 125
Menzies, Robert, 8
Milne, G. R., 84
Monsanto (company), 43
Morgan, M., 64, 65
Mount Franklin Water, 126
Movember campaign, 125

narrative theory, 26
National Bank of Australasia, 6
National Disability Insurance Scheme, 122
nationalisation of banks in Australia, 5, 6–8
natural disasters, 132–45, 158
  bushfires in Catalonia, 146–57
  effects of, 161
  phases of, 135–6
  preparation phase, 135, 144
  prevention phase, 135
  recovery phase, 135, 163
  resourcing of media teams, 143
  response phase, 135
  and social media, 144
networked journalism, 95
New Zealand
  100% Pure New Zealand branding, 43, 48–9
  'clean and green' image, 43, 50
  consumer trust in dairy products, 42
  food safety scare, 41–53
  importance of the dairy sector, 43
  Ministry for Primary Industries, 46, 47, 49
  'NZ Inc', 43
  regulatory framework for dairy products, 49
  reputation for food safety, 48
Newman, John Henry Cardinal, 24
news agenda, 96
news conferences, 21–2
news media
  democratisation of, 104
  dominance of celebrity and social news, 98
  effect on public panic and speculation, 67
  hard and soft news, 97
news subsidies, 96–7
news values, 97–8, 99–100
Ng, Danny, 75
Nicholls, S., 160
Norton, Chris, 18
not-for-profit organisations, 81
  adversarial organisations, 82
  advocacy organisations, 124
  authoritative source of information, 125
  consistency of organisational messages, 127
  cross-sector collaboration, 82, 83, 88
  decision-making hierarchies of, 125
  distinction between personal and professional communications, 125–6
  fundraising activities, 125
  maximisation of meaningful support, 109
  online communication and social media, 108
  related to health and wellbeing, 124
  reliance on volunteers, 121
  resources of, 121, 122–3, 128
  and risk aversion, 119–30
  risks faced by, 119
  and social media, 119, 120–6, 128, 129
  target publics of, 125
  types of, 82, 124–5

O'Neill, D., 98, 99
orangutans, 86
organisations
  decision-making in, 2
  internal and external responses to crises, 2
  and social media adoption and use, 120
  transparency of, 124
outrage management, 30–40
Oxfam Australia, 126
  The Grow Method campaign, 122
  use of social media, 122, 127

Palenchar, M, 3, 4, 7, 8
palm oil, 85, 88
Peloza, J., 109, 110, 112
Pew Research Internet Project, 114
political economy, 96
Pont, C., 148, 150, 152, 153, 155
Porter, M., 161
post-crisis period, 22–3
  assessment of PR damage, 22
  rebuilding during, 158–68
  recovery program, 22
  review of crisis preparation, 23
  review of crisis response, 23
  strategic changes, 23
private sector responsibility for issue management, 81, 82
product recalls, 42
Prostate Cancer Foundation of Australia, 125
public relations
  apologia theory, 23–6
  asymmetrical approaches to, 13
  criticisms of, 13
  definitions of, 13–14
  emergency management teams, 160
  models and procedures, 15–23, 26
  post-symmetrical theory of, 13
  and social media, 94
  symmetry in, 14, 23, 26
Public Relations Institute of Australia, 13
public relations profession, 1
  participation in newsmaking, 96
  and social media, 100, 103

Queensland, disaster communication in, 132–45
  Emergency Management Queensland, 138
  Get Ready Queensland initiative, 144

    Queensland Fire and Rescue Service, 139
    whole-of-government approach, 133

racial framing, 74
racism, 73–9
Red Cross, 141
reputation, definition, 107
reputation risks, 41–53, 121
reputational damage
    assessment of, 16
    quantification of, 44
resilience, 137
Responsible Care program, 34
Rice, Stephanie, 64
risk, 2–3
    assessment of, 5–6
    environmental risks, 30
    man-made disasters, 30
    and outrage, 34
    related to health and wellbeing, 124
    social risks, 30
risk audits, 15, 16
    desk research, 16
    internal and external, 16
    ranking of threats, 17
risk aversion, 119–30
risk communication, 1, 3, 30–40
    adjusting information, 135, 143
    choice of content, 136
    definition, 32
    image-based communication, 143
    instructing information, 135, 136, 142, 143
    interactive approach, 134
    internalising information, 136, 143
    lessons from the Bundaberg flood, 142–3
    multiple sources and channels of information, 136, 143
    during natural disasters, 132, 134–6, 142
    one-way communication, 134
    role of public relations in, 3
    two-way nature of, 3
    types of, 135
    use of experts, 33, 36–8
risk management, 1, 3, 52
risk perception, 32, 38, 134
Roberson, Kasie, 24
Romano, Gary, 47
Roundtable on Sustainable Palm Oil, 85
    membership, 85
Royal Commission on Banking, 7
Ruge, M., 97, 98
Russell, Jason, 115, 116

Sanderson, 63, 64
Sandman, Peter, 34, 35–5, 36, 38
Sanlu (company), 43
Saxton, G. D., 120, 125
Sea Shepherd Conservation Society, 82
search engine optimisation, 18
Sellnow, T. L., 136
sexualisation of young girls, 98, 100, 101
Sinar Mas (company), 112
situational crisis communication theory, 26
slacktivism, 107–18
    power of, 111–12
    role in online crisis and issues management, 108
    and token support, 111, 112, 113
Smith, C. 124
social identity theory, 63
social investment, 81
social media, 69, 123
    adoption and use of, 119–30
    archiving and storage of content, 95
    backlash against Target, 98, 100–4
    code of conduct, 128
    and community building, 123
    complexity of, 108
    control over, 123, 127
    cost of, 120
    and crisis management, 94
    etiquette on, 123
    evolution of, 121
    guidelines or policies and procedures for, 127
    importance of strategic messages and interaction, 122
    interactive and converged network systems, 152
    interactive communication on, 123
    monitoring tools, 20
    multiple sources and channels of information, 152
    and natural disasters, 138
    need for monitoring of, 101–4, 115
    noise and, 124
    opportunities presented by, 120, 127, 129
    paid posts on, 128
    professional and personal communication on, 120, 125–6
    relevance of different sites, 123–4
    and reputational risk, 122
    risks associated with, 129
    rules of engagement, 127
    and sports fans, 60, 62, 64
    target publics, audiences and stakeholders of, 108
    and token support, 110
    and traditional media, 61, 94–106, 114
    trends in, 98
    trolls, 122
    use by not-for-profit organisations, 126

Spierings, Theo, 42, 46, 47, 49, 50
sport and crisis communication, 60–72
sports fans, 60
  expectations of, 62–4
  and social media, 63
stakeholder expectations, 51, 80
  cognitive and normative expectations, 52
stakeholders, identification of, 80
Sturges, D. L., 135
subsidised news, 96–7, 100
Sumatran tigers, 113
Summers, J., 64, 65
supply chain slacktivism, 110–11, 112
sustainable palm oil, 85
symmetry in public relations, 13, 14, 26

Tajfel, Henri, 63
Target
  media crisis over girls' fashions, 94, 95–6, 98–9
  national news coverage of the issue of girls' fashions, 100
  response to social media criticism, 99
Terminals Chemical Storage Facility, 31
  Responsible Care program, 34
Tour de France, 62
traditional media and social media, 61, 94–106, 114
trolls, 122
Tropical Cyclone Oswald, 132
trust, 160
Twitter, 63, 69, 123
Tygart, Travis, 61

Underhill, Kerry, 48
Unilever, 80–91, 113
  collaboration with Greenpeace, 88
  Dove™ self-esteem fund, 87
  forests action against, 87
  Good Agricultural Practice Guidelines for Palm Oil, 85
  integrative relationships, 85
  issue management, 85, 88
  partnership initiatives, 86
  relationship portfolio, 85–8
  Roundtable on Sustainable Palm Oil, 85
  social and environmental investment, 85
  supply chain practices, 86
  sustainable palm oil, 85
  values of, 85
United States Anti-Doping Agency, 61, 62

Victoria, bushfires in, 147, 152, 155
  communication lessons from, 148
  convergent media and, 154

White, K., 109, 110, 112
Wide Bay – Burnett region of Queensland, 132
Wigley, S., 66
Winfrey, Oprah, 61, 65–6, 67, 114
World Anti-Doping Agency, 69
World Cancer Congress, 62
World Wide Fund for Nature, 112
Wronging Rights blog, 115

Zhao, William, 48